# INSIDER'S GUIDE to
# FINDING
# A JOB

EXPERT ADVICE FROM
AMERICA'S TOP EMPLOYERS
AND RECRUITERS

WENDY S. ENELOW, CCM, MRW, JCTC, CPRW
SHELLY GOLDMAN, CPCC, CEIP, CCM

JIST Works
America's Career Publisher

# Insider's Guide to Finding a Job

© 2005 by Wendy S. Enelow and Shelly Goldman

Published by JIST Works, an imprint of JIST Publishing, Inc.
8902 Otis Avenue
Indianapolis, IN 46216-1033
Phone: 1-800-648-JIST     Fax: 1-800-JIST-FAX     E-mail: info@jist.com

Visit our Web site at **www.jist.com** for information on JIST, free job search tips, book chapters, and ordering instructions for our many products! For free information on 14,000 job titles, visit **www.careeroink.com**.

---

See the back of this book for additional JIST titles and ordering information. Quantity discounts are available for JIST books. Please call our Sales Department at 1-800-648-5478 for a free catalog and more information.

---

Acquisitions and Development Editor: Lori Cates Hand
Interior and Cover Designer: designLab, Seattle
Proofreader: Jeanne Clark
Indexer: Henthorne House

Printed in Canada
08  07  06  05  04          9  8  7  6  5  4  3  2  1

Library of Congress Cataloging-in-Publication data is on file with the Library of Congress.

We have been careful to provide accurate information in this book, but it is possible that errors and omissions have been introduced. Please consider this in making any career plans or other important decisions. Trust your own judgment above all else and in all things.

ISBN 1-59357-077-5

# About This Book

As you read through this book, you will find interviews with 66 of America's top corporate human resources executives, recruiters, hiring managers, and career experts. They have shared their collective expertise so that we could provide you with the best strategic and tactical advice for building and managing your career—a career that is personally, professionally, and financially rewarding. We've taken the advice of these experts and focused it on each of the core components of career development, job search, and lifelong career management.

In addition to interviewing each of the 66 recruiters, human resources executives, hiring managers, and career experts, we also conducted a research study to collect data about the specific hiring, interviewing, resume reviewing, and related practices of these individuals. You will find our statistical results at the end of Chapters 2 through 7. To ensure that we captured data from a variety of types and sizes of companies, we were certain to interview people from a broad cross-section of organizations. As such, it is important to note that 35% of the responses came from individuals who work in companies with less than 100 employees, 15% in companies with 101 to 500 employees, and 50% in companies with 501+ employees.

Each chapter also features an "Authors' Best Advice…" section. These sections are a compilation of the best career advice based on the authors' expertise in combination with the valuable insights that each interviewee shared. They sum up the most important points for each career topic.

Only you have the power to create a successful career for yourself. Although the market is competitive and positions may seem few and far between, opportunities do abound. The trick is to play the new job search game well, understand its various components, and let it work for you. That is what our experts will show you how to do—create your own winning career plan and strategy, develop powerful job search materials, build a successful job search campaign, and get the offers you want.

## Acknowledgements

This book was possible because of only one thing: the willingness of each of the people we interviewed to give so freely of their time and expertise. Each was so open and candid, providing insights and information we never dreamed possible. For that, we are forever grateful and would like to acknowledge each and every one of them:

Lou Adler—The Adler Group/CJA
Christopher Bargeron—Silicon Graphics, Inc.
Viola W. Bostic—National Federation of Community Development Credit Unions
Jo Bredwell—JWT Specialized Communications
Charles W. Broach—Ford Motor Company
Steven Broadman—Convergenz
Joseph Cabral—New York Presbyterian Hospital
Jack Chapman—Lucrative Careers, Inc.
Michael Clement—Coretech Consulting Group
Patti Cotter—Nationwide Insurance
Gerry Crispin—CareerXroads
Rob Croner—Radian Group, Inc.
W. Herbert Crowder III—Darden Graduate School of Business Administration
Claire M. Donegan—Career Search
Drew Farren—Corning's Recruiting Center for Excellence
Anne Fisher—Fortune and Fortune.com
Dr. Clint Gortney—The Gortney Group
Joel Greengrass—Equinox Fitness
Joseph R. Hammill—Xerox Corporation
R. Douglas Hardin—IntelliDyne, LLC
Bea Hardman—Hyatt Hotels and Resorts
Cynthia A. Hartley—Sonoco Products Company
Wanda Jackson—National Urban League
Mark Jaffe—Wyatt & Jaffe
Dr. Beverly Kaye—Career Systems International
Valerie Kennerson—Corning, Incorporated
Timothy Q. Kime—Leadership Washington
Darryl L. King—Neoware Systems, Inc.
Mary Jane Koch—National Rural Telecommunications Cooperative
Robert B. Kuller—Process Powered Consulting

Tony Lee—CareerJournal.com/The Wall Street Journal
    Online Network
Frank Leonetti—Global Services, StorageTek
Stephen Lopez—National Board of Medical Examiners
Thomas J. Lynch—Mobilecube2, Inc.
Denise Males—Major League Baseball
John Martin—IQNavigator
Marie-Anne Martin—United Nations
Joseph Daniel McCool—Kennedy Information, Inc.
Jane McLaughlin—LifeCycle Software
Mary McMurtry—Southwest Airlines
Mark Mehler—CareerXroads
Tim Moran—Hallmark Cards, Inc.
Kurt Mosley—The MHA Group
Jeannine Nettles—State Farm Insurance
Jim Oddo—Oxford Health Plans, Inc.
Nels B. Olson—Korn/Ferry International
Rocky Parker—Nationwide Insurance
Chrisi Rogers—National Rural Telecommunications
    Cooperative
Weldon J. Rougeau—Congressional Black Caucus
    Foundation, Inc.
Coretha Rushing—The Coca-Cola Company
Raphael J. D. Sebastian—WorkplaceDiversity.com
Mary Jo Shackelford—Exselleration, LLC
Karen Shadders—Wegmans Food Markets
Rich Sierra—Health Care Recruitment
Lana Simcox—The Professional Golfers' Association of
    America
Andrea Sims—Match3 Productions, LLC
Coleen Smith—Colgate-Palmolive
Shaun Smith—Memorial Sloan-Kettering
Jack St.Genis—Molecular Separations, Inc.
Dr. John Sullivan—DJS & Associates
Katherine Virdi—IntelliDyne, LLC
Naray Viswanathan—Interview Exchange
Peter Weddle—WEDDLE's
Gwen Weld—Microsoft Corporation
Bill Welsh—Equinox Fitness
Michael Wirth—Talent+

We would both like to also acknowledge each other for our individual contributions to this book. Although as our first writing partnership it was an intensely collaborative effort, we each independently managed major parts of the process. The experience was so worthwhile for both of us that we anxiously look forward to other collaborations.

*To Shelly...Thank you! Your ability to reach out and connect with such wonderful people has made this an extraordinary experience for me. The questions that you developed and the vast amount of knowledge and information that you were able to collect through your interviews is what has made this book such a tremendously valuable tool to job seekers. (Wendy)*

*To Wendy...What can I say? You are the most talented writer I have ever known and it has been a total delight working with you. You were able to take my rough interview notes and create a masterpiece of which I am so very proud. What's more, as an experienced author, I learned so much from you about the strategy, process, and technique for writing a best-seller! Thank you so much for sharing and leading the process. This has been a wonderful experience for me. (Shelly)*

# CONTENTS

# CONTENTS

# CHAPTER 1 Take Control: It's Your Life and Your Career

The single most important lesson that every job seeker must learn and live by is that they—and they alone—control their own career destiny. The generally accepted principle in years past was that your employer controlled your career and whatever they decided was what would happen. As we've all lived through the past decade of layoffs, downsizings, rightsizings, reengineerings, and more, we have learned a crucial lesson: In order to sustain and accelerate our careers, we must have the control. No longer can we allow ourselves to be "at the mercy" of our employers, who make decisions based on the "bottom line" and not necessarily on what is good for each employee.

To help you better understand that concept, we've devoted this chapter to giving you the insights and the tools to make clear and decisive choices about your own career track. We'll address the benefits of working as an employee, a consultant, and/or an entrepreneur; the critical "three M's" of successful job search (mindset, merchandising, and multichannel); the key players in your job search community (for example, career coaches, career counselors, resume writers, outplacement consultants, and recruiters); building your job search support team (including mentors, colleagues, family, friends, managers, consultants, and others); and how to efficiently and proactively manage your search campaign. Read this chapter and you'll be much better prepared to launch your successful job search campaign that will open new doors and present you with wonderful new opportunities.

# Yearning for Years Gone By

We can remember being in our early 20s and applying for our first *real* jobs. It was just the start of our careers and, as such, these were not executive positions but, rather, administrative and publications management jobs. What we both remember most was how easy it was to get a job. Here was our five-step plan of action:

1. Look in Sunday's newspaper and select a few positions that sounded interesting.

2. Call on Monday to learn more about the job.

3. Submit a resume briefly outlining our job experience.

4. Interview for the position sometime that week.

5. Get the offer and start the job the following Monday.

The process was great—quick, easy, and efficient. But none of us realized just how great it was—until we compared it to the job search process as it exists today. Here's the 24-step plan of action that successful job seekers use today:

1. Assess your core skills and qualifications, interests, values, and more to determine the type of position and type of company you are most interested in working for.

2. Create a step-by-step career plan to guide your job search and career management efforts—today and for years to come.

3. Be sure to balance your career objectives with your life goals and plan: We are all now more focused on quality of life and life planning than ever before.

4. Write and design a powerful resume that focuses on your knowledge, achievements, credentials, and other distinguishing characteristics of your career. In fact, you might develop several resumes if you have several different career goals for which one resume won't cover all the bases.

5. Conduct extensive company research to identify the specific companies for which you would like to work, that best match your skills, and that align with your own personal values. Remember, cultural fit is vitally important today, particularly to companies that know what types of employees will thrive within their organizations.

6. Write customized cover letters that highlight the specific qualifications and experience you bring to each position that you
apply for.

7. Create a job search management system (on paper or your PC)
in order to keep track of all of your contacts, activities, interviews, follow-ups, and more. Managing all facets of your job
search requires a great deal of organization, so be sure to set
up a system that works for you.

8. Consider an e-mail campaign to recruiters who specialize in
your profession and your industry. This information is now
widely available on the Internet for a relatively small fee, so
you can easily contact recruiters who would be most interested in a candidate with your background and qualifications.

9. Consider a direct-mail campaign (e-mail or snail mail) to companies that would be most interested in someone with your
experience. Be sure to get contact names so that your go to
someone directly and not just to anyone. That way you will
also be sure to have someone to follow up with.

10. Consider a direct-mail campaign (e-mail or snail mail) to
venture-capital firms that would be most interested in someone with your industry experience. Be sure to get contact
names so that you can send your materials to someone directly and not just to anyone. Again, you will then have a contact
with which to follow up.

11. Post your resume on online job boards, but be careful. There
are hundreds and hundreds of job boards, and you can find
yourself spending endless hours posting your resume. This is
not necessarily a good use of your time, energy, and effort.
There are other activities that you can engage in (for example,
networking, follow-up calls, and interview training) that will
generally yield much better results. Posting your resume is a
passive process—you post and wait. Do your research, find the
job boards that are right for you, and then post your resume
only on those boards. Use the Internet wisely in your job search
and realize that it is not the answer to all of your prayers!

12. Search online job boards for opportunities. Again, we recommend that you do not spend a tremendous amount of time
online searching one job board after another. Find sites that
post positions that most closely match your career objectives
and then use those sites on a routine basis.

13. Respond to help-wanted advertisements in newspapers, professional journals, and other print publications. All too often job seekers ignore this tried-and-true method that still does work. Don't forget about these resources!

14. Attend job fairs, not necessarily expecting to get a position, but rather looking to establish new contacts with companies, recruiters, and other job seekers.

15. Take advantage of the services that your alumni career office offers. Very often one alum will contact the university to see whether a former classmate or another alum might be qualified for a position they are seeking to fill. This can be an invaluable and exclusive job search resource, so be sure to use it wisely.

16. Network, network, and then network some more. No matter how many times you hear it, it's still true: Networking is the single best way to find a new position. Yet networking is an activity that all too many job seekers try to avoid. How unfortunate! There is simply nothing that is more effective than networking, so bite the bullet and start moving forward.

17. Join a professional association or two where you will meet people in similar industries and professions. This can be a particularly effective way to expand your professional network and uncover new opportunities that might be precisely what you are looking for.

18. Join a job search group. In today's intensely competitive job search market, the going can get tough. Not only can job search groups provide you with leads and recommendations, their members will support and encourage you through difficult times.

19. Consider hiring a professional resume writer, career coach, or outplacement consultant. Don't go it alone if you need help, guidance, and support. These professionals can be of tremendous value to you in your search, from helping you identify your talents and career objectives to guiding you in effective salary negotiations and all of the other fine points in job search.

20. Learn how to effectively interview—in one-on-one interviews, panel interviews, group interviews, teleconference interviews, informational interviews, screening interviews, and more. Then learn how to tailor your responses and the presentation of your qualifications to each person you interview with by listening carefully to their needs and then highlighting your relevant skills, experiences, and contributions.

21. Learn the finer techniques of building interview rapport, using the right body language, making strong eye contact, asking good questions, and so much more. Interviewing has become intensely competitive and you must be able to play hardball.

22. Negotiate your compensation package. Although salary might be set for a specific job, there is often lots of room to negotiate for other types of compensation (such as stock options, flexible work schedules, vacation, year-end bonus, signing bonus, family insurance coverage, and automobile reimbursement).

23. Evaluate the employment offer and determine whether it is the right opportunity for you. Also determine whether you have the right motivations for accepting the position—you want the opportunity for success and not just the money and the perks! Then, either formally accept the position or verbally decline the offer and follow up with a letter declining the offer and thanking them for the opportunity.

24. After you have accepted a new position—*and this is critically important*—contact everyone in your network to alert them to your new position, your new company, and your new contact information.

Now, don't faint! Not all 24 steps are necessary for each job seeker. For example, if you're looking for an entry-level veterinarian technician position in the city in which you live, you probably don't need to do mass mailings to recruiters, companies, or venture capitalists. In fact, you might not even post your resume on the Internet or even review online job postings. Most likely, the position you're looking for won't be there. Your best chances for finding a position in this situation are your local newspaper; networking contacts; your local veterinary association; and direct contacts with veterinarians, breeders, groomers, and others who are right in your area.

On the other hand, if you are looking for a position as the Chief Financial Officer of a multimillion-dollar technology company, just about all of the 24 steps will be activities in which you will want to engage. Often, the higher the level of position you are seeking, the more diverse your job search needs to be and the more resources you'll need to use.

Your geographic preferences will also impact how many of these different job search tools you use. If you are looking to work only in Minneapolis/St. Paul and nowhere else, geographically dispersed e-mail campaigns and global Internet postings will not yield the results you want. Conversely, if you are a pharmaceutical sales representative willing to relocate anywhere in the U.S., those tools would be ideal for you.

In summary, today's job seeker must be savvy, know what he or she wants in a job and a company, know how to manage a multi-pronged job search campaign, excel at networking, and be a competent negotiator. The "easy" days of mailing a resume and getting a job in a week or two are long gone. Planning your search campaign requires a sound and appropriate strategy and not just haphazard distribution of your resume. Be sure you develop the strategy that will work best for you.

## Exploring Your Options—Employee, Consultant, or Entrepreneur?

With the emergence of today's complex job search process have also come unlimited opportunities for you to explore. In fact, never in the history of modern-day business have you—as a working adult—had so many different options for your career. Not only do you need to decide *what* you want to do—finance, sales, technology, human resources, general management, human services, and so on—you have to decide *how* you want to do it. You must decide which of the following you want to be:

- An **employee,** enjoying the safety, security (although somewhat questionable these days), and benefits of "corporate" employment. There are a great many positive things about getting a W-2, your pension plan, and all the other perks without worrying.

- A **consultant,** thriving in the world of projects, clients, and solutions. The diversity of a consulting career intrigues many senior managers and executives, allowing you to leverage your particular expertise and enjoy many different experiences and opportunities.

- An **entrepreneur,** defining and pursuing your own course of action. Entrepreneurship can be enticing and tremendously rewarding, but you must learn to live with the risk and potential for financial uncertainty. It can be a heavy load to carry, but you can also reap tremendous personal and professional rewards.

Each of these three choices offers you a host of advantages, but also some disadvantages. As such, it is critically important that you determine which is right for you.

# Working as an Employee

Despite the slow improvement of the financial markets, the recently poor performance of the technology sector, and our economy's struggle to recover, the opportunities for employment do exist—today and in the future. Finding them might take a bit more effort and creativity than in years past, but they are there and will continue to be there.

If you've made the decision to pursue employment, you must ask yourself the following questions:

- How will you find self-satisfaction and personal fulfillment in your job?
- How are you going to manage and advance your career, positioning yourself for continual increases in your compensation?

### Personal Fulfillment at Work

The single most important thing to remember as an employee is that no matter who writes your paycheck, ultimately you work for yourself and for your family. Therefore, your job must not only provide money, benefits, and the like, it must also provide you with a feeling of self-worth and personal identity. In a world where work often dominates our lives, personal feelings of value and contribution are vital to your own growth and sense of achievement. Just as critical and perhaps more so, your employer must find value and worth in what knowledge, skills, and contributions you bring to the organization.

### Managing and Advancing Your Career

Planning and preparation are key. We strongly recommend that you develop your own "career map," a tool that will allow you to envision where you will be a year from now, five years from now, 10 years from now, and so forth. With your career map in hand, you can chart your projected career growth and direction, knowing that it will change over time as you move forward, encounter new opportunities, expand your knowledge, and reposition yourself for continued growth.

When you have a plan in hand, you have control over your destiny, something that all too many employees feel they give up when they accept an employment opportunity. Many believe their careers are now in the hands of the company, and they sit by passively, waiting for the company to make the next move. But not you! You know that your objective is to move up another tier in the management structure of your company, or another company, within the next two years. In anticipation, you should engage in the following activities:

- Prepare and continually update your "achievement journal," highlighting each and every contribution, project, cost savings initiative, revenue increase, and more that you have delivered to the company. This will be a vital tool in negotiating your next promotion and accompanying salary increase.

- Develop a "networking resource file" that you can easily and quickly update with each new network contact, people who might be of value when planning and executing your next job search campaign.

- Prepare a "compensation chart" that specifically depicts your realistic projections for growth in salary, benefits, and other financial perks. Keep this with your career map and update them simultaneously.

As an employee, you strive to meet two independent, yet interrelated, agendas—your personal agenda and your employer's agenda. It is quite possible to achieve both as long as you are clear about what you want and can communicate that information and your supporting qualifications, achievements, and talents to your employer.

## Working as a Consultant

Ten years ago, there were few consultants, and those people most often worked for large, well-established consulting firms. Today, however, consulting is a rapidly growing profession that is advantageous for both the consultants and the companies who engage them.

Once you have established yourself as a consultant and built a solid reputation, you are free to pick and choose your assignments, concentrating in areas of professional interest and challenge to you. Further, you are often quite well paid for your expertise, and the opportunities can be unlimited. There are consultants who specialize in strategic planning, sales, marketing, IT, HR, productivity and efficiency improvement, corporate and investment finance, mergers and acquisitions, operations, and virtually every other profession and function you can think of.

Employers like hiring consultants because they can capture the best talent for a specific project or assignment, whether for two weeks or two years, and be *done* with that consultant when the project is complete. There is no long-term commitment as there exists between employer and employee, and this is what makes consulting particularly attractive to both individuals and companies.

If you are thinking of pursuing a consulting career, you must answer the following questions for yourself:

- Do you thrive in a constantly changing work environment? Consultants are often on the move, from client to client, working in a diversity of organizations. To succeed, you must be able to quickly adapt to your changing environment and get up to speed almost instantly.

- Can you handle the pressure of constant deadlines and commitments? More often than not, consultants work on time-sensitive projects and are constantly pressured to deliver, deliver, and deliver. Can you handle the stress?

- Do you have strong team-building and team-leadership skills? Teaming is the preferred method of operation in tens of thousands of companies today. Virtually no one works independently. Rather, you are engaged as a consultant to either participate on a team or lead that team. Do you have the requisite management, leadership, and communication skills to meet that requirement?

- Are you a talented marketer, confident, articulate, and self-motivated? Most consultants, other than those employed with the largest of consulting firms, must sell their consulting services as the first step in building new client relationships. As such, regardless of your area of specialization, you must be an astute marketer, able to quickly communicate your knowledge and expertise, and able to quickly demonstrate your value to a prospective client company that is considering engaging you for a particular assignment.

- Do you want to work as an independent consultant, or would you prefer to join an established consulting firm? This is perhaps the most critical of all questions.

If you choose a career as an independent consultant, you are choosing what many consider to be an entrepreneurial path. There will be no single employer writing your paycheck, no paid sick days, no paid holidays, and no benefits package. Rather, you will have to create your own opportunities through a combination of your marketing savvy, your client relationship-management skills, and your particular area of consulting expertise. What's more, you have to ask yourself whether you can live with the financial risk of self-employment and the roller-coaster of emotions that often follows along. You're "up" when you're working and "down" when you're not, and this can be particularly difficult for some individuals.

If, on the other hand, you choose to join a consulting firm, you are often getting the best of both worlds—the dynamic and constantly changing working environment that appeals to so many consultants, along with the stability of that biweekly paycheck from your employer (the consulting firm). Think long and hard about which consulting path will provide you with the best opportunities and the most satisfaction.

Today, consulting is a well-established and well-respected career path appealing to the professional, the manager, and the executive. Opportunities abound as companies have realized the tremendous financial and operational benefits consultants can bring to their organizations. It truly is a win-win situation for everyone involved. If you have the fortitude, the drive, and the expertise to position yourself as a consultant, you will find that the personal, professional, and financial rewards can be quite significant.

## Working as an Entrepreneur

Nations around the world have nurtured entrepreneurship in its various forms for centuries, but never before has there been such a phenomenal number of entrepreneurs, from small-business owners down the street to the Bill Gateses of today's technology revolution. It is vital that you be realistic in your expectations, knowing that the vast majority of entrepreneurs own small ventures and not mega-corporations. We are not seen on Oprah, not featured in *Time* magazine, and not rushing to the bank with our millions of dollars. Rather, we are hardworking individuals who have chosen an entrepreneurial career path for a diversity of personal and professional reasons.

Before you make the decision to launch an entrepreneurial venture, ask yourself the following questions:

- Are you a risk-taker?
- Can you live with the uncertainty of when you'll get your next paycheck? Do you have money saved?

- Can you work tirelessly for weeks and months on end? Do you have a high level of energy?

- Can you work through disappointments and lost opportunities, and continue to move forward?

- Are you confident, assertive, self-motivated, and self-reliant?

- Do you have the emotional support of your friends and family?

If you answered "yes" to these questions, you most certainly have the entrepreneurial grit, determination, and support system that are so vital for success. Without those qualities and an intense commitment, you'll face an almost insurmountable challenge.

Then ask yourself why you're considering entrepreneurship.

- If it's to escape the drudgery of a "9 to 5" job, *forget it!* "9 to 5" will seem like a vacation when you're self-employed.

- If it's to make a ton of money, *forget it!* No matter the business concept, no matter the marketing strategy, no matter your network of contacts, no matter anything, building a new venture costs money. It will take time—maybe six months, maybe three years, or maybe more—before you'll begin to see a steady stream of profits.

- If it's so that you can call your own shots, *forget it!* Although you might be profitably self-employed and think that you are running the show, the reality is that your customers or clients run the show. Now, instead of reporting to just your manager, you are reporting to each and every client that you work for. Your accountability increases, not decreases.

- If it's so that you can pick and choose which hours you want to work, *forget it!* You'll find that you're working all of them to meet client and project deadlines. Sure, it's easier to take a Friday off here and there, but only if your business continues to operate and respond to clients' needs in your absence.

- If it's to create a stable working environment, *forget it!* Entrepreneurship is a dynamic and forever-changing career path. You must be able to work fluidly, be willing to change as the market and your customers dictate, and be able to emotionally handle the constant flux in which you will find yourself.

Are you totally discouraged now? Don't be! Yes, there are uncertainties, long hours, lack of sleep, financial concerns, and tremendous commitments as an entrepreneur, but there are also tremendous advantages. As entrepreneurs and small-business owners ourselves, we cannot imagine doing anything else. Despite the many negatives, there is no other career path that would have been appropriate for either of us. Is it the same for you?

Work is such a huge part of our lives today that both personal and professional fulfillment are vital to the success of your career. Now, with such unlimited opportunities as an employee, consultant, or entrepreneur, you can pick and choose the path that is most closely aligned with your skills and long-term career objectives. Go forward with zest and determination, and make your career what you want it to be!

# The Three M's of Job Search Success

For true career fulfillment, you must focus yourself and your campaign on the three M's of job search success: *mindset, merchandising,* and *multichannel.*

## Mindset

Job search is sales, pure and simple. You have a product to promote (yourself) and you must create a strategic marketing campaign to sell that product. It is an active process to which you must commit your time, energy, and financial resources. No product is ever sold if it sits quietly on the shelf. It's all about market visibility—in the right places and at the right times.

Successful job search is also about having a clear vision of your value in the marketplace. With each passing day, the market becomes more competitive, and the candidates who manage their campaigns well are the candidates who receive the offers and opportunities. It is not necessarily the most qualified candidate who gets the position; it might instead be the individual who most effectively manages his or her search campaign. Therefore, you must clearly and concisely communicate your value because it is the foundation for your entire campaign and your market success. It is what prospective employers and recruiters will want to buy, so be clear in communicating what you are selling.

## Merchandising

Designing and writing powerful job search communications (for example, resumes, cover letters, career profiles, endorsements, follow-up letters, and thank-you letters) require a strong focus on merchandising your qualifications, achievements, successes, skills, and knowledge. In theory, you want to lay all of your experience on the table; then pick, choose, and merchandise those items that are most related to your current career objectives. Communicate *who you want to be* and not *who have you have been.*

Consider the following example for merchandising your resume. Assume you're a Chief Marketing Officer with three different objectives. Objective #1 is another CMO position; objective #2 is a COO/CEO position; objective #3 is an International Business Development position. How you merchandise your qualifications and expertise will vary significantly among the three versions so that you can bring to the forefront your core skills and experience most related to those three different objectives. For objective #1, your focus will be on your marketing expertise; for objective #2, on your leadership qualifications; and for objective #3, on your success in building international business relationships and ventures.

It is also critical that you appropriately merchandise your letters. Consider this: When writing your resume, you are taking your entire career and summarizing the most relevant points in a one- to two-page presentation. When that is complete, you will consolidate the high points of your resume and career into a two- to three-paragraph cover letter. Despite the fact that you are consolidating your skills and expertise, you must keep your focus on the core qualifications that will be most attractive to each prospective employer.

## Multichannel

An integrated job search campaign that uses multiple channels of distribution is a winning job search campaign. Use each and every channel that is appropriate for your search objectives. This should include networking, ad responses, targeted direct-mail and e-mail campaigns, Internet resume postings, Internet job postings, executive job lead reports, and much more. Think of your multichannel campaign as a wheel with many spokes, each of which is vital and each of which contributes to your overall ability to move your campaign forward.

Consider the three M's of job search success your new mantra and repeat the words over and over—*mindset, merchandising,* and *multichannel.* If you can effectively build your campaign around these concepts, you will be one of the fortunate ones whose search campaign is quick, efficient, and successful.

# Building Your Professional Job Search Community

When did it all become so confusing? It used to be just you and the company. Now, there are career coaches, career counselors, retained recruiters, contingent recruiters, resume writers, and outplacement consultants, to name just a few. It's like a traffic jam!

Building a strong job search community to support your efforts— today and in the future—is vital to your long-term career success. It is just as critical, however, to always remember that you are the leader of this initiative. Although you might receive a great deal of help and assistance from others, you are the one who must lead the way. The amount of energy, drive, and commitment that you invest in your job search and career is directly proportionate to the time and efforts others will contribute. To help you better understand who all the players are, what they do, and their potential value to your job search campaign, here is a brief summary of each of your potential job search partners.

## Career Coaches

The newest phenomenon in the employment industry, career coaching is an exciting and growing occupation. Just as professional athletes have coaches, so now can you. Career coaches push you on to victory, helping you to make the right decisions for yourself. They do not simply give you the answers, but rather they coach you to reach your own conclusions and take your own actions. They are there to

- Help you explore and better define your professional competencies
- Address personal issues that impact your career
- Help you clearly identify your career objectives
- Discuss and resolve obstacles to employment and career success
- Guide you in developing both short-term and long-range career strategies
- Assist you in developing, executing, and managing a successful job search campaign
- Prepare you to competitively interview for jobs, negotiate compensation, and evaluate job offers

In addition, many coaches offer services beyond your immediate job search and are available to support you throughout your career with ongoing guidance in long-term career planning, management, and advancement.

## Do You Need a Career Coach?

Are you clear about your objectives? Can you overcome the obstacles you are encountering? Are you marketing yourself effectively? If you answered no, you might consider hiring a career coach. Their services can be invaluable to facilitating your successful search campaign.

## What Should You Look for in a Coach?

When looking for a career coach, consider individuals with the following professional credentials:

Credentialed Career Master (CCM)
(see www.cminstitute.com)

Certified Career Management Coach (CCMC)
(see www.careercoachacademy.com)

Certified Career Coach (CCC)
(see www.careercoachinstitute.com)

Job & Career Transition Coach (JCTC)
(see www.careernetwork.org)

# Career Counselors

Career counseling is a well-established and well-respected industry that has existed far longer than career coaching. Career counselors tend to be

- Well-credentialed with graduate degrees, licenses, and professional certifications

- Qualified in the administration and interpretation of various career testing and assessment instruments (which provide valuable information as you plan your long-term career path)

- More focused on the "front end" of the search—career testing, assessment, analysis, and planning—than the "back end" of the search—resume writing and actual job search

- Highly skilled problem solvers, crisis managers, and facilitators, able to help you identify your career direction and proactively move forward

## Do You Need a Career Counselor?

Do you know what you're hard-wired to do? Do you know what motivates and excites you? Do you know your natural abilities, interests, behaviors, and values? Getting to know yourself can be a valuable tool for lifelong career success. Career counselors can help you find those answers.

## What Should You Look for in a Counselor?

When looking for a career counselor, consider individuals with the following professional credentials:

Nationally Certified Career Counselor (NCCC)

Nationally Certified Counselor (NCC)

Certified Professional Counselor (CPC)
(see www.napsweb.org)

Licensed Professional Counselor (LPC)
(designation offered by individual states)

> **NOTE:** The differentiation between career coaching and career counseling is becoming increasingly more vague, and there is significant crossover between these two areas of specialization. As such, we recommend that you speak with several coaches and/or counselors before making a choice as to who to work with. Most important is that you feel comfortable with that individual, they understand you and your needs, and they have the knowledge and resources to provide you with a realistic, step-by-step plan to career success and fulfillment.

# Retained (Executive) Recruiters

Always remember the guiding principle of job seeker and recruiter relationships: The recruiter is *never* working for you! The recruiter works for, and is paid by, the company that has hired them. As it should be, the recruiter's allegiance is to them. Never be fooled into thinking a recruiter is out there hustling on your behalf. This rarely happens.

With that said, retained recruiters are an outstanding addition to your job search community because they have the jobs! However, recruiters are of value to you only if you find the *right* recruiters, those that specialize in your profession or your industry. The closer the match, the better the chances of securing a new position with that recruiter's assistance. Remember, recruiters are hired to find a specific person with specific qualifications to perform specific tasks; they are not hired to find "you" a job.

### Do You Need Executive Recruiters?

If you are an executive job search candidate, the answer is yes! And the more you have in your corner, the better. There is no exclusivity in these relationships so work with as many recruiters as possible. The more who know about you, the greater the number of opportunities that may be presented to you.

### Finding Recruiters

To find recruiters who would be your best source of hiring leads, we recommend an extensive Internet search. Currently, there are more than 8,000 recruiters nationwide, so you need to do your homework in order for find the "right" recruiters for your job search—those that specialize in your particular industry and profession. One excellent resource is *Kennedy's Directory of Executive Recruiters* (www.kennedyinfo.com/db/db_der_bas.html), but we recommend that you do not limit yourself to just this one publication.

## Contingent Recruiters

Unlike executive recruiters, who are retained (and paid) by a company to manage their search process, contingent recruiters are paid only if they execute a successful placement. However, don't rule them out too quickly, even if you are a senior-level candidate. The world of recruitment has changed dramatically in the past few years, largely as a result of the Internet. One of the many changes is the crossover between contingent and retained recruiter assignments. Use any and all recruiters that specialize in your industry and profession. It makes no difference to you how they get paid!

## Resume Writers

Resume writers do more than just write resumes. They write cover letters, thank-you letters, career profiles, executive leadership profiles, broadcast letters, endorsements, and more. They are well-qualified professionals who are trained to get the attention of hiring managers, HR executives, and recruiters. A minor investment in having a professional prepare your resume can be worth thousands, sometimes even tens of thousands, of dollars by getting you in front of decision makers faster.

For the most impact, be sure that you work with a writer who has experience in your profession and industry. That way you will be certain that they know the *right* keywords, resume formats, and more that will get you noticed and not passed over.

### Do You Need a Resume Writer?

Does your resume focus on your career achievements and successes? Does it communicate your value? Does it have the *right* keywords and language? Can you "feel" the energy of the document? Is the visual presentation top-of-the-line? If you answered "no" to any of these questions, then, yes, you need a professional resume writer.

### What Should You Look for in a Resume Writer?

When looking for a resume writer, consider individuals with the following professional credentials:

Master Resume Writer (MRW)
(see www.cminstitute.com)

Certified Professional Resume Writer (CPRW)
(see www.parw.com)

Nationally Certified Resume Writer (NCRW)
(see www.nrwa.com)

Certified Resume Writer (CRW)
(see www.prwra.com)

Certified Electronic Resume Writer (CERW)
(see www.prwra.com)

## Outplacement Consultants

Outplacement was a relatively new industry that exploded onto the scene in the early and mid-1980s following the tremendous changes (downsizings and reorganizations) that occurred within the workplace. Best described as *one-stop shopping,* outplacement companies provide a wealth of services to transition the unemployed professional through the job search process to his or her new position. With an outplacement consultant, you get coaching and counseling as needed, resume writing assistance, training in interviewing and salary negotiations, contact information for companies and recruiters, and more. You might also get an office to work from, and receptionist and secretarial support services. For many senior-level job seekers, this is a service that can't be beat.

### Do You Need an Outplacement Consultant?

The answer to this question is not clear-cut because of the high price involved. What's more, many of the traditional outplacement services are no longer necessary for most executives, who now have their own PCs and are e-mail– and Internet-savvy. If your employer has offered to pay for your outplacement, ask yourself whether you actually need all that the outplacement company is offering. If yes, accept your employer's offer and take advantage of all that the outplacement company can do for you. If not, consider asking your employer to directly give you the money they would have invested in the outplacement company and allow you to use it as you feel appropriate in your own search campaign. If you decide to invest in outplacement yourself, be as certain as you can that the return will be well worth the investment.

### What Should You Look for in an Outplacement Consultant?

If you are considering hiring or working with a career services professional, check their qualifications and references to be sure that you are engaging an individual who

- Is well informed about your profession and your industry
- Has a track record of success working with other job search candidates with a similar background to yours
- Has solid credentials—professional certifications, licenses, publications, academic degrees, and more

## Building Your Job Search Success and Support Team

It is extremely difficult to achieve your goals in isolation. Knowing this, successful people constantly surround themselves with other successful and positive people to support the realization of their goals. Your job search is no different. You can either go it alone or benefit from the combined expertise and support of a team working with you to keep you positive and on track, to provide sound advice and honest feedback, and to help you set realistic goals and keep you accountable for them.

Your job search success team should be made up of individuals whose opinions you respect and who are positive, accessible, and straightforward. They should have insight, knowledge, or expertise that is in line with your career goals.

To begin, contact five to ten people you would like to have on your success team to discuss your situation and how you could benefit from their support. If they agree, simply arrange a mutually convenient time and regularly scheduled commitment to meet in person or via phone. They can review your resume and cover letter with an objective eye, make networking contacts on your behalf or share those leads with you, recommend alternative career options you might not have considered, provide valuable feedback, help you solve problems, and guide you toward action.

Who do you want on your success team?

- **Mentor.** If you have been fortunate enough to have developed a solid relationship with a mentor, this individual should serve as the foundation of your success team. Hopefully, this is someone who has known you well for years and is quite familiar with the depth and scope of your career, performance, knowledge, and achievements.

- **Past and present managers.** If you have had a particularly positive working relationship with any of your past managers, invite one to three of them to join your success team. Again, these individuals are familiar with your qualifications and can share career insights that might be obvious to them, yet not to you.

- **Professional peers.** This will generally be a large group of individuals from which you will need to select one to three people. When evaluating who to approach, consider the time they have available to assist you, other contacts they might have that could potentially be of value in your search campaign, and their particular style. Are they giving and supportive, or are they "all business" with little time left over?

- **Banker, accountant, or financial consultant.** These individuals can be valuable additions to your success team, particularly if they are well connected in the professional communities in which you plan to focus your search campaign. Further, because these individuals often work on a consulting or contractual basis with many clients, they might be aware of opportunities and career options that you might never have considered.

- **Vendors.** Vendors tend to know a great deal about what's going on internally at their client companies. Use this information to your advantage by inviting a vendor with whom you have a particularly strong working relationship to join your team and share his or her expertise with you.

- **Family and friends.** Think about who you know and who your family and friends know. The list might include people with whom you have never associated professionally, but know quite well from the golf course, country club, Rotary Club, condo association, day-care center, and the like. Carefully review this list of people to determine who would be valuable additions to your success team.

When assembling your success team, be sure you get a good mix of people. Your team will be of limited value if everyone comes from the same industry, same profession, or same geographic area. You want diversity of ideas and input. In addition, it is best to meet individually or in small groups of two to four. If you assemble everyone at once, it is often difficult to absorb all the valuable information each member has to share with you.

# Efficiency and Your Job Search

Managing your job search is just like managing any other project and business. You must create an administrative and organizational process that will allow you to operate efficiently and productively. Disorganization does not work for anything you do, and particularly not for your job search.

Following are some tips and strategies to consider as you create a system to manage the flow of contacts, resumes, follow-ups, interviews, and more as you proceed through your search campaign.

## Technology Is Not the Answer to Everything

Of course, it is an essential and tremendously valuable tool in your job search. In fact, managing a job search without technology is almost impossible in today's virtual market. However, not everything has to be automated! Wendy tells a story about an ongoing joke between her and one of her techie buddies that relates to the old-fashioned Rolodex that sits proudly on her desk. He hates it; she loves it. It takes her two seconds to find a phone number. Instead, he wants to automate it, so that every time she wants to look up a number, she has to go to her PC, open the program, type the name, and two minutes (not seconds) later, she'll have the phone number. Somehow, it just doesn't seem too efficient!

## Create Two Working Spaces Within the Same Room

Shelly uses two desks—one is her PC desk for all her writing, e-mail, Internet research, and so on; the other is where she talks on the phone, writes notes, keeps important files, and does administrative tasks. The desks are side-by-side, so she can easily reach from one to the other, but they are separate and distinct workstations. It allows her to keep all the stuff she needs to do on her PC separate from the stuff she needs to do at her desk. Each desk has a priority pile of items that must be addressed immediately (along with lots of other to-do piles that are not as time-sensitive). Try adopting this strategy or a similar strategy to help keep yourself well organized.

## Establish a Schedule

It is difficult to write a cover letter and e-mail a resume in response to a job posting when you are rushing madly so that you can make your 10 a.m. interview. To efficiently manage your time and obligations, you must establish and try to stick to a schedule. Consider this: Use the mornings as your quiet time when you can write cover letters and thank-you letters, send resumes, respond to e-mail messages, and other tasks that are best managed without any interruptions. Then set aside your afternoons for interviews, follow-up calls, networking, and other "outreach" activities. Or flip the schedules around if that works better for you. Whichever system you choose, try to set aside quiet time each day so that you can attend to whatever writing, editing, e-mailing, and other "distribution" activities you have to take care of. You will be amazed at how much more productive you will be.

But, remember, flexibility is vital. If you've established 3 p.m. to 5 p.m. as your designated writing time, yet you're invited for an interview at 4 p.m., I recommend you accept the invitation!

One other important note. If you are having difficulty reaching certain people, try calling at times other than the normal business day. You will be amazed how much easier it can be to reach someone at 7:30 a.m. or 6:00 p.m., when they are quietly sitting at their desks.

## Prioritize Your Incoming E-mail into Three Categories

Everyone is inundated with e-mail messages these days, and for many of us, it really is a problem. We get 50, 100, 200, or more e-mails each day to sort through. Why not try this system? Immediately delete all unsolicited e-mails, spam, and Viagra advertisements! Then quickly respond to those messages that you know will take only a minute or two to handle. Remember the organizational rule of peak performance: Handle it once and be done with it. Finally, work your way through the remaining messages, one by one, being sure to handle the top-priority ones first.

You probably have already developed some job search management strategies that work best for you. Try integrating some of the preceding suggestions into what you've already created and your search campaign will proceed even more efficiently. And the faster you move forward, the faster and more easily you'll find your next opportunity.

# Power Words and Thoughts to Drive Your Winning Job Search

The most important thing in your entire job search is having the right attitude. You must understand how to *play* the job search game, you must take control of the process, and you must move your career in the direction that you want. If you don't take control, someone else will. Then you will be left at the mercy of others, a place you definitely do not want to be. Putting yourself in that position can be disastrous, as anyone who's been laid off knows.

To help you find the right attitude and mindset that will lead you to success, we've outlined 20 power words and thoughts to drive your winning job search. These words summarize some of what we have discussed in this chapter, as well as some of the most critical information you will find in subsequent chapters.

### INDEPENDENCE: Who Do You Work For?

Yourself! Forever and always. No matter who writes your paycheck, consider yourself self-employed. Never be fooled into believing that your company considers you family. Those days are long gone.

### COMMITMENT: Job Search Is a Job!

The more time and energy you devote to your search campaign, the more resumes you get out, the more aggressively you network, and the more interviews you accept, the faster your search will proceed. If you're employed, commit yourself to 15 to 20 hours a week; if you're not currently working, 30 to 40 hours should be your minimum.

## MARKETING: Job Search Is Marketing

You have a product to sell—*yourself*. Approach your search as a marketing campaign, preparing accomplishment-oriented marketing communications (for example, resumes, cover letters, executive profiles, endorsements, thank-you letters, and broadcast letters) and using a multichannel distribution strategy (for example, networking, targeted e-mail campaigns, Internet postings, and ad responses).

## PREPAREDNESS: Start Now!

If you know that you are going to leave your current position, whether it will be in two weeks or nine months, start your search campaign now! Don't wait until you've already left your position. There will be too much downtime and too many lost opportunities.

## INTROSPECTION: Consult a Career Coach or Counselor

If you are uncertain as to your current career direction, your goals, your desires, and more, speak with a career coach or counselor. Before you launch your search campaign, take a step back and clearly define *who* you are and *what* you want. Your answers to those two questions are the entire foundation for your campaign. The more clear your objectives, the more clear your job search path and the faster your success.

## VERIFICATION: Get References on All Job Search Services

With the tremendous expansion in the job search industry, the number of firms offering job search services has exploded. Most are extremely reputable and provide consistently high-quality services. Others, however, have jumped on the bandwagon to take advantage of unsuspecting job seekers. Check references carefully to protect your dollars, integrity, and search campaign.

## STRUCTURE: Stick to a Schedule

Establish a schedule and stick to it. The more efficiently you manage the process of job search, the more quickly and easily you will find a new position—guaranteed!

## GLOBAL: Stress Your International Experience

The business world has globalized at an unprecedented pace and virtually every company wants to take advantage of each employee's experience working, living, traveling, and conducting business abroad. Be sure to highlight any and all international work experience, foreign-language skills, and cross-cultural background.

## VERSATILITY: Let Your Resume Work in Other Ways

Your resume is your personal marketing tool and has applicability well beyond your job search. Use it for consulting opportunities and interim positions, in business plans and capital financing proposals, or as part of your public speaking/press kit. You have already invested the time and energy to create a powerful marketing tool. Use it wisely and to your advantage!

## SELL, SELL, SELL: Sell It to Me...Don't Tell It to Me

In your resume, cover letters, interviews, and networking contacts, you have two options. You can (1) *tell* the facts or (2) *sell* the success. For example, you can *tell* your reader that you increased sales or you can *sell* the fact that you identified a new market, developed key accounts, and increased sales revenues by 45 percent within the first year!

## INNOVATION: There Are No Rules

The single most important concept in resume writing is that there are no rules, and that's precisely what makes the process so difficult. What you include and how you include it are entirely dependent on your current career objectives (and *not* your past career history). Your challenge is to create a resume that powerfully sells your skills, qualifications, and success for the type of position you are currently seeking.

## PERCEPTION: Paint the Right Picture

Our resume-writing motto is to *paint the picture of yourself that you want someone to see, while remaining in the realm of reality!* "Push" your reader in the right direction by highlighting the skills, experiences, and achievements you want to bring to the forefront and that are most relevant to your current career objectives. This might or might not be where most of your career experience has been!

## JUDGMENT: Age and Job Search

Do you include the fact that you graduated from college in 1964 when writing your resume? What about a job you held in 1962? Is your age closing the door before you get in for an interview? Remember, resumes are marketing tools and not career biographies. There are no rules stating that you must include the date you graduated from college or all of the positions you held early in your career. Use your judgment to determine what information gives you value on your resume and what detracts from your candidacy.

## THOROUGHNESS: Take Nothing for Granted

No one makes assumptions in job search. If you are attempting to communicate a specific message, spell it out. For example, don't assume that because you tell someone you managed international mergers and acquisitions, they will also know that you managed business relationships in eight different countries or personally negotiated a $12 million acquisition. Communicate everything that is vital and leave nothing to chance.

## TARGET: Targeted Direct Mail Can Work!

There is so much controversy about direct mail (paper, fax, or e-mail) that it is difficult to determine whether it is a reasonable search strategy. The answer is yes, it can work, but only if it's well targeted. Mailing thousands of resumes is *not* the answer. Mailings work only if you position yourself in front of the right companies and recruiters—people who would be interested in a candidate with your specific qualifications. This requires research and effort on your part to identify those target organizations, but the benefits can be phenomenal.

## REALITY: Let It Go!

You have all the qualifications for the position and know that you can do the job. However, for whatever reason, the company is not interested. Don't beat your head against the wall. Don't waste your time writing letters or making phone calls. There is nothing that you can do or say that will change their minds. Let it go and move on to more promising opportunities.

## PATIENCE: Interview #1

The *only* purpose of interview #1 is to get an invitation for interview #2. With the increased complexity of job search, it is extremely rare that you will ever be offered a position after only one interview. Your challenge, therefore, is to impress your interviewer, favorably position yourself against other candidates, and get on the short list. That's it!

## PROBLEM-SOLVING: Thank-You Letters That Solve and Sell

Are thank-you letters simply a formality? No! They are an excellent tool to demonstrate the value you bring to a company based on the specific needs and issues the hiring manager communicated to you during your interview. Use your letter to *sell* the fact that you can solve their problems, meet their challenges, and deliver impressive results.

## PERSPECTIVE: Life Is More Than Work

When you're in the midst of a job search and consumed by its activity, it is often difficult to remember that life is more than just your career. Take a deep breath and put it all back into perspective. A healthy mindset leads to a successful and profitable search campaign.

# CHAPTER 2 How to Plan Your Career

For most people, career planning is one of the most difficult challenges they will ever face. There are so many options today that it is often difficult to decide which career track is right for you. When we're young and idealistic, we have great expectations for what we want to do and what we want to accomplish. However, life often takes us down a different path than we originally intended, and many often find themselves in jobs and careers that they never planned to pursue.

We've always admired engineers, mathematicians, and other "analytical" types, most of whom knew right from the start where they were headed. You found them at age 6 tinkering with batteries and wires in the garage; you then find them at age 36 tinkering with larger and more expensive batteries and wires at work. It's as though they were programmed from birth to pursue a specific career path.

For many of the rest of us, it might not be that clear-cut or straight-forward. You might have studied economics in college and now work as a technology sales representative. Or maybe you majored in philosophy and now manage a territory of restaurants. Many people simply fall into their career tracks. They graduate from college and accept a job with some company—any company—to launch their career. Years later, perhaps with the same company or not, they might find themselves in a career track that is far removed from their original goals and they don't know how to get out. At that point, the money might be decent, they're accustomed to the lifestyle, and it's often difficult to make a career change.

All of that leads us back to the purpose of this chapter—giving you guidance, support, and advice on how to build a career that will bring you personal and professional rewards, fulfillment, and satisfaction. If you calculate the number of hours you will work over your lifetime, the total is staggering. Doesn't it make sense to spend all of that time doing what you enjoy instead of feeling as though you're an indentured servant? In today's fast-paced, global economy, if you don't take control of your career, who will? You certainly don't want to leave your career choices in the hands of your employer(s), who no longer have the long-term commitment to their employees that they had in years past.

If you're one of those fortunate people who really knows *who* you are and where you will thrive, you're already one step ahead of the game. If you understand what makes you tick, what excites you, and where you can best contribute, you will have positioned yourself for a long and successful career. If you are uncertain about your goals and objectives, it is critical that you devote time and energy to introspection and self-analysis. The information you glean will be the foundation for your lifelong career plan. You have to figure out who you are; no one else will.

As you read the following interviews with HR executives, hiring managers, and recruiters, you will be introduced to some of their best strategies and advice for taking control of your career and making great things happen.

□ □ □

# Developing a Successful Career Plan

**Tim Moran**

*Director—Corporate Staffing*

*Hallmark Cards, Inc., Kansas City, MO*

We first met Tim Moran when we were fortunate enough to hear him speak at the 2003 Career Masters Institute Conference in Kansas City. Listening to Tim for 90 minutes, we all sat in amazement as we heard wonderful stories about the remarkable corporate culture of Hallmark and the caliber of its workforce. Later, when we met with Tim to interview him for this book, we wanted to know what he considers to be the most critical facets of developing and managing a successful career plan. He summarized his comments around four key points:

- Introspection
- Assessment
- Company fit
- Motivation

## Introspection

Tim believes the most difficult part of career planning is introspection. Each person must closely and honestly evaluate themselves and what they enjoy doing. Tim has found that the best candidates he has selected, interviewed, and hired understand what makes them tick and what they have a talent and passion for. They understand what it will take to grow their careers. The best candidates don't stumble through the interview process with just the memorized answers to the questions. They are not intimidated; they are confident. It's not that they have to "get it right" the first time, either. It's that they try and do the best they can.

Take the time to understand who you are, what you like, and what you need to do in order to plan and move your career forward. Then, when you contact Tim or any other corporate recruiter or headhunter, be able to quickly and accurately articulate what you want. The most positive exchanges during the interview are when candidates take control, know what skills they bring to the table, and know what types of positions they are qualified for.

## Assessment

Tim is also a big proponent of assessment tools and believes the feedback can be quite valuable in clarifying who you are and what you want. There are scores of assessments available today—both online and on paper—that will provide you with information about your personality, occupational interests, skills, aptitudes, values, and much more. Everyone has special talents. Some people are great with numbers and focus their careers in finance and accounting. Others have outstanding interpersonal skills and can influence people. They become sales professionals, managers, and business leaders. Positively exploit your talents to the best of your ability and you will find yourself well positioned for a long and successful career.

## Company Fit

Another key component for planning and moving your career forward is finding the right company—a company that provides you with opportunities to do the things you like—a company that fits your background and abilities—a company with the same values. A 90 percent fit with an organization is great and will most likely ensure your success with the company. Conversely, if it's a 10 percent fit, you probably won't last long.

## Motivation

The final component in Tim's equation for successful career planning is your level of motivation. Are you continually updating your skills, attending training programs, being involved in professional associations, or participating in other activities that will expand your knowledge base and your network? Reading, learning, and networking will help you not only further clarify your core skills, but also demonstrate a strong level of motivation and interest in more than just your 9 to 5 job. Tim, like anyone else, wants to interview and hire people who are interested in doing their best and being the best they can be.

As time progresses and your career moves forward, you'll mature and build confidence in yourself. Where your career begins today is most likely *not* where it will be in 10 years or 20 years. Careers are evolutionary and, over time, you'll gain a much clearer understanding of where you belong in the working world and where you get the most personal and professional satisfaction.

□ □ □

# Creating a Personal-Inventory Career Plan

**Valerie Kennerson**
*Director—Global Staffing*
*Corning, Incorporated, Corning, NY*

A vital component to any successful career plan is a clear understanding of your personal interests, characteristics, attitudes, behaviors, values, and more. To help us better appreciate the importance of these items to long-term career planning, we spoke with Valerie Kennerson, who outlined some outstanding points that each and every job seeker should consider.

Valerie recommends you begin your career-planning efforts by developing a personal inventory that addresses each of the following items:

1. What do you feel, need, and desire in your next position? Are you looking to work in an environment where you are micromanaged, or macromanaged? What do you want in a boss or supervisor?

2. What type of organization do you want to work for? If you are currently interviewing, do you believe the company's vision can lead it into the future? Do you understand the culture of the company and the department in which you will be working? What do you need from the company that will make it a good fit for you?

3. What do you want to gain from your next position? Do you want more flexibility, better pay, less travel, a shorter commute, work/life balance, or what?

4. What are the "must-have's" that you cannot give up, and what are the things that you can be flexible about? You might be comfortable taking a lower level of compensation in a new position if the opportunity exists for rapid promotion. Only you know the right balance.

5. What are your personal and professional strengths and weaknesses? It is critical that you be able to accurately identify these. They are the foundation for your long-term career success.

6. What perceived threats exist in the position, the company, and the industry? The Internet has made it so easy to research this type of information. A quick Google search can uncover so much. Then ask yourself how these threats could potentially impact you and outline your proposed response to each situation. Inevitably, you probably won't come up with solutions that ensure a 100 percent comfort level, but rather, a solid margin of comfort and ease.

Once you've created your personal inventory, realize that it's always a work in progress and commit to updating it every 6 to 12 months. As time passes and your career grows, your personal inventory will also evolve.

Valerie brought to our attention another critical component of career planning—an individual's mindset. She firmly believes that in order to proactively manage your career, you must assume full responsibility. Although your company might provide opportunities for training, education, and career growth, it is entirely your own responsibility to analyze your career on a regular basis, identify any gaps, and determine what you can do to fill those in. You are the commander of your own career. Know what makes you tick, learn what you can, ask questions, and build your own value.

□ □ □

# Five Key Career-Planning Tools

**Joseph R. Hammill**
*Manager—Corporate Talent Acquisition*
*Xerox Corporation, Rochester, NY*

When we approached Xerox to interview one of its top human resources executives, we had no idea that we would have the privilege of interviewing Joe Hammill, who manages Corporate Talent Acquisition Initiatives. It was an engaging and thoughtful interview with insights from an organization that has been well known and well respected for generations.

Our interview with Joe focused on the five career-planning tools he believes are invaluable in identifying your right career path and finding satisfaction and fulfillment.

## Job Fit and Organizational Fit

The balance between job fit and organizational fit is most important when determining what types of positions you are most qualified for. You need to be clear about your skill sets and motivating factors in order to find a company whose culture, people, and values are most closely aligned with yours. If this fit can be optimized, you will find yourself in a truly great career position.

## Workplace Adaptation

Workplace adaptation, successful orientation to the new organization, has also emerged as a critical facet of effective corporate hiring. In years past, a recruiter's job was to find a candidate and simply facilitate a successful hire. With the new emphasis on adaptation, recruiting organizations now are challenged to help facilitate each new employee's success within the organization. Often referred to as "on-boarding," it's big stakes these days whenever you're hiring, and particularly when you're hiring for a top-level management or executive position.

## Corporate Web Sites

More and more companies are investing in their corporate Web sites. As a result, they can provide a wealth of critical information to any job seeker. You can read about products, services, financial and stock performance, the executive team, business operations, and so much more. This information will give you an excellent perspective of the company and what they need/want in their employees. Then use that information to evaluate how your skills, experience, and background complement their organization. You can also register, and apply for, positions through a corporate Web site and exercise various options on building a relationship with a prospective employer or employee.

Company Web sites are no longer static; they are moving and living entities able to communicate a wealth of valuable information and establish candidate/employer relationships.

## Intra-Organizational Networking

For candidates looking to work for a specific company, the single best approach is to network and talk to people within the company of interest. Building a meaningful network of people who have an understanding of the organizational culture and of your character can be invaluable in opening doors and getting interviews far ahead of others who might be applying by sending resumes online or through the mail. What's more, those contacts can often give you valuable information about the company and its objectives, values, hiring requirements, and more.

## Work/Life Balance

Xerox is well respected for its dedication to work/life balance and well known for its unique policies to uphold its commitment. These flexible policies have created a wonderful attitude and culture throughout the company. Whenever you are looking for a new position, you must consider the impact it will have on your own work/life balance. The level of commitment varies greatly from one company to another, and you must work to find an organization that matches your own particular needs. Some companies offer flexible schedules, innovative working arrangements, and other incentives that encourage work/life balance. Other companies might want their employees to work 10, 12, or more hours a day, yet compensate them extremely well. All successful companies look for strong and dedicated contributors. You need to find the balance that is just right for you and your family.

□ □ □

# Knowing Your Skills and Competencies

**Stephen Lopez**
*Vice President—Support Services*
*National Board of Medical Examiners, Philadelphia, PA*

Knowing who you are and what you can do is one of the most critical factors in planning a successful career path. To understand the real importance of truly appreciating your skills, competencies, capabilities, and assets, we turned to Steve Lopez for his insights.

When planning your career, take the time necessary to do a complete inventory of your skills and competencies. Steve used this strategy himself when, early in his career, he realized that his people skills were as strong as his technical qualifications. What's more, he realized that it was his people skills that would accelerate his career within the technology industry. By clearly focusing on his skills checklist—what he had and what he did not have—he was able to move his career along much more easily and more rapidly than most. He understood how to parlay his strengths into career advantages.

Early on, when people fall into specific academic curricula or career paths, they tend to think that they are tied to that one career track. Frequently, they plateau and get bored. Understanding your skills and doing a periodic inventory can help you better understand where you are in your career and where you want to go. It takes a great deal of time, but will be well worth the effort.

Once you have clearly identified your core skills, identify those additional skills you will need to meet both your short-term and long-term career goals. If you need additional training or academic credentials to move forward, plan how, when, and where you are going to acquire these skills. Try to identify new roles that will be available in your company, understand what you will need to do to be qualified for those positions, and then work to develop these skills and qualifications.

Steve has also benefited greatly from his coaching and mentoring relationship. When he reached his senior role in his company, the organization arranged for him to work with a professional coach. Steve found this to be a particularly rewarding experience, learning that others might not perceive your skills in the same manner in which you do. He recommends that you learn to balance your skills assessment with how others perceive your skills. You can also use your performance reviews as a way in which to identify how the company views your skills, strengths, and weaknesses. Then, add in an occasional conversation with your boss about your skills and performance, and you will have a wealth of feedback upon which to draw.

A quick warning to any recent graduates and young professionals reading this book: Younger people in the workforce often believe they can tackle anything. Their limitations are not always readily apparent to them early in their careers. This is natural because their skills and capabilities have not been fully tested. Steve recommends that they give themselves time to develop a true understanding of their skills, capabilities, and interests, and how and where to best apply them.

□ □ □

# You and Your "Right" Career Track

**Dr. Beverly Kaye**
*Founder and CEO*
*Career Systems International, Sherman Oaks, CA*

We are honored to have had the opportunity to interview Dr. Beverly Kaye for this book. Twenty-five years ago, Dr. Kaye developed a career model while working on her doctoral dissertation, which looked at how organizations view careers and how they help their employees develop their careers. Since then, she has been using this model with great success while working with companies across the country. Her model can be referred to as the "5 P's" for career success:

- Person
- Perspective
- Place
- Possibilities
- Plan

## Person

People have to be able to articulate their skills, competencies, interests, and values. They need to understand and explain the way they like to work, the culture that is right for them, and how they perform at work. The better you understand these things about yourself and are able to describe them with enthusiasm, the easier your career-planning process will be.

## Perspective

It's wonderful to get to know yourself and see yourself through the eyes of others. You can say, "I think I'm good at _____ . Do you see me that way?" Ask many people lots of different questions and you'll get a great *perception check* of yourself. Otherwise, how do you know?

## Place

You must understand the greater world of work and how you fit into it. You must appreciate the fact that things keep changing—industries, jobs, your profession, and more. Ask yourself whether you have developed the right skills to handle all of these changes.

## Possibilities

Think about multiple options. "If I can't do this, then I can do that." A savvy careerist in a company needs to think about the six options that enable people to successfully leverage their careers:

- Lateral
- Enrichment
- Versatile
- Explanatory
- Realignment
- Relocation

You must always be thinking about these things and not be caught by surprise. If you do your homework, the shifting in an organization will be easier for you to manage and you won't be disheartened by organizational changes.

## Plan

Ask yourself, "What do I have to do to pursue these possibilities?" Then create a plan of action and follow through. There is nothing more valuable in your career-management effort than a strong foundation and plan. If you are a loner, sit down and put together your strategy. Or buy a career book and work your way through the exercises. If you are not a loner, find a support group willing to help and guide you.

When developing your plan, here are some questions you might consider:

- Ask your boss and peers what you could do more of, or continue doing, to serve them better.
- Tell your colleagues that you have been thinking about your competencies and have outlined them as your strongest skills. What do they think of your list?
- Appreciate the fact that others may see you differently than you see yourself. Ask them for more information so that you can get a better sense of how others perceive you. This information can be invaluable in your long-term career planning and discovery efforts.

Dr. Kaye has developed workshops, training seminars, and an entire coaching practice based on these 5 P's, and they seem to work no matter what changes are happening. The lesson here is to do your homework and mind your 5 P's!

□ □ □

# Selecting a Position and Culture That Are Right for You

**Joel Greengrass**
*Vice President—People and Learning*
*Equinox Fitness, New York, NY*

Joel Greengrass shared his insights about how best to select a profession and pursue your occupation. His insights are invaluable for selecting a corporate culture and position that are right for you.

The very first step in planning your career—identifying and writing down your career goals—is one that many people simply gloss over and ignore altogether. That's a huge mistake! Knowing your goals is critically important and can serve as the framework for your entire career. Start by writing down what you like and dislike about your current job (or a job under consideration). If you are interviewing, your interviewer will want to know that you are committed to the company and to the position. If the company does not embrace who you are, they most likely do not share your values. Not every job is right for you and you are not right for every job. It is much better to discover this during the interview process than after you've started the new position.

Weigh your career possibilities and put what you want in writing so that you have a tool to help guide your career growth. This list is for you and not for a prospective employer. When an offer or multiple offers come in, you can then evaluate them against your list. How long will the commute be? What are the responsibilities of the position and the long-term opportunities with the company? Attempt to measure the offer, company, and position against what you love to do and what you would like to do in the future.

Here's a strategy that you can use to review specific offers. Identify something you want to do and then write down your strengths and skills and the skills required for the position. Is there a gap? Even if there is a gap, don't totally dismiss the opportunity immediately. Rather, carefully evaluate the gap and think about how you could close it and whether you would want to invest in closing it. Then you can make a rational decision about whether the opportunity is right for you.

Another important consideration when determining what career path to pursue, and where to pursue it, is your set of values. It is critically important that your values match the company's values, or there will be conflict or a total disconnect at some point during your employment. When attempting to identify your specific values, look at life outside of work. Consider your home, your lifestyle, books and magazines you read, television shows you enjoy, and other things that inspire and represent you. You might even consider making a display of these items, which will allow you to actually visualize your values. Consistent patterns may evolve that you never realized until you had the chance to actually see your visual values representation.

Now, take that information and go interview. Be sure to interview with at least three to five people at each company. The more you get to know the people, the more the culture and values of the organization will emerge. A company that really lives its mission and values will pass those values through to its employees. As such, the company's values must be congruent with yours in order to ensure a good fit and long-term employment.

□ □ □

# Focusing Your Career on Your Values and Principles

**Mary Jane Koch**
*Senior Vice President—Strategic Business Resources*
*National Rural Telecommunications Cooperative, Herndon, VA*

We asked Mary Jane to share her insights about the critical topics of values and principles and how they impact a person's lifelong career planning and satisfaction.

Mary Jane believes that things that you value *are* your principles and that your behavior must be in line with your values. People should ask themselves what their dreams are, what makes them happy, what they want to do, and where they want to live. If a great career opportunity is waiting for you in Michigan, but you don't like cold weather, will you enjoy living in Michigan even if the job is great?

Begin planning your career by taking an inventory of yourself. What do you bring to the table, what attitudes do you convey, are you willing to try new things, and are you willing to do whatever it takes? Do you come across to others as genuine and caring, or more like a prima donna?

Hiring managers consider many factors in the selection process. One of the most critical is to determine what types of players he or she wants in the organization or on his or her team. A team player who has less education or fewer skills and might need to be developed more for the position, but has a great attitude and a burning desire to succeed, might be the preferred hire over a prima donna who has a stronger skill set but a less-than-promising attitude. If the candidate needs additional training, a company will often provide it. When these individuals work hard, they gain more knowledge and develop the capacity to function at a higher level. In turn, they are generally loyal employees because the company has invested in them.

Most people know about good and bad; it's an inherent part of many people's internal make-up since they were young children. We were all taught about the "Golden Rule" as children as we learned what was acceptable and "good" behavior and what was not. However, values and principles need to be learned and are an integral part of everyone's personal growth. Focus on the "Golden Rule" and live the values and principles in the way you behave, what you do, and how you interact with others.

Mary Jane values the following principles:

- **Trustworthiness and integrity.** Do what you say you will do. If you say that you are honest, Mary Jane doesn't want to hear that you massaged your expense report!

- **Fairness and consistency.** Treat everyone by the same rules. Unless someone has proven themselves to be unfair or inconsistent, you should treat them with the same level of respect you would anyone else.

When you think about values, think about what trust means. Do others trust you? Are people afraid of you? If people are afraid of you, they will not be able to trust you. If a person does not foster trust and is not consistent with positive behavior, his or her employment may be short-lived.

A leader with strong principles and values helps people grow and develop. A strong leader believes in accountability and will hold others to it. Many times a person who is intimidating can even be perceived that way by their boss, who may, at times, back off because the person is so strong. A person who creates fear can be like a kicking horse that creates a circle of freedom around themselves. A good boss needs to be willing to break into that circle and stop the behavior, because a person who divides others is not an asset to any organization. Their skills might be needed, but not their negative influence.

If you are currently in an active job search, be sure to pay attention to the values of each organization with which you interview. Walk around and talk to employees. Does the culture feel right for you? Does the company offer a trusting environment that rewards teamwork? What are the internal values of the organization? What is important to the organization? What is it like to work there? Then be sure to communicate to your interviewer what you are looking for in a company—open communication, opportunities for growth, a commitment to excellence, and whatever other values are essential to your success.

Prior to her current position with the National Rural Telecommunications Cooperative, Mary Jane worked with Stephen Covey and learned very clearly how important it is to appreciate and live *The 7 Habits of Highly Effective People.* Here they are briefly:

Habit 1: Be Proactive

Habit 2: Begin with the End in Mind

Habit 3: Put First Things First

Habit 4: Think Win/Win

Habit 5: Seek First to Understand, Then to Be Understood

Habit 6: Synergize

Habit 7: Sharpen the Saw

Mary Jane strongly recommends the 7 Habits to everyone, believing that if people live by these strong values and principles, they will be much more successful in their jobs and in their careers.

□ □ □

# Using Your Past Accomplishments to Pave the Way to Future Success

**Darryl L. King**

*Vice President—Business Development*

*Neoware Systems, Inc., King of Prussia, PA*

With more than 40 years of combined experience in the careers and employment industry, we both know how important past achievements are in predicting future success. If you have already proven yourself a winner, there is no reason for anyone to think you will do any less than win again. It is a marvelous position to be in. And, to best demonstrate how your past accomplishments can work for you, we spoke to Darryl King, who shared his personal background and how critical it has been to his career success.

Darryl attended Rice University in Houston, where he excelled in track and field. He was the first Black American to be inducted into the Hall of Fame for track and field, was All American, won three conference championships, and was ranked #4 in the nation for the high hurdle. When asked why he was so successful, he shared seven personality traits he considered vital:

- Persistence
- Determination
- Sense of who you are
- Optimism
- Dependability
- Positive attitude
- Flexibility

Darryl believes his sports career positioned him early to be motivated and focus on being the best he could be. He feels that people need to be driven and highly motivated to truly succeed in any venture, project, effort, or activity. One must truly believe in oneself and great things can happen. When Darryl first started competing, he was told he was too skinny, too slow, and did not have the "right" muscle type. What he did have was heart and the drive to achieve. As the first-ever Black American to be inducted into Rice University's Hall of Fame, he certainly proved the critics wrong.

"If people have a purpose and a single-mindedness, it allows them to achieve despite challenges and disappointments. In fact, disappointments and small failures can help keep you focused on your goals and what is needed to achieve," Darryl commented.

In his business career, this type of focus and determination has been the foundation for his success. He has always kept his eyes on his goals, working harder, longer, and smarter. In essence, he has taken his natural abilities, channeled them in a new direction, and enjoyed equal success and recognition.

In closing, Darryl felt it was important to mention that he had encountered many people in business who were smarter and more talented than he, but without a sense of determination, an optimistic view, and specific goals, they were not able to achieve. Defining your purpose will keep you on track through the good times and the bad.

□ □ □

# Movin' On Up

### Christopher Bargeron
*Director of Employee Communications and Development*
*Silicon Graphics, Inc., Eagan, MN*

All too often, job seekers believe that in order to advance in their careers, they need to leave their current employers and find opportunities elsewhere. Knowing that great positions can exist within an employee's current company, we wanted to find out how a candidate can best position himself or herself to achieve their career goals within their current organization. For that information, we turned to Christopher for his expertise in employee development and advancement.

Christopher began his interview by stressing the fact that *change brings opportunity*. So many companies are experiencing dramatic internal changes these days, but that does not negate the fact that it is also a great time for people within companies to look at opportunities to develop their careers within those organizations.

There are many ways for people to structure their career growth to take on new opportunities and to move their career paths forward. Changes in the economy and in industries can result in jobs being eliminated and, as such, there is a certain degree of risk. However, that change can also result in new opportunities within an organization, not simply a reduction in force. When people have a clear vision of themselves and know where they are headed 5 to 10 years from now, they can look at the specific action steps needed in order to develop their careers. When people know themselves, they can see their goals more clearly and, in turn, they can *own* their careers.

The time is long gone when someone worked for an organization for their entire career and then got their gold watch. It is now up to each individual professional to figure out what they want and how to get there. If someone is dissatisfied in their career, frustration can keep them from seeing the opportunities that are right in front of them. Time spent focusing on being frustrated and unhappy will not advance anyone's career!

To ensure that does not happen to you, consider Christopher's sage advice:

1. **Start with a reality check.** Planning your future is a subjective experience, so the more realistic you are, the more quickly you will advance in your career. People move at different rates in learning and career advancement. Look at skill-based learning opportunities to develop the core competencies you will need to move forward. Plan how you would like to experience and achieve that growth.

2. **Create your vision.** Simply put, this means determining what role you would like at work and how you will get there.

3. **Evaluate your capabilities.** Consider the capabilities that you think you need to have to get to that career path successfully. Look at the people who have the job that you want. Ask for an informational interview to learn more about the position and specific responsibilities. Then determine what skills you will need to acquire in order to advance into that position and start developing those specific skill sets immediately.

4. **Take advantage of training opportunities within your organi-zation.** Today, many companies offer employee-development programs to help their personnel develop and advance. If your company does not, consider outside training programs, formal educational programs, certificate programs, volunteer work, and more. Some employers offer tuition reimbursement, but be prepared to spend some of your own money if necessary to acquire that additional training to ensure that you develop the skills to prepare you for your next promotion.

5. **Build relationships.** Building relationships is extremely important. Good relationships with bosses and supervisors are key because they are often the gatekeepers to additional opportunities. In addition, develop a relationship with someone in human resources who works with your piece of the organization. Be sure they get to know you, your skills, and your long-term career goals.

6. **Think beyond your boss.** If your immediate boss is not supportive of your career goals, there may be other relationships you can develop to help counterbalance how your boss perceives you. Consider developing a relationship with a manager one level up from your boss. Many senior leaders want to know the people within their organization. If you have a meeting scheduled with your next-level manager, make sure that meeting is not just, "I wanted to say hi and get to know you." Rather, make your time with this person valuable for both of you by having a focused agenda. Know what you want the meeting to focus on and be prepared to share your knowledge of the organization, your core skills and competencies, and areas in which you can make a difference.

7. **Find a mentor.** Mentors are an important part of career growth, more so now than ever before. Some companies do not have formal classes to assist in career growth; in this situation, mentors can be especially helpful in moving your career forward.

8. **Deal with your problems now.** If you are facing challenges in your personal or professional life that are impacting your career, address them. It is better to let someone know that you are facing a difficult situation sooner than later. Obviously, it is best to find solutions to your problems before they affect your work performance. If possible, go to your boss and explain the situation. If for some reason you cannot do this, go to the human resources manager. How you deal with problems will have a great effect on how successfully your career will evolve and mature.

In closing, Christopher reminded us that internal candidates often have a great advantage over external candidates, even external candidates with stronger skills. The organization already knows you, and this can place you in an extremely advantageous position. If you work to develop your skills, increase your visibility within the organization, and build strong relationships across all levels of your company, you will find that you are a prime candidate for future career opportunities!

□ □ □

# Personal Career Management

**Peter Weddle**
*Editor and Publisher*
*WEDDLE's, Stamford, CT*

Peter Weddle's name is familiar to many. He is a well-respected authority on career management, with a particular expertise in online job search. Our discussion with him was fascinating and focused on what he considers the most essential component in long-range career development: a personal career management plan.

Peter began his interview by outlining one essential concept—the fact that everyone has two distinct jobs:

- Performing your profession, craft, or trade
- Proactively managing your career

The global economy is changing at a remarkable rate, faster than ever before in the history of our nation or any other nation. As a result, business has changed. We have all felt the repercussions of company downsizings, reorganizations, mergers, acquisitions, expansions, turnarounds, recoveries, and more. As organizations adjust to keep pace in our competitive market, so do jobs, workforce requirements, skill requirements, and more.

Today's working environment is fraught with volatility. Both companies and individuals need to strategize how they can best respond to this volatility. The people and organizations who are the most adaptive will be the ones that survive. You must recognize that change is a constant and that in order to survive and thrive, you must take charge of your career. If you do not proactively manage your career, it will manage you, with potentially devastating consequences.

Perhaps the most dramatic change in each individual's ability to manage their career has resulted from the emergence of the Internet and the abundance of information that is available to everyone. Years ago, career-related information was difficult to acquire.

Today, with a quick search of the Internet, you can find a wealth of information about companies, services, products, technologies, job openings, and so much more. Now, for the first time in history, people can efficiently have access to all this information and, in turn, take real control of their careers.

## Your Personal Career Management Plan

Now, here's where the concept of the personal career management plan comes into play. This is how Peter defines it:

- Understanding what gives you joy and satisfaction at work
- Appreciating what you can do and accomplish within the constraints of what you are good at
- Knowing your motivations, skills, and abilities

After 20 to 35 years working, all too many people get to a point in their careers where they find they are unhappy and hate their work. It is often the first time that they really start to think about what they are doing and what they really want to do. After years and years of being in a position that was not satisfying or fulfilling, they need courage and support to move in a different direction and pursue what they really want to do. They need to develop a plan and a strategy and understand the dynamics of the career field that they have selected and the opportunities that are available. In today's employment market, perhaps more so than ever before, it's important to give yourself permission to look at new careers and new opportunities.

Peter also strongly recommends that you acquire as much help as possible in defining your career and developing your own personal career management plan. You can hire a professional career coach or counselor, talk with your friends and colleagues, network, contact your college alumni office, and get as much feedback as possible. Test, probe, and push outside your comfort zone to see all that is available. Proactive career management is a financial, psychological, and emotional investment. Unlike the money we spend on cars, vacations, and videos, however, the ROI on your career planning and management efforts can be a lifetime of satisfaction, growth, fulfillment, and reward.

If you are fortunate enough to work in an environment where your manager is encouraging and supportive, you can often find a great ally to help move your career forward and meet your personal career management plan objectives. This is a win-win situation for both parties; the company and manager want to keep talented employees in their organization, while you want to advance your career.

While on the job, be the best you can be and work to achieve the highest and most fulfilling levels of performance in your chosen field. That applies to all jobs—including janitors, retail sales clerks, and construction workers—not just the high-paying ones. Over the course of your life, the time you will spend working is considerable. Just think how much more satisfied you will be if you are working in a position that you enjoy and find rewarding. To do that, however, you have to know yourself and select your career path accordingly.

## Tactical Issues

Once your personal career management plan is in place, you must address some tactical issues. You must acquire the necessary skills to support your career change, network with your colleagues and with others outside your normal sphere of relationships, use the Internet to research opportunities and collect information, have your references in order, prepare your resumes and cover letters, and be interview-ready.

The best jobs come and go at a fast pace, and recruiters want you to be ready to interview on the spur of the moment. This is where your personal career management plan—your 24/7 toolkit for success—comes into play. Although a good plan is a living (and, therefore, changing) document, it should always be complete enough to help you take care of your professional life and move your career in the direction you want.

Bear in mind that there are different dimensions of being in charge of your career. When leaving college, you might not know where you are headed, and your job choices might be experimental. As you mature and spend more and more time working, you will begin to get a much clearer understanding of what type of work and what type of organization gives you the most satisfaction. Even then change is possible, even likely, so use the plan to stay prepared.

The worst time to plan your career is during a crisis situation. Having your plan at the ready, in contrast, will keep you in control of that change instead of being its victim. It will be the platform for success that leads you to memorable and rewarding career opportunities.

▢ ▢ ▢

# Balancing Your Life Objectives with Your Career Goals

### Charles W. Broach

*Human Resources Business Partner*
*Ford Motor Company, Norfolk, VA*

One of the most daunting tasks in planning and managing your career is finding a position that allows you to merge your career goals with your life objectives. To better understand this concept and how to achieve it, we turned to one of Ford Motor Company's human resources professionals. Here are some of his insights.

First and foremost, Charles believes you must follow your interests and your heart. This will give you the best chance of succeeding in your career and pushing the extra mile. And pushing the extra mile is what will set you apart from other people in your organization and get you recognized within your company. It is a lot easier to work extra hours when you are doing something that you love.

Following your heart will also allow you to move fluidly through your career and stick with it over the long haul. If you do not follow your heart and your interests, you will suffer through the years and always wonder "what if?"

When evaluating your various career opportunities and interests, follow your first instinct and think about what makes you happy, fulfilled, and comfortable. Frequently, people focus their career choices on salary, take a job that is not right for them, and shortly end up looking for other opportunities. Determine what is important to you, your family, and your work/life balance, and let those characteristics be a key component in your career planning efforts.

If you are able to achieve work/life balance, the quality of your work will improve noticeably. Employers seek out employees who have balance, are willing to work hard and perform exceptionally well, and yet are committed to their home and family lives. Certain career choices will help you find the level of balance that is important to you. For Charles, getting home to his family each evening is what pushes him to work hard and be productive for the company.

Career goals and personal/life goals are inexplicably intertwined. If you can find the right balance that meets both sets of goals, you will be well on your way to a long, productive, and rewarding career. What's more, you will know that you are one of only a small percentage of individuals who are fortunate enough to have found that balance and fulfillment.

□ □ □

# Finding Career Peace and Satisfaction

**Weldon J. Rougeau**
*President*
*Congressional Black Caucus Foundation, Inc., Washington, DC*

For our last interview in this chapter, we wanted to speak with a hiring authority who "walks the talk" and deeply understands how vital long-term career peace and satisfaction are. As such, we turned to Weldon Rougeau for his comments and some fascinating insights.

In the long run, finding career satisfaction is what it is all about. Yet people often do not take into consideration their particular personality styles and types when making career decisions. This can lead to a lifetime of career dissatisfaction. You must remind yourself that it is not just about money. What an individual values must be their primary focus.

Some of Weldon's classmates from law school are still practicing law in New York, Chicago, and Los Angeles. They are wealthy now, but after 31 years, many are saying that they made a terrible career decision and should have practiced in another area of law. Now that they are older and more experienced, they realize how important their own personalities and values are to them—values that would have altered their original choice of specialization.

Conversely, Weldon's choices have worked for him. His career has been diverse, yet focused on his core interests in government, academia, and the not-for-profit sector. He has experienced phenomenal career satisfaction and communicates with intense energy and enthusiasm.

What does this tell you? It's simple: Plan and build your career around those things that inspire you, motivate you, and excite you. If you can accomplish this, you will experience a lifetime of career fulfillment and peace with the decisions that you have made.

If a person is not certain about what career to pursue, Weldon recommends they find help through two important channels. First, he advises they find a mentor who can help guide them in their analysis, evaluation, and decision making. Your mentor should be someone who can help break your life down into small pieces and look carefully at each piece. He or she should also be someone who has made mistakes and learned valuable lessons from them.

Second, Weldon recommends that career seekers speak to a lot of people in their field of interest. When Weldon was considering law school, he spoke to many attorneys he trusted and respected. Now, he still speaks with those same people all these years later. Find people in your chosen field who can guide and advise you throughout your entire career.

And, finally, be patient with yourself. Sometimes it takes a while to discover what you truly want to do, and that's okay. You might be in a prestigious job with a prestigious company, yet still not sure that you are doing what you truly want to do. Take the time to explore, discover who you really are, and search for a job that will make you happy. Cast a wide net and get lots of opinions before making any important decisions. Take risks and do not be afraid to fail. Everyone does; it is part of the process as your career grows, evolves, and becomes all you want it to be.

□ □ □

## Authors' Best Advice for Planning Your Career

1. **Knowing *who* you are is the foundation for all of your career-planning efforts.** Career planning really begins with introspection and a clear understanding of what interests, motivates, and excites you. Use this information as the baseline data for identifying optimum career paths that will lead to the right positions and opportunities.

2. **Take career assessments.** Career assessments are wonderful tools that can provide you with a wealth of information about your skills, core competencies, motivators, and work preferences. What's more, many of them are now available online for just a small fee. Use these assessments to help you better understand yourself and your prominent skills as part of your career-planning process.

3. **Get feedback from others.** Often the way that you perceive yourself is not how others perceive you. Understanding what they see in you, what they like about you, and what they believe about you can be instrumental in helping you determine who *the professional you* should be.

4. **Understand what motivates you.** Are you motivated by prestige, a big office, and a huge compensation package? Or are you more motivated to make a difference and contribute to an organization? There is no right answer to this question, only the answer that is right for you. Be sure to understand your underlying motivators so that you are sure to put yourself on a career track that will fulfill those needs and provide the inspiration that you desire.

5. **Be the driver of your own career destiny.** Today, more than ever before, you must take control of your career and where it is headed. Twenty years ago, you could accept a position with a large corporation and know, to some degree, that you would work there throughout your entire career. You would advance up the corporate ladder as the company saw fit and you would tackle new challenges as the company presented them. In essence, the company drove your career. Now, everything has changed and you must take control. Chances are that you will work for five, six, seven, or even more companies over your career and none of them will take you under its wing. Instead, you need to decide what career track you want to follow, put a plan of action in place, and work that plan to ensure that your career takes you where you want to go.

6. **Look closely at organizational and cultural fit.** Never before in the history of the industrialized world have the concepts of organizational and cultural fit been so critical. As companies worldwide have streamlined their workforces to reduce expenses and improve their profitability, organizational and cultural fit have emerged as two critical factors in hiring and retaining the *right* talent. Consider your values and principles carefully to determine whether you will be comfortable working for a particular organization and whether you will fit into their culture. It is instrumental to your long-term success with that company.

*(continued)*

(continued)

7. **Find a mentor.** Mentors can be wonderful allies with great information and ideas that can be tremendously valuable to you in planning and moving your career forward. For the relationship to work, you have to find the right mentor—an individual with an interest in helping you move forward, the insights to guide you, and the contacts to help make things happen for you. Consider current or past supervisors and managers, college professors, industry contracts, business leaders, and others whom you admire and respect. If they are willing to take you under their wing, great things can happen!

8. **Be open to exploration and discovery.** Your work life is all about change, growth, and new opportunities. And, in order to make that happen, you have to be an explorer and discoverer, willing to attempt new things, enjoy new experiences, meet new people, learn new things, and be open to whatever may present itself to you. Often you will find that your career takes you in directions that you never imagined and never planned for, and that's okay!

9. **Balance your work life with your personal life.** For those of you in your twenties and thirties, you may find that a huge percentage of your life is dedicated to work and, in many instances, that's fine. You are just beginning your career and you must give it 110 percent. However, many people over 40 have come to the place in their lives where life is *not* all about work. Rather, personal issues, interests, and commitments might begin to move to the forefront and you must find an even balance between work and your personal life. This can be a tremendous challenge; however, when you have found that right balance, you will also find tremendous joy and self-satisfaction.

10. **Let yourself off the hook.** We cannot tell you how many people we have spoken to over the years who have beat themselves up because of their lack of satisfaction with their careers. Well, that's in the past and there is nothing that you can do about it. Or is there? You can take control now—today—and start paving the way to a career that will fulfill you, will satisfy you, and will allow you to look back with pride. Do it and do it now!

## Career and Job Search Survey Results

### Question:

Are you more inclined to hire a candidate who has worked for the same company for an extended period of time, or a candidate with several different employers?

### Results:

70 percent commented that it did not impact their decision.

20 percent are more inclined to hire a candidate with several employers.

10 percent are more inclined to hire a candidate with only one employer.

### Conclusion:

The number of past employers a candidate has had does not generally impact the decision as to whether a company will be interested in hiring the candidate.

# CHAPTER 3

# How to Write Your Resume and Cover Letter

Welcome to the world of resume and cover letter writing! It is a subject that is particularly near and dear to our hearts and one that is critical to your success in today's competitive job search market. It is also an area in which there are no rules, making resume writing one of the most challenging components of your job search. Sure, there are certain things that you are supposed to include in your resume (for example, employment experience, college degrees, foreign-language skills, technology skills, professional memberships, publications, and public-speaking engagements), but how you include that information, where you include it, and what additional information you include is entirely up to you. It all depends on your current career objectives and how you can best utilize your past experiences to support your current goals.

If you are over the age of 45, you probably can remember a time early in your career when writing your resume was quick and easy.

All you had to do was list your employment experience and education credentials on a short, concise, one-page, typewritten document and you were ready to go. No problem at all; no time at all. In fact, the whole world of job search was different then. You would send out a few resumes, get a few interviews, and get an offer. Life was so much less complicated!

Today's world of resume writing is a totally different place. To stand out from the crowd of other candidates vying for the same positions that you are, your resume has to shine. Your challenge is to write and design a resume that *sells* your skills, qualifications, accomplishments, and value to an organization. Writing a resume is not about writing an autobiographical document. Rather, it is about writing a marketing piece that sells you and what you have achieved.

Your resume should not be grandiose or overstate your qualifications. Rather, it should *merchandise* them well, showcasing the breadth of your responsibilities, major projects in which you have been involved, quantifiable achievements, professional recognition you've earned, and more. Consider this: Resume writing is not about listing your responsibilities. Instead, you want to highlight your achievements in handling those responsibilities. Don't tell your reader, "This is what I did." Rather, tell the reader, "This is what I did and this is how well I did it!"

If you are able to create a resume that truly does sell and merchandise your qualifications and accomplishments, it will have a unique energy and intensity to it that will attract prospective employers and encourage people to interview you. And isn't that what the purpose of your resume is? Remember, a well-written and well-designed resume will get you interviews, not jobs!

Before we move on to the expert advice we have gotten from HR executives, hiring managers, and recruiters to help guide you in developing your own powerful resume and cover letters, it is important to note that you might want to consider hiring a professional resume writer if writing is not one of your strong skills. Just as in any other profession, there are tricks of the trade, nuances, strategies, and the like that resume writers know and you probably do not. Take advantage of their expertise to be sure that you are positioning yourself well.

Now, let's move on to the advice of our experts.

□ □ □

# How to Write a Great Resume

**Lana Simcox**
*Manager—PGA Employment Services*
*The Professional Golfers' Association of America,*
*Palm Beach Gardens, FL*

We turned to a real employment pro and asked for Lana's input on what makes a great resume. Because of her years of experience advising PGA members on how to best present their qualifications and write winning resumes, we knew that she could give us a real insider's view of what makes a resume stand out, get noticed, and encourage calls. Here's what she shared with us.

## Resume Types

When preparing your resume, you have three distinct resume formats to choose from:

- **The chronological resume,** which is the most widely recognized and easiest to read. It highlights work experience in an easy-to-follow progression throughout your career—starting with your current or most recent position and working back from there.

- **The functional resume** focuses on your primary skill sets. Although it's *not* the most widely accepted format, it can be just the right answer in situations where there are employment gaps (for example, a mom returning to work), limited work experience (for example, a graduating student), or lots of short jobs in quick succession. These resumes focus on skills and competencies while downplaying actual work experience. Be advised, however, that you do want to include a brief listing of your work experience, most likely at the end of the resume. Lana does not believe that functional resumes work particularly well because they are often interpreted as trying to hide something (which might, in fact, be the case). However, if they are well-written and well-presented, functional resumes can be just the right answer in specific circumstances.

- **The combination resume** can be the best of both worlds. Your most notable skills, achievements, and credentials are included at the beginning—in a career summary or career profile—leading into your chronological resume, which highlights your specific work history and accomplishments.

You need to determine which type of resume is right for you based on your particular work experience, current situation, and specific career objectives. Resume writing is not a one-size-fits-all proposition!

One of the things that is most important to Lana is that resumes be creative. The job seeker needs to know what they do well and be able to get that message across on paper—concisely and professionally. It can be a difficult process for many people, especially if you have never written a resume before. To expedite the writing process, Lana recommends that you write your resume in sections—one section at a time. Then take all of your sections, put them together, polish them, and you will have your resume.

Your resume should clearly communicate *who* you are and *what* you can do. Although most job seekers tend to want to include everything they have ever done in their resumes, Lana thinks this is the wrong strategy. Your resume should highlight your skills, experiences, and accomplishments as they relate to the specific position at hand. You want it to have impact and create excitement; you want it to hit the interviewer between the eyes right from the very beginning. Then you'll be sure the interviewer will review or scan the entire document. Remember to sell what the employer wants to buy and not just what you want to sell!

## Resume Tips

Lana reminds us that it is human nature for hiring managers to want to get excited about a candidate. And, as the job seeker, it is your responsibility to create that excitement and have the employer say, "Yes, we need this person!" Here are several specific resume writing tips that Lana shared with us:

1. Begin your resume with your **name, address, e-mail, and all contact phone numbers.** Make certain that your e-mail address is professional and not something personal that your entire family uses. If you want to enhance the visual presentation, consider using professional-looking lines, light shadows, or boxes, which will give your resume a distinctive and attractive look. Other type enhancements—bold, underlining, and italics—can also be used to highlight certain headings, words, phrases, and accomplishments. Use these enhancements sparingly; if you overdo it, nothing will stand out.

2. Whether you use an **objective** is up to you. Many recruiters and hiring managers like objectives simply because it is immediately clear as to the type of position you are seeking. If you are going to use an objective, be sure that it is succinct and on point (for example, "Seeking a position as a regional sales manager"). Do not write an objective that says, "Seeking a position offering challenge and opportunities for advancement." That objective is very me-oriented and is just wasted words. State what you can do for the employer.

3. Over the years, the trend has shifted from starting your resume with an objective to starting with a **summary of qualifications.** Consider this: An objective states "this is what I want from you, the company." Conversely, a summary states "this is what I can do for you." Although in both instances you might be talking about finance, customer service, retail, or any one of hundreds of different jobs and industries, the summary is much more powerful than an objective. It is the section where you can really catch your reader's attention with the *best of the best* of your skills, competencies, qualifications, and achievements as they relate to that employer's specific needs and expectations. Research the company, learn about the people and the organization, understand its products and services, and then write your summary to reflect the desired skills and experiences. Sell yourself for that job!

> **NOTE:** Some job seekers choose to use both an objective statement and a summary. This can provide you with the best of both worlds!

4. The next section that will most likely follow on your resume is the **experience** section, where you will list (preferably in reverse-chronological order—most recent to past) your work history. Lana prefers a style that quickly communicates a summary of your overall responsibilities and then the top six to eight achievements of your most recent position or the top one to three achievements of your older jobs. Ten million other people list duties and responsibilities on their resumes. Accomplishments are what will make your resume unique and make you stand out from the crowd of other candidates. Be sure to focus your achievements on the things that will be

important to each prospective employer. In fact, you might want to write a list of all of your achievements in each and every one of your positions. Then rank them in order of importance for each prospective employer and include only those that are most relevant.

Lana recommends that all job seekers (especially those 50+ years of age) concentrate on the last 10 to 12 years of their experience and their accomplishments within that time frame. Remember, your resume is not an autobiography. Rather, it is a career marketing document designed to sell you into your next job. It is not necessary to include everything you have ever done in your career.

5. Your **education** section should be comprehensive and include all your college degrees (or college attendance if you do not have a degree), certifications, professional licenses, and more. If you have attended a lot of professional training programs, highlight those that are most relevant to the position for which you are applying. If you are 50+ years of age, you probably do not want to include the date you graduated from college. Why include information that might be used to immediately exclude you from consideration?

Your resume is a powerful career tool. Not only will it open doors and get you interviews, it should also help guide the interview itself. A good resume will give your interviewer a path to follow through the interview process and allow you the opportunity to expand on those things that are most relevant to that company, which you highlighted in your resume.

In closing, Lana stressed the importance of keeping your resume up-to-date. The hardest thing to do is develop a resume under pressure. Keep a tickler file that reminds you once each year to update your resume. Throughout the year, put notes, training certificates, recognition letters, revenue and profit numbers, accomplishments, project highlights, and other information you have into that folder so that when you sit down to update your resume next year, you will be able to remember everything you did this year. Make the process easy for yourself and you will find that you are prepared and ready to send out your resume at a moment's notice.

□ □ □

# Best Resume Advice

### Jeannine Nettles
*Agency Recruiter/Human Resources Specialist*
*State Farm Insurance, White Plains, NY*

The best place to continue our discussion of resume and cover letter writing is with expert advice on what makes a winning resume. We turned to Jeannine Nettles, who has years of hiring experience, and asked her what she considers the most important characteristics of an effective resume. Here are Jeannine's top five strategies for creating your best resume:

1. Try to keep your resume to one page if possible. Two pages is fine, as long as you have enough information to include—information that is important to the particular position for which you are applying.

2. Use action verbs to describe your job responsibilities, but be careful not to use the same action verbs over and over. You want your resume to flow smoothly and read easily.

3. If you have an objective on your resume, be sure that you change it each time to match the position for which you are applying. If the objective does not match the job title, Jeannine believes the candidate is not serious about the position and, therefore, she is not interested in the candidate. If a resume appears too generic—as though the candidate is sending it out to everyone—it makes the person less attractive to Jeannine. She wants to know that the candidate has taken the time to research her company and understands the job description and responsibilities.

4. If you have been out of work for a while, the use of personal experience is more than acceptable. This might include community service, volunteer work, or active participation in an organization or association. By including this type of information, you are communicating that you have not just been sitting idly, but rather contributing, learning, and growing. Most likely, some of the skills you acquired through these experiences will be transferable to a new position.

5. Format is very important. Your resume should be visually attractive, with a typestyle and format that make it easy to read. Spacing should be adequate to enhance readability. Jeannine prefers to receive resumes as Microsoft Word documents, as do the vast majority of companies and recruiters, so be sure to create a version of your resume in Word.

□ □ □

# Overcoming Challenges

**Wendy Enelow**
*President*
*Career Masters Institute, Coleman Falls, VA*

As one of the authors of this book, I felt it was appropriate that I share some of the knowledge I have gained in my 20 years as a resume writer and as the author of 16 books on resume and cover letter writing. In particular, I wanted to address some of the most frequent challenges that executives face when writing their resumes.

## Creating the Right Perception

When you come right down to it, resume writing is all about creating the *right* perception of who you are to support your *current* search objectives. Read that sentence again, for it is vitally important to understanding the strategy behind resume writing.

If you are a Vice President of Sales looking for another sales management position, the resume writing process is reasonably straightforward. Your resume highlights your career progression, notable sales achievements, key account wins, and more—all things that were relevant to your past positions and relevant to your current objectives. However, if you are that same VP of Sales who is now looking to transition into a general management role, your resume will be entirely different. Although you will continue to highlight your strong revenue performance, you'll want equal emphasis on your management achievements, roles, and responsibilities. You must create a resume strategy and structure that *paints the picture* as you want someone to perceive you and understand your value.

Remember, the single most important consideration in resume writing is to create an accurate picture of how you want to be perceived now and not in the past. Using your objective as the overall framework for your resume, how can you integrate your experiences to support that objective? You will find that the answer might not be the traditional chronological resume format, but perhaps a more unique strategy that positions you for the type of position you are currently seeking.

## Resume Challenges and Solutions

Following are four common resume strategies that might help you overcome specific issues or challenges you might be facing.

### Your Company Has Changed Hands

CHALLENGE: To create a picture of cohesive employment despite the fact that your company has changed ownership four times in the last 10 years.

SOLUTION: Use the following recommended format. Note that it communicates the perception of long-time employment with the same organization and not the picture of someone who hops from one job to another.

---

**VERIZON**, Albany, New York                                                   1991 to Present
*(Originally recruited to NYNEX Telephone System in 1991. Company was acquired by Bell Systems in 1994; then by Alltel in 1998; and most recently by Verizon in 2005.)*
    **Managing Director—U.S. Cellular Division** (1999 to Present)
    **Director—U.S. Cellular Division** (1998 to 1999)
    **Manager—Cellular Site Provisioning** (1996 to 1998)
    **Manager—Purchasing & Outsourcing Contracts** (1993 to 1996)
    **Purchasing Agent—Government Division** (1991 to 1993)

---

Follow up here with your job descriptions and achievements.

### Applying for Several Jobs in the Same Industry

CHALLENGE: To create a resume that you can use for *both* general management and senior management positions within a particular area of expertise.

SOLUTION: Use the following recommended format. Note that this candidate wants to remain in the financial services and banking industry, but is considering both general management and financial management positions.

---

*FINANCIAL SERVICES & BANKING INDUSTRY EXECUTIVE*

**U.S. & International Markets**

**MBA Degree—NYU Stern School of Business**

| **Leadership & Organizational Expertise** | **Financial & Investment Expertise** |
| --- | --- |
| Strategic Planning & Profit/Loss Management | Foreign Exchange & Treasury Operations |
| New-Business Development & Marketing | Corporate Credit Analysis & Risk Management |
| Cross-Border Trade & Finance Transactions | Debt & Equity Financings |
| Information Systems & Technology | Mergers, Acquisitions & Divestitures |

---

## Changing Industries

**CHALLENGE:** To position yourself for a career change into the technology industry when your entire experience has been in another industry.

**SOLUTION:** *Connect* yourself to the technology industry with a format similar to the following, which was written for an executive whose entire career had been in the plastics manufacturing industry. Note the description of his company.

---

**PROFESSIONAL EXPERIENCE:**

**Vice President & General Manager**                    2001 to Present
BLOCK MANUFACTURING CORPORATION, Butte, Montana
*($40 million manufacturer with state-of-the-art technology & automation center)*

---

Be sure to write job descriptions that are an equal blend of general management *and* technology functions, including such keywords as *e-commerce, networking,* and *advanced automation.*

## Consultant Wanting to Appear as an Insider

**CHALLENGE:** To create the perception that you are a corporate insider when the reality is that you have worked for small consulting firms throughout your career.

**SOLUTION:** Include a listing of your major corporate clients in the very first section of your resume. This clearly communicates that you have played with the big boys and immediately positions you as an insider.

> **SALES PROCESS, PRODUCTIVITY & PERFORMANCE IMPROVEMENT EXECUTIVE**
>
> Armour, Chevron, Citibank, Coors, Frito-Lay, Nabisco, Pepsico, Wells Fargo
>
> **U.S. & Global Business Markets**

When using this format, be 100 percent upfront in your job descriptions about the fact that you worked in a consulting capacity with these companies.

> **NOTE:** There are no absolutes in resume writing. These recommendations are simply examples of alternative strategies that might or might not be applicable in your particular situation. Use them to help you rethink your resume writing strategy to be sure that you are writing to support your specific search objectives.

□ □ □

# The Buzz About Keywords

**Wendy Enelow**
*President*
*Career Masters Institute, Coleman Falls, VA*

While I was on a roll and sharing some of my best resume advice, I thought it only appropriate to include a brief discussion of the importance of keywords in resume and cover letter writing. Here are some critical thoughts you will want to consider.

Ten years ago, no one had even heard of keywords, yet they are nothing new. Previously known as buzzwords, keywords are words that are specific to a particular industry or profession. Keywords have two vital purposes in your job search:

- **A single keyword communicates multiple skills and qualifications.** When a prospective employer reads the keyword *sales*, he or she will assume that you have experience in new business development, product/service presentation, negotiations, sales closings, customer relationship management, new product introduction, and more. Just one keyword can have tremendous power and deliver a huge message.

- **Keywords are the backbone for resume scanning technology.**
  If a company is seeking a Chief Financial Officer, they might
  do a keyword search through their database of hundreds of
  electronic resumes to find candidates with experience in tax,
  treasury, cash management, currency hedging, and foreign
  exchange. If you do not have those words in your resume, you
  will be passed over.

To better understand the concept of keywords, here are a few typical ones for business managers and executives:

| | |
|---|---|
| Strategic Planning | Organizational Leadership |
| P&L Responsibility | Profit Improvement |
| Performance Optimization | Multi-Site Operations |
| New-Business Development | Joint Ventures & Alliances |
| Budgeting & Finance | Consensus Building |
| Corporate Administration | Decision Making |
| World-Class Organization | Press Relations |
| Best Practices & Benchmarking | |

---

**NOTE:** Although you might assume that keywords are individual
words, keywords can be multiple words or short phrases, as demonstrated in the preceding list.

---

Now that you understand what keywords are, the next question is
how and where to use them. To be most effective, you must use keywords in all of your job search marketing communications—
resumes, cover letters, interview follow-up letters, and more.
Carefully integrate them into the text, when and where appropriate,
to be sure you are communicating a complete message of *who you
are* and what value/knowledge you bring to that organization.

Here are a few ideas for how and where to incorporate keywords
into your resume:

- **In the Career Summary at the beginning of your resume.**
  Summaries are the ideal section in which to highlight your
  most notable keywords. You can do this either in a paragraph
  format or a listing of bulleted items. By doing so, you are
  quickly communicating your core qualifications (keywords)
  for immediate impact.

- **In your job descriptions.** Use keywords to write powerful action statements, project highlights, achievement statements, and more.

- **In a separate section.** Although this is optional, you might choose to summarize your keywords in a separate section titled Professional Qualifications or Executive Qualifications. Today's resume scanning technology can find your keywords anywhere in your resume and cover letter, so a separate section is not required but might be a good presentation in your particular circumstance.

Now, get a copy of your resume and review it carefully. Have you incorporated all of the keywords that are most relevant to your profession and your industry (if your search is industry-specific)? If not, go back through and integrate the appropriate keywords so that your resume clearly communicates "This is who I am."

□ □ □

# The Unique You

### Michael Clement
*Staffing Manager*
*Coretech Consulting Group, King of Prussia, PA*

One of the primary purposes of your resume is to position yourself as a uniquely qualified candidate for a particular position. To better understand how to achieve that, we turned to Michael Clement for his guidance on how to create a unique perception of yourself and stand out from the crowd of other candidates. Here's what Mike shared with us.

First and foremost, you must be able to qualify exactly why you are a good fit for the position. Some people simply apply for any and all jobs, hoping anything will stick. They use the same resume and form cover letter for every job, and it can be a real turnoff for hiring managers. In fact, Mike has received cover letters before that were addressed to someone other than him! Obviously, these candidates are never interviewed. Mike wants to feel that the person sending the resume and cover letter is not just looking for a job, but that they know that they are a good fit for the specific position for which they are applying. He recommends to all job seekers that they include specifics on their background, accomplishments, and what makes them a fit for his particular job.

## Cover Letters That Work

When Mike posts an ad, he will often get 300 to 400 responses within just a few days. Surprisingly, an average of 75 percent of the applicants do not fit the position (it's as though they didn't even read the ad!) and are immediately deleted from consideration. Of the remaining 75 to 100 resumes, 30 to 40 of them have written excellent cover letters, which immediately catch his attention. Characteristics of these letters include the following:

- **They are specific about what position the candidate is applying for and why he or she is a good fit.** Job search is intensely competitive these days and it is critical that candidates proactively position themselves. When explaining why you are a good fit for the position, consider communicating something like this: "I have six years experience communicating with upper management and have developed the people skills you seek in a qualified candidate." In other words, spell it out so that your reader clearly understands your skills and how they meet the organization's specific needs. If your cover letter is interesting and to the point, the chances are much greater that the employer will then actually read your resume.

- **Great cover letters force the reader to *look behind the curtain* and can work wonders.** If you use a template for your cover letters, it's okay, but be sure to take the time to make them sound and look customized. People think that the person who reviews the cover letter will automatically review the resume. In many instances, that is not the case. Mike wants cover letters to grab him. If a candidate can excite him, he will be sure to read the resume.

- **Great cover letters are honest.** If a particular position requires a certain skill set and you have all but one or two of those skills, it is fine to tell Mike that you do not have experience in those one or two areas. However, be sure to follow that with information about what you are doing to acquire those skills—reading a book, taking a training class, or earning a certification. It is best to be honest up front so that there are no surprises or disappointments during the interview.

Mike finished his discussion of cover letters with a quick list of cover letter "don'ts":

- Don't use a generic cover letter.

- Don't shorten the cover letter to the point that important information is excluded.

- Don't use poor grammar. Have others review your cover letters just to be sure they are perfect.

- Be sure the date on the cover letter is correct. If not, it will be obvious that the cover letter is old and was used previously.

- Don't use another employer's name in the cover letter. Be sure you have addressed your letter to the right person. If you do not know the name of the person you which to contact, you can address your letter to "hiring manager," "recruiter," or "human resources professional."

- Don't be too general or vague. Communicate your message clearly and boldly.

## Characteristics of a Well-Written Resume

Once Mike finished discussing what is important for him to see in a cover letter, we moved on to our discussion of resumes. Here is what he considers to be the most important characteristics of a well-written resume that will uniquely position a candidate as a front-runner for a position:

- **Buzzwords, now often referred to as keywords, are very important.** You must be sure that your resume has the *right* words for a particular position, the words that tie directly into what the company is seeking in a qualified candidate. Further, it is important to remember that both recruiters and companies often use keywords as the search mechanism by which to select candidates they will interview from various Web sites, databases, and other technology tools.

- **Be 100 percent honest and direct when writing your resume.** No bluffing! If you stretch the truth too far, it will only serve as a double negative against you later if a phone screen or interview is granted.

- **Having more than one version of your resume can be a good idea, if appropriate in your particular situation.** Some people have multifaceted skills and experience (for example, sales, recruiting, HR, customer service), so they honestly can apply for a variety of positions. Craft each resume around the position you are applying for, target it as closely to that position as possible, and include as much relevant information as you can.

- **Be consistent with the date system you use on your resume.** Mike prefers that you include both months and years; others say that years only is enough. Whichever you choose, pick a system and stick with it.

- **Use a font style and size that is easy on the eyes.** Generally, a 10-, 11-, or 12-point font size is best; anything smaller is too difficult to read. You might want to put your name at the top in 14-point type. You can use an attractive typestyle, but nothing that is over the top. Look at magazines or newspapers and pick a font similar to ones that they use. Their objective is readability; so is yours.

- **Write a chronological resume.** Mike, like many other recruiters and hiring managers, much prefers the chronological resume style (focusing on employment history) over the functional resume style (focusing on skills with minimal emphasis on work history). Chronological resumes give your reader much more specific information with which they can make an informed decision.

- **Use bold print to highlight specific skills, qualifications, and buzzwords.** For example, if you are a computer programmer and the position you are applying for requires experience in Visual Basic and C++, highlight those items in your resume by using a bold print so that they pop off the page when someone sees the resume.

- **Be sure to include your educational credentials.** Mike recommends that you include all of your degrees and certifications, whether relevant to the position or not. Best to overstate versus understate in this situation. You can include these at the beginning or the end of your resume.

□ □ □

# Catching Their Attention

### Timothy Q. Kime
*President/CEO*
*Leadership Washington, Washington, DC*

We asked Tim Kime, a well-recognized business leader in the Washington, DC, metro area, what is the one thing that someone could do in their resume and cover letter that would almost always catch his attention and almost always result in an interview. Here's what he had to say.

Tim's most important advice is to design your resume for each particular job. Research and learn about the company and its culture. Tim's organization is flexible, and as such, he likes when people are creative in the wording and presentation of their resumes.

Tim warns not to send resumes that do not fit the job. He wants to feel as though you are sending your resume to him personally and not to hundreds of other companies. You need to understand who the company is and what they need so that you can respond to that. With the ease of computer technology, you can quickly edit and move things around on your resume with virtually no effort. Make your resume as relevant to each position as possible. This might mean changing just a few words or rewriting the entire summary.

Tim told us that one of the most valuable lessons he ever learned was that the cover letter can be a powerful tool. Do not simply reiterate what is already presented in your resume. Rather, use your cover letter to talk about you: who you are, what you offer, what you value, and more. Your cover letter can also help position you for jobs in which you have no experience. For example, a flight attendant was pursuing a career change into the financial services industry. Although the flight attendant had no real experience working in the financial world, she and her family were extremely well versed in the investment market through their own efforts. In turn, she was able to write an intelligent and insightful cover letter that immediately caught each reader's attention. The lesson here is to show that you can use much more than your basic work history to demonstrate the qualifications you bring to a position.

The other critical point that Tim addressed was the power that a referral name can have when used in your cover letter. If you are able to reference someone's name when making your approach, you can often stop someone in their tracks. "Wow! Bob knows this fellow and he's recommending him. This must be a great candidate!" Work your network of contacts, get referrals, and let those referrals work for you.

□ □ □

# Standing Out from the Crowd

**Andrea Sims**
*Partner*
*Match3 Productions, LLC, McLean, VA*

With more than 30 years of experience in the entertainment industry, Andrea Sims has hired hundreds of employees, from hourly production assistants to creative production teams, from administrative clerks to highly skilled media executives. What's more, she truly is a skilled interviewer, able to quickly and accurately assess the viability of a particular candidate, what skills they can bring to her organization, and whether they will be a good cultural fit.

Andrea's comments focus on the world we live in today…a world of great fluctuation and uncertainty in virtually every industry and, in particular, the media and entertainment industries. As such, it is critical that an employee in the new world order understand the importance of networking and marketing his or her unique talents. Each employee, no matter what field they are in, needs to set themselves apart from the masses, thereby getting the requisite "face time" needed to get that special job.

Andrea states that there are really three important things that a prospective employee can do to catch her attention and pique her interest. These are all particularly important in an environment such as Andrea's, where employers are wading through hundreds of resumes each week and each candidate has only a moment to get noticed.

1. **Every successful job-search candidate must have a *you can't live without me* resume, cover letter, and attitude!** Every time I read a cover letter that communicates energy and excitement, I can't wait to read the resume. The cover letter is my window into their world. Since I have so little time to focus on each and every resume, I look for compelling reasons to read the resume. If the cover letter is creative and has the right buzzwords, it immediately tells me the candidate is a cut above the others. These kinds of powerful and actionable communications let me know that the job seeker has just the spark necessary to fit into our corporate culture.

2. **Every successful job search candidate must demonstrate that they have the knowledge that I need.** Specifically, they should have done their homework about my company, who I am, and the specific project at hand. This requires creativity and shows me that they spent some real time getting to know about us. If they are willing to put forth so much effort to begin with, then I know, to some degree of certainty, that they will put forth that kind of effort in their new position with us.

3. **Every successful job search candidate must know how to network and understand its intrinsic value to their career.** They can demonstrate their networking savvy in their cover letter by telling me (in the first paragraph) who referred them to me, organizations they may have contacted in order to locate me, or other means by which they networked to find me.

Andrea states that if she has a candidate who presents all three of the preceding items—a winning resume and cover letter, the background knowledge of the company, and a strong professional network—then she knows she has a winner and almost always will make an offer (assuming that an appropriate position exists for the candidate). Follow her advice and you will be able to competitively position yourself above the crowd of other applicants; get those all-important, face-to-face interviews; and land a great new job.

□ □ □

# Positioning Yourself for Global Opportunities

**Shelly Goldman, CPCC, CEIP, CCM**
*President*
*The Goldman Group Advantage, Reston, VA*

Opportunities for international employment abound today, and many Americans are considering a tour of duty in a foreign country. It can be a great adventure and educational experience for the entire family, while offering you unique professional challenges and opportunities. After 20 years of coaching clients through resume writing, job search, and more, I have consulted with scores of clients seeking to relocate abroad. If you have ever considered working abroad, you *must* know the following about resume writing:

■ Resumes and CVs (curriculum vitae), although often used interchangeably, are *not* the same thing. A CV is typically longer, with more detail about publications, speaking engagements, affiliations, continuing education, and the like. And, in fact, in many foreign countries, it is also customary to include personal information on a CV. Be sure to research the country in which you will be applying to see whether a resume or CV is your most appropriate job search tool.

■ While you are researching resume writing practices in each country, be sure to identify their standards for how to present your employment experience—in chronological order (from past to present) or reverse-chronological (most recent to past). The latter is most often used in the U.S.; the former is preferred in many other countries worldwide. If no specific guidelines are recommended for a particular country, use reverse-chronology.

■ Detail your educational credentials, licenses, certifications, and background if there is any potential that these items will not be clearly understood in another country. This means including course/program name, university, location, number of course hours, and specific course highlights.

■ Be sure to use industry-specific and job-specific terminology that will be known the world over.

■ If you are submitting your resume in English, be sure to find out whether the country in which you are applying uses American English or British English. There is a significant difference in the spelling of many words. Note that U.S. companies use American English in all of their offices worldwide.

■ Include all of your foreign-language skills as well as foreign experiences (for example, traveling, working, or living abroad). If you prepare your resume in a foreign language, be sure to also prepare one in English. Many companies will expect you to be able to conduct business in both their native language and in English.

■ If your resume is written in a language other than English, be sure to have a native speaker of that language carefully review your resume. This will help you avoid the potential for major errors and ensure that your document is culturally correct.

- Computer and technology skills are always important, no matter the job, company, or country. Be sure to include yours in detail.

- Know that different countries use different size paper. For example, the paper standard in the U.S. is $8\frac{1}{2} \times 11$ inches; the paper standard in Europe is $210 \times 297$mm (known as A-4). Use the page set-up function in your word-processing software to select the correct size paper and automatically reformat your document.

- Work permits and visa regulations vary greatly from country to country, and might take months to acquire. Be thorough in investigating requirements for specific countries by contacting each country's embassy in the U.S. for detailed information. This process will be expedited if (1) the country has a shortage of professionals with your particular skill set or (2) you are transferred to that country by your current employer.

Working abroad offers you a tremendous opportunity to strengthen and expand your professional skills and qualifications, while offering you and your family an outstanding cultural exchange experience. If you decide to pursue an international career track, know that flexibility, patience, and the willing acceptance of differing cultural and business norms will be vital to your success.

□ □ □

# Getting the Interview

### W. Herbert Crowder III
*Director—Alumni Career Services*
*Darden Graduate School of Business Administration,*
*Charlottesville, VA*

When we had the opportunity to interview Herb Crowder, we were thrilled. Herb directs the career services organization supporting MBA alumni from Darden, alumni who work in virtually every industry and in every type and size of company imaginable. This broad exposure gives Herb unique insights into the employment industry, careers, and, in particular, resume writing. Here is his sage advice on how to write a resume that will get you noticed and get an interview.

## Who Do You Want to Be?

Herb finds that most resumes tell him who people used to be and rarely focus on who they want to be. This is critical when changing careers or industries. You must create a resume that focuses on *who you want to be* and not on *who you were*.

When Herb counsels his alumni about resume writing, he starts at the other end of the equation by closely examining the desired position and industry. Using a structured process for resume development, he begins by asking each job seeker to find and print 12 to 15 job postings that they would be most interested in and to closely examine the skills and experience that are required. Then he has them take a blank sheet of paper and on the left side write words, phrases, skills, and more that describe the requirements in each of the job postings. Then he tells them to use the right side of the page to list their skills and experiences and identify those that are transferable. This is the information that becomes the foundation of the resume. If you are able to mirror the keywords and phrases in your resume that are required in the market, you will have clearly communicated to your reader why you are a perfect fit for the job.

All too many job seekers forget this important first step in the resume writing process. Instead, they use their resume as a photo album of their career life, telling everything and hoping that the reader will find a few keywords or phrases that appeal to them. This is a terrible strategy! People generally spend only about 10 to 15 seconds reviewing a resume to decide whether the basic fit is there. If relevant information does not jump out at them, your resume will end up in the circular file. The lesson here: Delete extraneous information and include only what is most relevant to that prospective employer.

## Focus on Achievements

The second-most critical mistake that many job seekers make is that they focus their resumes on attributes they have, activities they have been involved in, and functions they have done. In turn, they do not spend enough time talking about their achievements, and achievements are what will sell you. Talk about revenue results, market share results, cost savings, efficiency improvements, customer satisfaction rankings, and more to create a resume that is powerful and engaging.

## Begin with a Summary

Resume format is another topic that Herb addresses quite frequently with his alumni. He recommends that you begin your resume with a career summary (which describes who you are, your skills, values, credentials, and notable accomplishments) and not a career objective (what you want from the company—a job). When employers see what you have achieved for others and the results that you have delivered, they can see what is in it for them. And that is what job search is all about—solving a company's problems.

Here is a great example of a powerful and direct career summary that begins with a headline that clearly communicates *who* the candidate is and the knowledge he or she can bring to an organization:

---

**SENIOR MARKETING EXECUTIVE**
**Consumer Products / Pharmaceutical Products**
*Follow this headline with the text (paragraph or bullets) of your career summary.*

---

A headline allows your reader to immediately *see* who you are without having to read a single word on your resume. It is clear, concise, and a great marketing strategy. Many times the person initially reviewing your resume is a fairly junior-level person, and as such, it is definitely in your best interest to spell it out and not leave the question of who you are open to interpretation.

## Preferred Format

Herb believes that the chronological resume is the best resume format to use. This resume type lists your work experience from most recent to past and is clear and easy to interpret. People hire you because of what you have accomplished over the last three to five years, and chronological resumes best depict that. Conversely, functional resumes that focus on skills and competencies, while downplaying past work experience, make it much more difficult to understand your background. As such, many of your readers will think that you are trying to hide something in your background. The only time that Herb recommends a functional resume is when there has been a large gap in employment (for example, a mom returning to work, an extended illness, or a layoff).

Herb also mentioned that he prefers two-page resumes and rarely recommends anything longer, except in particularly unusual circumstances. He likes short resumes that are clear and concise, and easy to scan and read. Remember, your resume is a teaser, designed to entice your reader to call you in for an interview. It does not have to include each and every thing you have ever done. What it does need to include are your relevant skills, experiences, and accomplishments. As Herb pointed out early in his interview, step one is researching the position and the industry to be sure that you are using the right keywords, phrases, and information for the job. You must speak the buyer's language and show them what you bring to the table.

When discussing job descriptions, Herb commented that he prefers them to be three to four lines in length, followed by a bulleted listing of accomplishments. The first and second bullets are the ones most often read, so be sure to include the achievements that are most important to the position you seek as the first two, and not necessarily the ones that you consider to be the most significant. Herb also mentioned that if the companies you have worked for are not well-known, it is best to include a one- to two-line description of each company and what it does.

## Assess Yourself

As we finished the interview, Herb brought us back to where we started—a discussion of how important it is to define who you are and what you are looking for. If you do not know what you're looking for, how can you possibly make yourself attractive on paper? You can't! In order to effectively profile who you are, you must first know what you want to do.

Before you ever start writing your resume, take a step back and go through a self-assessment process. Learn what you want in your life as well as your career. In essence, create a life template that addresses your goals for career, company culture, preferred work style, location, and more. Once you have this template, you can then determine what positions and what companies will be right for you.

Herb strongly encourages everyone in career transition to go through this self-assessment process. Until you know the key drivers in your job search, you cannot start an effective campaign. People who are not aware of this, or do not devote the necessary time to it, often flounder in the job search market. Don't let that happen to you!

□ □ □

# Ensuring That You Will Never Get an Interview!

### Kurt Mosley
*Vice President—Business Development*
*The MHA Group, Irving, TX*

We decided to take a contrarian view while talking to Kurt Mosley and asked him what someone could do in their resume that would almost always ensure that they would *not* get an interview. Here's what he had to say:

- Grammatical errors in your resume or cover letter are sure to guarantee that you will not get an interview. Kurt once received a resume from a candidate who spelled the word "position" as "positron." You must be sure that your spelling, grammar, and punctuation are 100 percent correct.

- A pet peeve of Kurt's is when people talk about themselves in the third person and when they include inappropriate things in their resume or cover letter. For example, this statement in John Jones' cover letter would really turn Kurt off: "John Jones wants to work for your company since he is moving to the Seattle area and is anxious to secure any type of employment." Not only is this sentence written in the third person, it also clearly communicates that he wants a job—any job with any company—a sure turnoff to a prospective employer.

- A "flowery" cover letter—full of superlatives, overstatements, and useless words that don't really communicate any real information about your skills and qualifications—is a real turnoff. So is a resume that looks like a booklet, a screenplay, or any other gimmick.

- Incomplete contact information means that a company will not contact you. So, what was the point of sending your resume and cover letter?

- Putting your chronological work history in the wrong order is strongly not recommended. Instead of listing your current or most recent position as the first one on your resume, some people start from the beginning of their careers because those positions are more relevant to their current objectives. This makes it much more difficult for Kurt to read and interpret, and therefore, he strongly discourages this practice.

- An e-mail address without the name of of the Internet service provider (for example, SallySmith@____) makes it impossible for people to contact you and communicates that you are not too interested in them being able to. Generally, this happens simply because of carelessness or because someone has not carefully proofread their resume. Obviously, that certainly is not the impression you want to create when you are sending your resume for a position that you are interested in.

- Resumes without enough information are virtually worthless. Resumes without complete descriptions and accompanying accomplishments really miss the boat in Kurt's opinion. He wants to know what people did and how well they did it.

- A cover letter that is too personal is also a real turnoff. Suppose your cover letter started with a statement about joining a young, enterprising company like theirs. It is as if you are saying you would like to date a tall blonde and, in Kurt's opinion, shows a lack of professional maturity. He recommends that unless you really know something about a company, do not say anything.

- Overuse of the same adjectives makes your resume boring and unappealing. You want your resume to be sharp and crisp, and one of the best ways to accomplish this is by avoiding repetitive language.

To be sure that he ended on a positive note, Kurt also shared this sound advice with us. He recommends that when you submit your resume and cover letter, be sure to include a time frame for when you can begin with the company. When the employer knows this information up front, it can help them to make effective hiring and staffing decisions. If they bring you in for an interview or tell someone else in the company about you and, at a later date find out that you cannot start for four months, it can be a real embarrassment to them and a real negative for you. If you are candid about this information and the person who receives your resume is impressed, they will call you to talk or call you in the future when a position opens up in the appropriate time frame. Be upfront and remember that it is the hiring manager's reputation on the line!

□ □ □

# The Age-Old Issue of Age

**Wendy Enelow**
*President*
*Career Masters Institute, Coleman Falls, VA*

One of the topics I believe is most important to include in this chapter is a discussion of age as it relates to resume and cover letter writing. This topic frequently comes up in conversation, particularly with candidates over the age of 50. Following are some critical points to consider if you are an over-50 candidate who is in the process of preparing your resume.

## Age Is Not Always a Negative!

For years and years, I have spoken to candidates who believe that once they've hit the age of 50, their chances of employment drop dramatically. That simply is not the case. Suppose you are on the board of directors of a pharmaceutical company and you need to hire a new president. You want a candidate with a wealth of experience in the industry, along with strong skills in leadership, organizational management, and new business development. Are you more likely to hire a 32-year-old who has had some good experience and management accomplishments, or a seasoned executive who can quickly take control of the company and guide it to the next level? The answer is obvious, and clear proof that the over-50 candidate need not feel as though his or her chances for employment are virtually nil. There are tremendous opportunities for qualified executives over 50. It is just that you might have to look a bit harder these days to find the right opportunity.

Here's another example. Five years ago you launched a high-tech company. Now, at age 29, you need financing in order to take the company public. However, everyone on your current management team is under the age of 30 and you have found some resistance on Wall Street. As such, you decide to hire a new CFO to take the helm of all financial affairs. Are you more likely to hire another under-30 executive or a more seasoned and more experienced CFO who can represent you well to the Wall Street community? Again, the answer is obvious.

# Writing Your Resume

As an over-50 candidate, you will have to make a decision about how far back in time to go on your resume. Is it necessary to include each and every position that you have ever held? No! A resume is not an autobiography and you do not have to include every job you have had since you began working. However, you certainly do not want to omit any valuable information from years past, particularly information that might be worthwhile in helping you land your next great opportunity.

A good rule of thumb to follow (knowing that there really are no rules in resume writing) is to go back somewhere between 10 and 15 years in your employment history, depending on how relevant the experience is to your current career objectives. Those 10 to 15 years will give your resume size and substance, and demonstrate that you are an accomplished professional.

If you are in a situation where you believe your older experience is worth briefly mentioning on your resume, there are three great strategies you can use to highlight the strength and reputation of your past employers, your rapid career progression, or your notable career achievements. Which of these strategies you decide to use will depend largely on where you can get the most mileage. Here are examples of all three:

## If You Want to Draw Attention to Your Past Employers

Previous health care administration experience includes positions with Sloan Kettering, The Johns Hopkins Hospital, and the Mayo Clinic.

## If You Want to Draw Attention to Your Record of Rapid Promotion

Promoted rapidly through a series of increasingly responsible sales, territory management, and sales training positions during early career.

## If You Want to Draw Attention to Your Early Career Accomplishments

Advanced through several key management positions with Kellogg's based on double-digit gains in productivity, efficiency, and quality ratings at the company's flagship manufacturing plant.

## Dating Your Education

I cannot tell you how many times I have read that you should never date your education on your resume. Sometimes, that's true, but just as often, it's not. Suppose you have gone back 15 years in listing your employment experience and you received your degree 16 years ago. In that situation, be sure to date your education. If not, people will assume that there is a bigger gap between when you graduated and the employment listed on your resume, therefore making you appear older than you are! Conversely, if you have gone back those same 15 years in listing your employment but got your degree 10 years prior to that, do not include your date of graduation. In this situation, it is better to be a bit vague instead of instantly adding 10 years to your age.

If you are an over-50 candidate, everything about writing your resume is a judgment call based on your specific experience and where, when, and how successfully it was acquired. Look carefully at the perception you are trying to create in your resume and make your decisions accordingly.

□ □ □

# Including Personal Information on Your Resume—Yea or Nay?

**Bill Welsh**
*Controller*
*Equinox Fitness, New York, NY*

For years and years, people have discussed the appropriateness, or lack thereof, of including personal information on a resume. Here's what one of our experts, Bill Welsh, had to say.

Bill believes that including personal information on a resume is important. As a hiring manager, Bill is starting with an blank slate and wants to learn as much as possible about each prospective candidate. He believes that the more he knows about someone—professionally and personally—the more informed his hiring decision will be.

When hiring an employee for the long term, it is difficult to measure compatibility through a resume and two-hour interview. However, it is often the case that determining whether a candidate's skill set is aligned with the corporate culture and company dynamics can be achieved through the discussion of personal interests and goals.

For example, if a candidate likes martial arts and he or she includes that on the resume, it gives Bill a point of discussion in the interview. As the candidate talks about his or her interest, characteristics such as focus and discipline, which are essential in a corporate finance environment, may be conveyed. Conversely, the candidate might go on to state that they must attend classes two nights out of the week. Rigidly scheduled extracurricular activities may establish a clear conflict between the candidate's interests and the inherent demands of the position for which they are being interviewed. Bill's working environment can often require long hours, and employees might not be able to leave work early on certain nights with little or no prior notice. A fast-paced, demanding company might not be the right place for them. Better to raise the issue in the interview than after three or four months of employment.

Personal information can also have a positive and lasting impact. Suppose a candidate includes the fact that they are active with a local charity or organization that the company is affiliated with or supports. Already it is a good match and common ground has been established.

Other important information to include, if you have not included it elsewhere on your resume, would be foreign-language skills, international travel, and international residency. Remember, our world truly is global now; so, if appropriate, show that you are part of that global community.

Just remember, the more information the hiring manager has, the better.

□ □ □

## Authors' Best Resume and Cover Letter Writing Advice

1. **There are no rules in resume writing!** This, in and of itself, is what makes the resume writing process so challenging. Although there are common sections of information you must include in your resume (for example, experience and education), the way in which you present this information is entirely up to you.

*(continued)*

*(continued)*

2. **There is no one-page resume writing rule!** Do not let the number of pages drive your resume writing process. Rather, write the document and then see if it fits onto one page or two. Either is fine as long as the information is important and relevant. Resumes that are more than two pages are normally recommended only for professionals in health care and education, and are more often referred to as curricula vitae (CVs; academic-type resumes).

3. **Sell it to me, don't tell it to me.** What does that mean? It means that when you are writing your resume and your cover letter, you do not want to tell someone what you have done. Rather, you want to sell it by using action-oriented language and accomplishments to demonstrate your proficiency and success.

4. **Use industry-specific and profession-appropriate keywords.** Keywords are the newest craze in job search and everyone is talking about them. Be sure to integrate the right keywords and keyword phrases into your documents to demonstrate your knowledge of the industry and profession for which you are applying.

5. **Use the "big-to-little" strategy.** When writing your resume, focus on the big projects and associated achievements and not on the details of each and every task that you performed. Save that little stuff for the interview.

6. **Make your resume interviewable.** After your resume has helped you land an interview, you want your interviewer to be able to use it to actually guide your discussions. Be sure to highlight your prominent achievements, projects, and responsibilities at the beginning of your resume, leave lots of white space for reading ease, and eliminate information that is irrelevant or that you do not want to discuss.

7. **Do not oversell your qualifications or overstate your accomplishments.** Although resume writing is all about selling, you do not want to misrepresent yourself. The worst thing that can happen is to be hired for a position that you are not qualified for and then find yourself out in the market again. Be honest and upfront!

8. **Create multiple versions of your resume.** In today's electronic age of job search and career marketing, you will need not only your nicely designed, printed resume, but you will also need scannable and ASCII text versions. Multiple versions will allow you to transmit your resume in whatever format an employer requests.

9. **Design your resume to stand out from the crowd.** This does not mean that you should create a resume on bright yellow paper with icons all over it! Rather, use a distinct typestyle (for example, Tahoma, Bookman, Soutane, or Krone) rather than the most-often used Times New Roman and Arial. Consider including a few graphic lines here and there, or a box to highlight critical information. Upscale, conservative, and distinctive should be your guiding principles.

10. **Use your cover letters as sales letters.** You have a product to sell—*you*—and your letter is your sales brochure. Highlight the benefits and value of the product as it relates directly to that customer and you will be able to close the deal!

## Career and Job Search Survey Results

### Question #1:

Which element makes a resume stand out more—the visual presentation or the content?

### Results:

57 percent reported that a combination of both made a resume stand out.

32 percent reported content as the element that most made a resume stand out.

11 percent reported visual presentation as the element that most made a resume stand out.

### Conclusion:

The resumes that stand out the most from other resumes are those that combine excellent content with a strong visual presentation.

*(continued)*

*(continued)*

## Question #2:

Think of the resumes you have discarded immediately. What did you dislike about them?

### Results:

Results for this question are subjective and cannot be quantified. Here are the most common responses:

- Misspelled words and poor grammar.
- Not targeted to the specific job.
- Sloppy with a poor visual presentation.
- Inability to express ideas clearly.
- Not a fit for the advertised position.
- Lack of detail.
- Hard to read because of too much content.
- Not highlighting strengths and skills.
- Too much fluff.

### Conclusion:

To ensure that your resume is not immediately discarded, it must be neat and clean with no grammatical or typographical errors; it must include adequate detail to highlight your skills and competencies without being too full of extraneous data; and it must be targeted to the specific job for which you are applying.

# CHAPTER 4 — How to Manage Your Job Search

In decades past, job search was a snap. You would see a few ads in the paper, mail in a few resumes or make a few calls, go on several interviews, and get an offer. Generally, it was pretty painless! Jobs abounded and there was never really any talk of layoffs, downsizings, reorganizations, mergers, or divestitures.

Today, things have changed dramatically and layoffs, downsizings, mergers, acquisitions, consolidations, take-overs, company closings, and the like are a routine part of our world. What's more, with the emergence of all the online resources that now support the job search industry, you are faced with using both traditional and new, high-tech job search methods. In turn, the process of job search has become increasingly complex as companies want to hire only individuals who they believe will make measurable contributions to their organizations and their bottom lines. No longer will mailing out just a few resumes in response to advertisements do it for you. Rather, you have to create a truly integrated job search plan that will allow you to tap into all the avenues where you might find your next job.

When we speak of an integrated job search plan, we are talking about a specific plan of action designed to get your resume in front of decision makers who can offer you an interview. In order to make that happen, you will want to consider using a combination of the following job search tools and resources:

- Networking

- Responding to print advertisements in newspapers, trade journals, and other publications

- Responding to online job postings on company Web sites, public Web sites, and fee-paid Web sites

- Researching print and online advertisements to collect information about specific companies

- Reading online resume postings on company Web sites, public Web sites, and fee-paid Web sites

- Launching targeted mailing campaigns to recruiters (e-mail only)

- Launching targeted mailing campaigns to companies (e-mail or print)

- Launching targeted mailing campaigns to venture-capital firms (e-mail or print)

- Attending job fairs

- Joining and participating in industry, trade, alumni, and professional associations

- Joining and participating in civic associations and volunteer organizations

- Writing articles for online and print publications

Now, not every tool is right for everyone. You must consider your job objectives, willingness to relocate, salary requirements, and more to determine which of these job search channels might uncover the best opportunities for you. Consider this scenario: You live in Detroit and are not willing to relocate. Ask yourself whether it makes sense to spend money posting your resume on job boards with global distribution. Probably not! It's best to post your resumes only on job boards that are frequently used by companies in the Detroit market and its surroundings. Be a wise job seeker and use only the job search tools that will open the right doors for you.

Now, to give you some really outstanding advice, we turned to our experts to hear what they had to say about how to plan and manage a successful job search. Their insights are enlightening and will be extremely valuable to you as you plan your own campaign.

□ □ □

# Job Search 101

**W. Herbert Crowder III**
*Director—Alumni Career Services*
*Darden Graduate School of Business Administration,*
*Charlottesville, VA*

To provide an excellent overview of the basics of job search, we turned to Herb Crowder for the insights he has gained after working with hundreds and hundreds of job seekers pursuing professional, management, and executive opportunities. Here are his top tips for developing an effective job search campaign:

- **Use public windows to market yourself.** This includes posting your resume on appropriate sites on the Internet, reviewing job-posting sites to identify opportunities, and responding to advertisements in trade journals, newspapers, and other print publications. Use these opportunities to see what is available in the market, but be sure to devote much more time to networking. Only a very small percentage of senior-level jobs ever make it to these public windows.

- **Carefully consider the value of direct-mail campaigns.** Most mass mailings are expensive and ineffective. Even people who are in the mass-mailing business tell you to expect only a 2 to 3 percent response rate. However, when a company or recruiter does respond, it is generally because they do see you as a qualified candidate who meets the needs of the company. It will at least serve to get you in the door for an interview.

- **Contact recruiters who specialize in your industry and profession.** Again, these types of mass campaigns are not the most effective, but if you have the right qualifications for a particular search assignment, the results can be exceptional.

- **Nothing beats networking!** Everyone agrees that the single most important activity in your job search is networking. In an average market, 85 percent of your search should be focused on networking. In a more difficult job search market, 90 to 95 percent of opportunities will be uncovered through networking. It is the most challenging of all job search activities; but, by far, it's the most effective. You can do it in person or over the phone, but in order to be effective, you must devote a significant amount of time and effort to the task.

- **Think of networking as building relationships.** For people you know well, this process is easy. For those you do not know, it will take time and multiple interactions because you will rarely get the information you need on the first call. Develop a system and process, make multiple calls, build your credibility, and establish rapport with each person. By doing this, you will build relationships that will lead to people making suggestions, sharing thoughts, and leading you to great contacts.

Building a network is hard work! Look at networking as a transaction and make it as purposeful as possible. Developing these types of long-lasting relationships will become easier as you get to know each person and understand the value you can deliver to each other. Remember, networking is a two-way street where each party needs to give back to the other.

Here is Herb's breakdown on how much time to devote to each the preceding job search activities:

- Public windows: 5 percent
- Letter-writing campaigns: 5 percent
- Recruiter campaigns: 5 percent
- Networking: 85 percent

If you follow his plan, Herb can almost guarantee that you will be successful in opening new doors and finding great new opportunities.

□ □ □

# The Multi-Pronged Approach

**Joseph Daniel McCool**
*Vice President and Editor-in-Chief*
*Kennedy Information, Inc., Peterborough, NH*

When we wanted to interview someone who truly has a wealth of experience in understanding how successful job search campaigns work, Joe McCool instantly came to mind. We wanted an individual who would be able to give us information from both sides of the fence—the job seeker and the employer.

Joe said that job seekers often do not realize that the successful search process requires a multi-pronged approach. All too often they rely on newspaper classified advertisements, online job boards, family, or friends. This is how many job seekers think they will find their next dream jobs. However, in most instances, this is not the case because the hiring market has changed.

To truly succeed, Joe says that job seekers should use the strategies he has outlined, along with many other activities. Smart job seekers integrate a wide variety of strategies to propel their job search campaigns and a range of approaches to get their foot in the door with prospective employers.

## The Changing Face of Recruiting and Hiring

The business of recruiting is changing and job seekers need to know how recruiters and human resources departments work today. The people who hire are forced to demonstrate the impact their hires have on the company. Before, HR professionals and recruiters were thought of as non-strategic to the organization—serving functions that did not have an impact on the bottom line. That is changing rapidly, and the hiring of human capital is now considered part of the overall corporate strategy and critical to the bottom line. In essence, HR professionals and recruiters are being held accountable for who they bring in and the retention of the best employees. What's more, the buyer of talent (the hiring company) is now being held to new standards, and HR and recruiters need to demonstrate the same metrics and results as any other department within an organization. This means that recruitment is changing forever.

### Doing Their Own Recruiting

For corporations that once relied on external search consultants, outside staffing agencies, and job boards for the bulk of their hiring, they now know that the future for them is to do more internal hiring on their own. Companies are aware that there is a real cost savings for them if they do more of their own recruitment. They rely less now on the big job boards and more on the investment in their own corporation's career Web sites. Not only is this more cost effective but, more importantly, no one can communicate the culture of the hiring organization better than the company itself.

This is particularly true when a company is searching for executive talent who must be able to mesh with the culture of the organization. Certainly, they need the skills for the job, but culture, personality, and the driving objectives of the organization and its mission are key to a successful executive hire. In fact, when hiring companies are faced with choosing one candidate over another, they are most likely to hire the candidate whose cultural integration will be easier, despite the fact that his or her skill set might not be quite up to par with the other candidate's.

## Spelling It Out on the Web

Companies say a lot about the culture of their organizations on their Web pages. They know the investment in their own Web sites really does work. They put job specifications and announcements on their Web sites. They communicate the culture, mission, and driving principles through employee branding and by communicating what it's like to work for them. Companies do not want to use their Web sites to get more and more candidates. Rather, they want to bring in the right candidates who understand the company and are excited about the prospect of working for them.

## The Importance of Cultural Fit

Job seekers have more choices, and will have even more in the future. Candidates do not need to meet each and every one of a company's requirements in a job description. Rather, it is often more critical that they have the right cultural fit. And, in fact, companies are now willing to accept candidates outside of their industry when the cultural fit is right. Companies know that people can learn and develop new skills and have longer tenure when joining an organization where there is a strong cultural match.

## Employee Development

Companies are now vested in helping their executives develop, learn, and grow, as well as discussing areas of improvement with them. There is no longer a stigma that halts executives from talking about their professional development and improvement. Today, companies are supporting their executives' work with career coaches, leadership coaches, executive coaches, and others who can help them be more successful on the job now and in the future.

Executives look for mentors who can help managers expand their skill sets on the job. In years past, if a manager was not measuring up to the company's standards and expectations, he or she was often penalized, or someone else was called in to help correct the problem. Companies want to facilitate the career development of their executives, build on weaknesses, further strengthen skills, and pave their way up through the ranks. Managers are well served by checking their egos at the door!

## Using New Resources and Channels

To truly learn and understand the job search process, job seekers must understand how things have changed. Today, they will most likely have less contact with the middle man, job boards, executive recruiters, and human resources professionals. Instead, applicants will have more one-on-one contact with the hiring organization and the hiring manager directly.

As a candidate, the likelihood is that you will find your next job through a reference, referral, or recommendation from someone who knows you. Companies are viewing their employees as their very best recruiters. They talk up the company and its benefits, the great career tracks that are available, and the overall advantages of working for the organization. Current employees are a company's best resource for finding and bringing in top-quality talent. People want to work with people who hold the same values as they do, and current employees are an organization's best spokespeople to find and bring in that talent.

Today's job search process is made easier by technology. E-mail, videoteleconferencing, and web conferencing are now available and quick to use. These emerging technologies will continue to grow in popularity and will be essential to managing an effective job search in the 21st century. Utilizing technology and having an integrated job search will be each job seeker's answer for success. And, remember, not only can today's technology help you manage your job search and maintain communications with a potential employer, it can also help you manage yourself and your time much more efficiently.

To create and manage a truly integrated job search campaign, applicants need to reach out and use as many resources and channels as possible. As a job seeker, you should

- Review the local and daily newspapers in your area, read the classified section, and identify opportunities for which you are a strong candidate.

- Use the Internet and scour the job boards.

- Compile a list of companies you would like to work for.

- Connect with friends, family, co-workers, and referrals. This is not the time to be shy!

- Create a short list of companies that seem exciting to you and then research each company to learn as much as you can. Visit their Web sites, read articles about them, review their current listings of job openings, and more. The more information you amass about a prospective company, the better equipped you will be to determine whether the company is the right company for you.

- Be visible and network. Networking is a powerful tool. Hiring managers put more stock and faith into employee referrals than any other avenue for bringing new talent into an organization. In fact, many employers give their employees referral bonuses.

- Physically present yourself to people who can refer you to others. Let them get to know you and your talents. Then, hopefully, they can start working for you.

- Attend networking events, be active in professional and civic organizations, and let everyone know that you are looking for your next opportunity.

- Be strong and consistent in your follow-up efforts. Recruiters have never been shy about sharing information on the candidates they remember. In fact, they talk up about one out of six candidates—the one person who calls every month about opportunities and seems truly committed to his or her search.

For executive-level positions, the job search is different! Do not post your resume and credentials haphazardly online. Rather, show some discretion. Cultivating the roster of people in your network is a much more powerful tool for the executive candidate. People at the executive level often have relationships that they have developed over 20 or more years. Use those people to your advantage.

When you're in career transition, whether it was your choice or your employer's, attitude is extremely important and emotions often come into play. If you have a spouse and children, and particularly if you are the sole breadwinner in your family, it can be an extremely emotional time. Your family, friends, and past business colleagues are so important to your successful job search. When you have a positive attitude about your life—both personal and professional—it quickly communicates a positive message to a prospective employer. It is an important indicator to the company of how you handle stress and what can be expected of you within their organization.

Be positive in your search, use a multi-pronged approach, and you will succeed!

□ □ □

# Winning Job Search Strategies

**Naray Viswanathan, Ph.D.**
*President*
*Interview Exchange, Shrewsbury, MA*

We had the pleasure of meeting Naray at the 2003 Kennedy Information Expo in New York City. He graciously offered to share his insights on what the best and worst strategies are for finding a new position, information he has acquired through his years of experience managing Interview Exchange, a prominent recruiting firm. Here's what he had to say.

## The Technology-Based Job Search

Ten years ago, job search was a paper process. Today, the entire market has changed and many, many companies use Web-based applicant-screening software and tools to facilitate the evaluation and selection of candidates to interview. In fact, public and company-specific job boards are one of the advantages of today's technology-based job search process. If you are an entry-level to mid-level candidate, you should spend about one hour a day on the job boards. If you are a more senior-level candidate, recruiters might be a more useful resource for you, but Naray does recommend that you spend about 30 minutes a day on the boards.

Naray believes that many job seekers are loyal to certain job boards. As such, smart employers list their job postings on multiple job boards in order to ensure that they are getting the word out to a broad range of job seekers. However, many companies are also loyal to certain job boards. As a job seeker, you must use multiple boards or, potentially, you will be missing out on what could be great opportunities.

## Recruiters

A recruiter or executive search firm might be a better connection for you because they will give you good feedback on the job and how well your skills and experience match the hiring company's requirements. In addition, they can provide you with information about the company culture and vision, which are also important considerations. That is how recruiters make their money—by making good matches. They will tell you what you need to know and, in turn, you will be much better prepared for each job interview.

## Know the Company You Want to Work For—And the One You Work for Now

As a job seeker, it is imperative that you understand the company that you are applying to. Talk to anyone who can give you information about the company, its organizational structure, major projects, key products and services, and more. Use the Internet to research company information, talk to company employees, read newspapers, or participate in any other activities where you believe you can gain valuable information. Once you get the information, you can then prepare yourself for the interview, or you might decide that company is not the right place for you.

When you are working for a company, you also need to spend time understanding what is going on around you. It is often quite easy to isolate yourself in your position and not be part of the larger picture. For any savvy job seeker, this is not the route to follow. To get additional information on your company, consider using the Internet, where you can find out all kinds of information about the organization, its financial situation, its long-term projections, its new products and services, and more.

## Networking

Naray also recommends that job seekers work their alumni contacts. This network can be an invaluable resource for learning about new opportunities. Communicating via e-mail with these people is easy, so be sure to update your resume and pass it along. You never know when someone you know might be aware of the perfect opportunity for you!

Professional associations are also a must. These types of contacts can be extremely beneficial for individuals who maintain good standing relationships with association members. In fact, whether or not you're in a job search mode, you should always belong to, and participate in, associations that are related to your profession and your industry. You never know when you might need your fellow members to help you expedite a job search campaign.

Naray summed up networking with one powerful statement. "Networking is a must." It's that simple, yet that complex, because relatively few people enjoy the process. However, it is a critical process of which every job seeker must take advantage.

## Want Ads and Job Fairs

Help-wanted advertisements in newspapers and professional journals can also be a great source for identifying new opportunities. With the explosion of Internet resources, many job seekers overlook the tried-and-true help-wanted ads. Be sure that you don't forget!

Naray believes that job fairs are of value only for entry-level people. The more senior level you are, the less effective they are. It is not unusual for a company to participate in a job fair, even though they are not currently hiring. They are simply testing the market to see who might be available. As such, do not invest too much time or effort in these events.

## The Role of Your Resume

Naray was adamant about the fact that direct-mail campaigns (also known as mass mailings) are almost always ineffective. Although you might land a job, it might not be the right fit because you did not spend the time to get to know the company and its values. Naray also does not recommend that you pay a resume-distribution service to send your resume to thousands of companies. When you use this type of campaign, you will not have the opportunity to research each organization. Again, you might get an offer, but it might not be the right offer. What's more, if you are attempting to change careers, these types of campaigns are even less effective because many of these companies use electronic keyword scanning technology. If you are new to the industry, your resume might not have the right keywords and phrases to get you noticed.

Most important in your long-term career-management efforts is to keep your resume updated. You never know when you might need it. When you land a new job, you will be inspired to learn new skills on a daily basis. Be sure that you incorporate those new skills and achievements into your resume so that you are always prepared to send out an updated resume should the need or the opportunity arise.

## Summing It Up

In summary, Naray believes that an effective job search incorporates the following:

- Finding a job that is appropriate for you
- Getting the job that you want
- Putting your experience to work for you
- Adding value to your new employer
- Helping your new employer flourish by doing what it is that you do best

□ □ □

# Setting Your Plan in Motion

**Jim Oddo**
*Staffing Manager*
*Oxford Health Plans, Inc., Trumbull, CT*

Understanding the intricacies of job search can be a complex process. To help us simplify the process, we turned to Jim Oddo, who shared his strategy for creating an effective job search plan, setting that plan in motion, and securing a great new position. Here's what he told us.

## Before You Start Your Search

Jim believes that step one in any job seeker's campaign is to set realistic expectations. When you find yourself in the job market, particularly after being in a job for some time, you need to establish a strategy and create a job search plan with realistic expectations. This can be particularly challenging for individuals who are currently employed and focused on their current jobs, not thinking about the day they might need to find a new job.

To help make this transition and the first step easier, you must be conscientious! Even if you are in a stable job with a stable company, you should always be thinking, "If I lose my job, what do I need to do to get a job?" This will help set your strategy in motion. Remember, you never know what is going to happen tomorrow, so you always need to be prepared today.

Always focus on your competition, economic news, political news, and other things that impact the economy. Keep a tickler file and, at least once each quarter, add new information to your resume that reflects your most recent responsibilities, projects, and achievements. If you do not do this in advance, you might find yourself in a situation where you need to look for a job tomorrow and, with that kind of pressure, it is often difficult to remember all the specifics about what you did on the job and how well. Be prepared in advance so that you can immediately launch your search campaign.

Utilize the resources that are available to you. You can do a great deal of research by phone and on the Internet while you are currently working, and be sure to keep your eyes open to current market conditions. For your research to really work for you, know the type of opportunity you are looking for and have your goals in place. Then ask yourself whether you are open to relocation. If so, expand your search. The more flexible you are regarding geographic location, the more quickly you will land your next opportunity.

Establish priorities and carefully review location, compensation requirements, the opportunity itself, and the various intangibles that go along with it (for example, people, culture, potential for long-term promotion and growth, and long-term compensation opportunities). Then ask how this job would affect your family and your personal life because these are also key considerations when accepting a new opportunity.

## Job Search Resources

A wealth of job search resources is available to you today:

- Networking (a must-do for every job seeker!)
- Alumni contacts (a must-do for every job seeker!)
- Online job boards
- Resume-posting services
- Classified ads

- Job fairs
- Direct mail
- Association contacts
- Recruiters

To determine which of these resources is most appropriate for you, you must know your goals. This will help you invest your time and money in the right areas that will be most effective for you.

In today's market conditions, it might be more difficult for some professionals to get the attention of and get results from recruiters and search firms. Jim has found that companies are not as open to working with search firms today as they were in the past, and candidates must be aware of this. Companies today have many more resources for hiring top talent on their own and saving the organization thousands of administrative dollars that help their bottom line. You certainly want to contact recruiters who specialize in your profession and industry, but you do not want to put all of your eggs in one basket. Contact recruiters, but also actively engage in all of the other job search activities that are appropriate for a candidate with your background.

If you do decide to work with recruiters, make sure you contact the right firm(s). If possible, get the recommendation of one of your colleagues and look for a firm that has stability in the marketplace, good contacts, and good relationships with the companies they work with. The most valuable recruiters that Jim works with will take the effort to identify Jim's needs and the needs of his company. It takes time to establish a trusting relationship. Jim prefers to work with agencies that have taken the time to understand Oxford's culture. By knowing them well, the agency will be able to submit candidates who are above and beyond Oxford's expectations. Further, Jim wants to work with recruiters who really understand each candidate's background, performance, style, and skills. This is the foundation for a positive working relationship among the company, the recruiter, and the candidate.

The Internet has emerged as an amazing tool for companies and candidates. Consider this: Three years ago, the Internet was not a good source to recruit for nurses and other health care professionals. Today, about 50 to 60 percent of health care professionals are putting their resumes online. As such, companies such as Oxford now place their ads online in anticipation of finding the right candidate without having to pay a 20 to 25 percent fee to a recruiter. The cost savings to companies is phenomenal.

Corporations are now obligated to have professional career sections as part of their Web sites. Individuals are now searching the Internet for employment opportunities, and companies must have professional Web sites that are easy to use and that provide key information about the company, its mission, its position in the marketplace, its products and services, and its employment opportunities. For most people, using the Internet is a core strategy in their job search plan. As such, companies need to be responsive to that trend and provide relevant online information.

Jim found that when hiring top talent (and when interviewing multiple candidates for a position), he will often hire based on a referral from someone who knows the candidate. Networking is key when seeking employment. If there are several candidates interviewing for the same job and they are all good, Jim will select the candidate whose work and performance can be validated by a third party (a network contact) because they are a known quantity.

In summary, Jim believes that a multifaceted job search campaign is the way to proceed. Utilizing all the appropriate resources at your disposal and all of the various job search channels Jim outlined previously, you can take control of your search and find your next great opportunity.

□ □ □

# Finding the Right Company

### Jo Bredwell
*Senior Partner*
*JWT Specialized Communications, New York, NY*

Candidates know that companies spend time and money to reach the appropriate candidates. What's more, companies realize that they have a product—the companies themselves and what they offer—and they must make it attractive enough to get the right people to work for them. That's where Jo Bredwell comes into action as part of an advertising agency that guides companies in the development of their marketing/communications tools to attract quality candidates. In fact, according to Jo, companies spent $4 billion on newspaper ads alone in 2002 to attract new employees.

## Finding Information About Companies

Companies want candidates to read information about them that is available on their Web sites, through articles and other publications, in advertising and marketing literature, and elsewhere. Before you waste the company's time, be sure that it is a good fit for you. Consider the company that is seeking entrepreneurial candidates because they know this type of person will be successful in the company. If a particular candidate does not thrive in an entrepreneurial environment with constant change and innovation, he or she most likely should not apply for a position in a company like this. It makes perfect sense; apply only where you will fit in and thrive.

A candidate can get a good sense of what a company is about through its brochures, advertisements, and other documents. In an ideal situation, the company hopes that candidates will read their information and can then communicate how what they feel the employer is all about relates to them. When a company spends money to advertise itself, there will be a style and energy to that advertising. Be sure that you, as the candidate, focus on that message and do everything that you can to demonstrate that your skills, qualifications, and expertise fit their needs and organization precisely.

## The Importance of Branding

Jo then brought up how important the concept of branding is—for both companies and candidates. Companies create a distinctive brand of who they are, what they stand for, what they do, and how they operate. What's more, they also know which candidates will be most successful in their organizations. Candidates also develop their own brand with similar characteristics. When the branding is similar on both sides (when the fit is good), the most successful employment relationships develop.

Companies describe themselves both verbally and graphically when discussing the types of people who work there. Many times, an organization's advertisements will show photographs of people working. These photos are carefully chosen to visually depict the types of work being done and create a specific image and feeling. Candidates should look at those photos carefully and the design of company ads, brochures, and other printed materials. Is the feeling formal and conservative? Is the photo electrifying, with a sense of energy and power? Does the company project a willingness to do new things? The graphics and design of these documents can be a real window into the company and its true self. The brochure of an insurance company will have a totally different feel than that of a cutting-edge software-development firm. Companies express their personalities just like people do.

## What Does Your Ideal Employer Look Like?

Candidates should define what their ideal employer looks like. Walk through the process of analysis and give careful thought to what positions would be most comfortable with what types of employers. Will your ideal company be large, small, or midsize? The size of a company is something Jo feels people have an instant reaction to based on what is important to them. Consider these questions:

- Is the company global?
- What is its reputation?
- Do people in the local office appear happy and satisfied?
- What is the longevity of the firm and its history?
- What is the stability of the organization?
- Does the organization appear to be looking for risk-takers?

Make a checklist, evaluate each company, and be honest about what you are looking for. Jo firmly believes that the money will come if you select an employer that will offer you opportunities that meet your needs, goals, and expectations.

When you are out of a job, it is more difficult to wait for the ideal situation. You are often feeling stressed, and it is easy to jump at the first opportunity. However, the reality is that if you continue to be honest about what is right for you, you will find a job that you really like, and both you and the employer will be happy. Patience is a very tough virtue to have in job search, but one that is truly valuable.

□ □ □

# Overcoming the Negative of Being Fired

**Patti Cotter**
*Vice President—Recruiting and Training*
*Nationwide Insurance, Columbus, OH*

If you were fired from your last job, we're sure you have already encountered some degree of difficulty in revealing that information to a prospective employer. How can you shine a positive light on the fact that you were let go from your last position? It can be an extremely difficult conversation. For tips on how to best manage this situation, we turned to Patti, who shared what she considers to be the best strategies for positively managing this conversation with a prospective employer.

## Tell the Truth

First and foremost, Patti always encourages candidates to be truthful and straightforward. It is important for her to know whether the candidate was fired due to displacement of the position or the company, as a result of a corporate downsizing, or because of poor job performance. Candidates must be clear and upfront about the circumstances.

If a candidate was fired because of a poor fit or poor performance, he or she should not attempt to hide that fact. Rather, they should face up to it and admit that the situation (for example, wrong job, poor cultural fit) simply was not right for them. In today's culture, few people have not lost a job for one reason or another. Honesty is the only way to proceed because Patti will verify that what the candidate is telling her is indeed the actual situation.

## Work Through the Issues Before the Interview

Before interviewing, take the time to prepare yourself, work through it all in your mind, and come to terms with the issues of being let go. This will help you immensely in the interview process because you will have to share that information. Most likely, you will not have divulged this information on your resume, so the first time that you are going to present it is during your interview. Be prepared to discuss it as positively as possible.

It is an amazing thing when a candidate works through the issues of being let go and gets through the question of "Why me?" If they can come to terms with it, pass through the stages of anger and denial, and then accept it, they will be able to share the issues around it in a positive and constructive manner during an interview.

□ □ □

# Insider Tips on Handling Rejection

**Tony Lee**
*Editor-in-Chief and General Manager*
*CareerJournal.com/The Wall Street Journal Online Network,*
*Princeton, NJ*

We originally met Tony Lee when he was editor of *National Business Employment Weekly*, a Dow Jones publication. When the Internet revolutionized job search, *NBEW* responded and reinvented itself as CareerJournal.com. When we needed an expert on job search to provide us with information on how to handle rejection (it happens to every job seeker!), we turned to Tony for his guidance. Here's what he shared with us.

## Don't Take It Personally

First and foremost, you cannot take rejection personally. More often than not, rejection in a job search is more about the company than it is about you. What's more, the higher the level of position you are seeking, the more likely you are to face rejection. For a senior-level candidate, it can be a rude awakening. The people you contact often will not care about you, your family, or your needs. Instead, you need to bring and prove value to them.

## Build a Support Network

It is critically important that you build a support network (for example, your spouse, a networking group, a career counselor you can trust) while you're looking for a job. You do not want to feel isolated from the world, so you must keep socializing, exercising, and being with people. Join organizations and network. You need to keep reminding yourself that you are a good, smart, and capable person, and your support network can help you do this. Managing a positive job search is all about retaining your self-esteem.

## Take Assessments

Another great strategy is to use self assessments to decide on the right jobs to pursue. People attempt to recreate what they know, and sometimes that is the most logical step to take. Get a legal pad and on the left side list all the things you liked about your job. On the right side, list those that you did not like. When you are finished, you will have a visual representation of what you enjoy and what excites you. Then use this tool to help you focus your job search in the areas where you have strengths and are most satisfied.

This strategy will make your entire job search move forward more smoothly and more quickly, and reduce your incidence of rejection.

## Do Your Research

It is also important to demonstrate that you know what you are talking about. This will require that you research the company and the position. If you are interested in transitioning your skills into a new career field, some people might feel as though you are being unrealistic. You can comfortably address that by saying, "I understand what you're saying, but what I've seen is _____." You still might not get the job, but you will feel more confident if you understand some key points about the company and the position and can talk about them during the interview.

## Get Feedback

Getting feedback from your interviews is also quite important. Most interviewers are not interested in talking with you afterwards if they are not planning to call you back for a second interview or make you an offer. If you know this is the case, use the interview to get all the feedback you can so that you will interview better and more effectively the next time.

## Anticipate the Interviewer's Concerns

If you know what some of the concerns of a new employer might be, you can address them before they are ever raised. For example, you might be thinking that although you do not have direct experience in the field in which you are applying, you do have transferable skills that you have acquired through other experiences, both paid and volunteer. Or you might be able to explain why you are the right candidate for the position, and this can sometimes turn the tables in your favor.

Here's a great example. John Johnson is a CPA and has just left a position with a public accounting firm. While at the firm, John had some experience working as a liaison with the public relations department. John has now decided that he no longer wants to pursue an accounting career and, instead, would like to transition into the public relations field. In fact, to further develop his PR skills, he volunteered with a local non-profit association to be its PR person. Although he knew that a professional career change would not be easy and that rejection was bound to be part of the process, he networked effectively and made a point of learning something from each rejection. If people said that he did not have the right skills for a PR job, he would say, "Help me! How would you do it? What guidance can you offer to help me get the job I want?" John had numerous interviews and was willing to accept a lower salary than what he had been making. It was a two-year process, but he did land a new position—a great new position in PR!

## Keep a Positive Attitude

Most important, you must maintain a positive attitude throughout your entire job search. Some days you might need to take a mental-health day off from your search and get your mind onto more positive things. Constantly remind yourself to take advantage of the things that you enjoy in your life. This will help you put the rejection in perspective and maintain a healthy outlook.

□ □ □

# Maybe Next Time

### Wanda Jackson
*Vice President—Human Resources*
*National Urban League, New York, NY*

We have often been asked what a job seeker should do if they were in the running for a position and considered a good candidate, but were ultimately not selected. What can they do to keep positive contact for future consideration? To answer this question, we turned to Wanda Jackson who, with years of hiring experience, shed some interesting light on this subject. Her response was short and sweet, but definitely communicates a critical message.

First and foremost, Wanda encourages you to stay in touch for possible opportunities in the future. As step one, you should send a thank-you note acknowledging that, although you did not get the job, you still have a decided interest in the company, enjoyed the interview experience, and would definitely like to be considered for future openings. Wanda also suggests that you send a handwritten note instead of e-mail. She gets so many e-mails that they blur together. A handwritten note will definitely help you stand out from the crowd. Then Wanda recommends that you check in with the company from time to time to see what is happening and when another position may become available. If you are viewed as a qualified candidate, this will keep you on the radar screen.

Selecting the best company is not always about the name of the company or its revenue. Rather, it's all about fit. When you are interviewing and do not get the job, your ego might be bruised. It's only human nature to feel badly when rejected. However, do not close doors, but rather look at it from a different perspective and learn from the experience. If you really liked the company and its culture, keep the relationship alive by staying in regular contact with your interviewer while you are pursuing other opportunities. You never know when the company might be ready to hire someone else—two weeks, three months, or a year. If you have remained in touch with someone at the company, chances are that they will immediately be in touch with you. Just think how much easier it would be for them to hire you, who they already know and are impressed with, instead of having to start the entire recruitment and interviewing process again. It truly is a win-win for both you and the company!

□ □ □

# Pack It Up and Move It

**Joseph Cabral**
*Director—Corporate Human Resources*
*New York Presbyterian Hospital, New York, NY*

There is often much discussion about how much of a potential disadvantage candidates who are seeking to relocate might have. To get a corporate human resources executive's opinion on how they view relocating candidates, what the candidates can do to make themselves attractive, and what obstacles the candidates might have to overcome, we turned to Joe and asked him to share his experiences with us.

## Local Candidates Have the Edge

Employers clearly look for and prefer candidates who are local. There are no two ways about it. In fact, many times when companies post openings on job boards, they state that only local candidates should apply. There is a definite preference for local talent. Some of the underlying reasons for this might be the following:

- The concern that if an organization hires an out-of-state candidate, that candidate might decide at the last minute not to take the job and make the move. Moving is one of the greatest stresses a person can experience. As such, these types of hires are a bigger risk for a company.

- Organizations might have concerns about how serious a candidate is about making a move. What is their motivation for wanting to relocate? Do they really want to work for that hiring organization (that's what the hiring company would like to hear!) or is this the only opportunity they have?

- Companies might not be in a position to pay for relocation costs or might not be willing to do so. Obviously, in this situation, no matter how qualified you are for the position, if the company is not willing to pay your moving expenses, they will not make you an offer (unless you offer in advance to cover your own relocation expenses).

## What Can You Contribute?

Before accepting an interview with an out-of-state company, candidates need to think about what they can do to contribute to the hiring organization's team or business unit. Then they need to be able to clearly, succinctly, and powerfully communicate that information. Bottom line, why should an organization be willing to take a risk on hiring them?

In Joe's industry—health care—there is a huge need for highly qualified nurses, pharmacists, and technicians, and they are hard to find. In turn, Joe will be open to relocating candidates if they fall into any of these professions. Conversely, Joe is much less inclined to hire a relocating information systems manager because there are plenty of qualified professionals in that career field in his immediate area.

## Overcoming the Distance

Candidates are savvy these days. They frequently ask family and friends who already reside in the area in which they would like to move whether they can use their address on their resumes. Many organizations are now using applicant-tracking systems that sort by location. So, unless a candidate lives in the area where the job is, his or her resume will not make it to the desk of the person responsible for phone screenings, interview scheduling, or hiring—unless the resume has a local address.

If candidates are relocating and do not have a local address to use, the cover letter becomes increasingly important. Joe recommends that job seekers use their cover letters to set the stage and highlight the value they bring to each organization. It is critical for the candidate to get in front of the hiring manager, even if the company is not paying for relocation, and the cover letter can be a powerful tool to help candidates achieve just that.

If a candidate is fortunate enough to get an in-person interview with the hiring manager, Joe strongly recommends that he or she bring up the subject of relocation by letting the interviewer know how many apartments the candidate has seen or by asking questions about the best places to live in the area. In addition, candidates should let their interviewers know their timelines for relocation (for example, "I'll be living in the area in 30 days."). A candidate's ability to communicate that they are serious about the move will have a great deal of impact on how interested the hiring manager will be. And, finally, Joe recommends that the candidate ask whether there are any concerns about hiring an out-of-state candidate so that he or she can immediately respond to and dispel them.

Joe concluded his interview by stressing how important the concept of cultural fit is when relocating to change jobs. Candidates will be able to learn about the organization's culture by the things the interviewer says, the questions that are asked, the way people behave and interact with one another, and the statements that they make. He warns job seekers to be as sure as possible that they are relocating for a position within an organization where they will fit—professionally, culturally, and personally.

□ □ □

# Pushing Beyond the Barriers of Fear and Procrastination

**Shelly Goldman, CPCC, CEIP, CCM**
*President*
*The Goldman Group Advantage, Reston, VA*

In reviewing all of the excellent information we received, we noticed two key issues of job search that were not addressed in their entirety—the issues of fear and procrastination—and what a negative impact they can have on your campaign. I'll address how to overcome these issues and put power back into your job search.

During my 20-plus years in recruitment and career coaching, I've had many talented clients with excellent work histories, successes, and accomplishments, yet they were stalled in taking the steps needed for effective job search because of fear, which, in turn, prompted their procrastination. For some, the issue may have been that they set unrealistic expectations. As such, they did not know where to start in their search, or their sense of self may have been compromised. For others, they may have simply been overwhelmed with the enormity of the entire job search process and could not identify the specific steps needed to go from point A to point B. There can be many reasons a job seeker finds him- or herself stuck in the process, and the purpose of this information is to help them regain control and move forward.

## Self-Discovery

There are many questions you need to ask yourself as you begin the process of discovery. Start by asking yourself the following questions:

1. What am I really afraid of?

2. What is really stopping me from starting an effective job search campaign?

3. What are my top three goals that I would like to achieve in the next three to six months?

4. What will be the outcome of delaying my search?

5. What do I need to do to get on track and have a successful job search strategy and campaign?

6. What type of support system do I need in place?

Whether it is fear or any other reason that is holding you back, the key is to face the issue as openly as possible so that you can address it, resolve it, and move on. If you allow yourself to shy away from the truth, you will achieve nothing but increased frustration and stress. Perhaps the very thought of networking makes you panic, or the reality that you are going to experience change has immobilized you. If you can identify the underlying reasons why your search campaign is stalled and why you are experiencing fear, you will be able to push through that fear, set your strategy, carry out your plans, and achieve success.

Many times, the job search activities people avoid are exactly the things that need to be done in order to succeed. Over the years, I have met many people with enormous talent and capabilities. However, at times, some of these gifted people are not as successful over the long haul as others who have less ability and natural talent. Why? Because they are not consistent in doing the things needed to reach their professional and personal goals. The message is clear: You must have a plan, or at least be diligent about finding out what is needed to develop a clear plan, and execute that plan consistently and reliably.

When you are honest with yourself, you will find the energy and strength needed to overcome the barriers to a successful search. The reality is that your fears will not evaporate, but rather, you will have the awareness and knowledge to manage them. By confronting the truth, you will start to feel better in a relatively short period of time because you are taking control of your life and your career. It's a great morale and ego booster and creates the positive momentum that you need. And it is amazing how much good luck will come your way when you put yourself in the driver's seat.

## How to Get Started with Your Search

Often people just do not know how to get a job search started, and so they avoid the process completely or move forward haphazardly. Fear of the unknown can be paralyzing. If you are concerned that you will not be viewed favorably by others and believe that job search will be dreadful, you will resist and the entire process will become distasteful. And, for those of you who may be perfectionists who do not want to begin your search until all the pieces are in place, forget it! Job search is much more of an art than a science and cannot be easily packaged. Consider it a continual work in progress.

To begin to move past your fear, start by making a list of your career accomplishments. Look at each work situation and identify what you did, how you did it, and what the result was. How did it affect you, your co-workers, your organization, your family, and others around you? What did you learn? What could have been done differently? How have you grown and changed as a result of the experience? What will this mean for the new organization you join? How will these experiences make you a more valuable resource to the team?

If you have been successful before, chances are good that you will succeed again. If you have had limited success in your past, look honestly at the reasons why. By doing so, you will begin the steps needed to have more success in the future. Everyone can and should experience success in their career unless they have some extreme emotional or physical limitations. And, even then, many have found ways to overcome these difficulties and find tremendous success.

## Dealing with Fear

To deal with your feelings of fear and uncertainty, you may need to learn new ways to tolerate emotional discomfort and change some beliefs you have about yourself. As your world changes around you, you will need to evolve if you want to keep in step and be successful. So much of how we deal with the stress of fear has to do with the way we learned to deal with fear as children. We all have triggers, and when we're in stressful situations, those triggers are activated. The way in which we experience a situation has much to do with the way we view the world. If we are sensitive to this, we can all make positive changes in our lives.

There may be times when you will find yourself disorganized as a direct result of the stress of fear and procrastination. This obstacle is easy to overcome with a simple data tracking system and calendar. Break things down into manageable tasks, establish realistic daily and weekly goals, set deadlines for yourself, and then reward yourself for meeting those deadlines. However, don't be overly ambitious or you will set yourself up for instant failure. Most important, hold yourself accountable to your commitments.

On occasion, you might find yourself distracted and allow other things to take you away from the focus needed for a successful job search. This behavior can really thwart your success. You must set boundaries for yourself, your family, and your friends and let them know the importance of your job search and the time you must devote to it.

There are times you may need the assistance of not only a certified career coach or counselor, but a trained psychotherapist to help you move beyond your fears. Various levels of fear and procrastination may be a sign of deeper things to be addressed. You could be experiencing clinical depression, Adult Attention-Deficit Disorder, or other psychological or organic physical conditions that may be adding to your difficulty in your job search.

Many years ago, while working with a group of psychotherapists, we talked about how pain is a wonderful opportunity for growth. It is in this place, where we see the benefits of confronting the deeper causes of how we deal with stress, that we can create the opportunity for significant life-altering experiences and create fertile ground for positive transformation. The new insight and tools you can gain from these coaching and counseling experiences can help guide you into new, positive ways of thinking and being, now and for always.

It is much easier to face your fears and push through procrastination when you know the outcome of reaching your goals. Take some time and visualize the wonderful ways in which your life will change when you find that great new job or when you recognize the things you need to do to eventually move into your new career role. Your determination and endurance during your career search will pay great dividends to you, your family, and significant others, but only if you stay on course, are open to learning new ways of being you, stick to your plan, and truly give yourself the time and opportunity to know yourself and what your passion is. If you have the courage to reach for what you want, it *will* come to you!

□ □ □

# The Ten Most Important Things I Have Learned

**Jack St.Genis**
*Chairman and CEO*
*Molecular Separations, Inc., Sarasota, FL*

To finish our discussion of job search, we wanted to interview someone who could give us a perspective on career management from both sides of the fence—both as a hiring executive and as a job seeker. We turned to Jack St.Genis, a former senior executive with such big-name companies as Matsushita, Pioneer, NEC, Raytheon, and others. Although he had been in the inner circle of several major U.S. corporations, Jack was hard hit by the downsizings and consolidations across several industries, so he has also been active as an executive job seeker. Here's what he told us were the top ten things that are most important in any candidate's successful search campaign:

1. **Do not shop when you are hungry.** It is better to negotiate when you have a job or another offer. Like most divorces, people who are let go say they never saw it coming. In most instances, however, that is not the case. There are many signs when your job, or company, is not doing well and things are going to change. Reduced funding or staffing, less communication from senior management, rumors on the street, changing relationships with your management, and more are all telling signs of a negative situation. Get out before they push you out! These days, most senior managers are charged with reducing overhead to meet budgets and *not* with preserving talent.

2. **Stage your job hunt so that all your offers come at one time.**
   Six years ago, I sent out 4,000 resumes and had six final negotiations going on in the same month. It was great! Prior to
   that, I had managed a search where I sent 500 resumes out
   each week over a period of several months using a great technology setup I had in my home office. During that search, it
   took six months to go through all of the negotiations and settle on the ideal position. You will get a better picture of the
   market if the offers all come to you at once.

3. **If you can, stage your campaigns in the fall before Thanksgiving,
   then again after the Super Bowl, and once again after Memorial
   Day.** The American vacation is alive and well in most corporations, and getting hiring approvals during the summer vacation
   times and holidays can be prolonged.

4. **Do not take a job below your current salary or level of authority unless you are doing it for unusual personal reasons** (for
   example, to care for children or elderly parents, or after the
   death of a spouse). Although you might be comfortable for a
   short period of time, generally it will not last long and your
   disappointment will soon be reflected in your performance.

5. **Do not commute a long distance; you can only take it for so
   long.** When we tracked this at one corporation, 60 percent of
   our commuters resigned in six months. Like a lower salary or
   authority level, it will begin to take its toll on you over time,
   and you may soon find yourself in the job market again.

6. **Do not go into an industry that you already know you do not
   like.** Again, over time, you will become disheartened and dissatisfied. All too many people who have worked for major corporations (for example, GE, IBM, Ford, GM, state and federal
   governments) stayed with those organizations because they
   were safe. My father worked as an executive in the automobile
   industry for 39 years and hated everything about the car business, but he loved the medical coverage and pension plan. That
   is because he came out of the Depression and wanted security
   rather than a career. Most of us have had these same unfortunate circumstances, so don't let his misery happen to you!

7. **Do not sell out for benefits.** Job seekers pass on great long-term opportunities because they got free dental coverage at a less attractive, more stifling, company. A complete benefits package is usually worth less than $8,000 annually, much of which is now taxed, so do not let it drive your decision-making process. You are better off with more money and paying your own perks.

8. **Make your decision based on the hiring company offer.** Most corporations have every job neatly placed into a salary range, and hiring managers do not have the authority to deviate from what has been established. As such, many great opportunities are not offered because of a demand by the candidate that the hiring manager is not authorized to approve. The question you should be asking is whether the company has the potential to meet your current and long-range career needs. If so, get in, prove yourself, develop a mentor, and the money and perks will improve.

9. **Do not lie about your past compensation.** Companies have people who do nothing but get the salary scales from their competitors and from like industries. In fact, prospective employers will often pick up the phone and verify your salary. Hiring managers, especially in the same industry, will almost always know someone at your previous employer. If you get caught, your credibility is shot before you ever get to the offer stage.

10. **Approach companies with the fact that you are the solution to their operating and financial problems based on your previous identifiable successes.** This approach is less about you and more about how you are a tool—a precision tool—that will pay the hiring company back many times after its initial investment in you.

□ □ □

# Authors' Best Job Search Advice

1. **Execute an integrated job search campaign.** At the beginning of this chapter, we outlined the numerous job search tools and resources available to you to create a truly integrated search campaign. Carefully review all of these resources to determine which are right for you based on your specific job objectives. Then create a plan of action and establish a timetable to achieve all of those goals.

2. **Network, network, and network until you drop!** There is no better strategy for finding a new job than networking with who you know and who they know. We have all learned the difficult lesson, at some point in our lives, that it really is all about who you know. Ask your network of contacts for their assistance and for names of additional contacts. The whole key to successful networking is exponentially building your network larger and larger and larger by getting additional contact names from each person you connect with.

3. **Be able to quickly communicate who you are.** When active in your job search, you will often find yourself in a position where someone is inquiring about you and your candidacy. They will want to know right up front who you are and what you can do. Make sure you are prepared to answer that question with authority, dignity, and confidence.

4. **Research the companies you are applying to.** There is nothing more frustrating to a company than a job candidate who does not know anything about the company. Be sure to do your research before you apply so that you know it is a company that you want to work for, a company that looks for candidates with your qualifications, a company that holds the same principles and values that you do, and a company that can provide you with the opportunities you are seeking. Be an informed job seeker!

5. **Be visible!** The people whose job search campaigns often move forward the most easily and effectively are those individuals who make themselves visible by attending networking events, joining associations, communicating with alumni, writing articles for publication, speaking at events, and more. If people do not know what merchandise is

*(continued)*

**119**

(continued)

available, how can they buy it? Be sure you are out there and visible.

6. **Send out lots of resumes.** All too often we hear job seekers remark that they did not send a resume here or there for whatever reason. Your resume is not made of gold! The more you send out (to the appropriate companies, recruiters, and other organizations), the more responses you will get. Don't be shy...distribute!

7. **Join a job search group.** Job search can be a lonely process if you try to go it alone. Consider joining a job search support group where you meet regularly with other individuals in transition to share ideas, referrals, successes, and opportunities. These types of relationships can be extremely important in keeping you motivated and on track throughout your entire search campaign.

8. **Follow up consistently.** After you have sent a resume—whether in response to an advertisement or to a recruiter, or simply because you would like to work for a particular company—follow up. By doing so, you are reiterating your interest in the company or position and getting your name in front of the hiring authority one more time. Plus, follow-up letters, e-mails, and calls give you another opportunity to highlight your most relevant skills and accomplishments as they pertain to that particular job or company. Remember, it's your responsibility to follow up, move the process along, and get interviews.

9. **Be prepared to handle rejection.** Rejection is a normal part of the job search process and you cannot allow it to deflate your ego. In many instances, the reason for not getting an offer will have nothing to do with you. It may be that the company promoted an internal candidate, changed its business model and eliminated the position, hired the president's grandson, or whatever—all of which had nothing to do with your competence and expertise. Just let it go and move on.

10. **Be realistic.** In today's market, job search is competitive and might take some time. The more realistic you are about this, the better prepared you will be to effectively manage your search. If you expect to get an interview each and

every time you send a resume, you are setting yourself up for disappointment. Better to be realistic and understand that your job search might require 50 resumes or 500. No matter the volume, the opportunities are out there and you will find your ideal job.

## Career and Job Search Survey Results

### Question #1:

Do you review unsolicited resumes?

### Results:

87 percent reported they did review unsolicited resumes.

13 percent reported they did not review unsolicited resumes.

### Conclusion:

If you send an unsolicited resume, chances are it will be reviewed by a human resources professional, hiring manager, or recruiter.

### Question #2:

What resources do you use to identify qualified candidates?

### Results:

Respondents were asked to identify which of ten different resources they used to identify qualified candidates. All of the ten resources were utilized by at least 50 percent of the survey population. Here are the ten:

- Recruiters
- Employment agencies and temporary staffing firms
- Help-wanted advertisements
- Online job posting boards
- Career centers of colleges, universities, and technical schools
- Networking
- Postings on company Web sites
- Alumni contacts
- Job fairs
- Employee recommendations

*(continued)*

*(continued)*

**Conclusion:**

A job search strategy that utilizes a diversity of resources to identify employment opportunities and build your visibility within the employ-ment market will yield the greatest exposure and most interviews.

# CHAPTER 5 — How to Network with the Best

Together, we have worked with thousands of job seekers over the past 20 years and rarely have we ever come across an individual who was excited about the prospect of networking. The normal response we receive is something like this:

> "I've done everything that I can think of to propel my job search—responding to ads, contacting recruiters and companies, posting my resume on the Internet, reviewing online job postings, and more. The only thing I haven't done—and simply cannot do—is network. I worry that if I ask my colleagues for help, it will appear that I'm desperate!"

Wrong! Networking is a natural and accepted part of the job search process. And, in fact, it's the most valuable part. If you are not working your network, you are closing the door on potentially great new contacts and great new opportunities. Statistics have proven over and over that more positions are filled through networking than through any other job search strategy.

Networking is not a one-way street where you ask for someone's help and they (hopefully) will provide it. Rather, networking is a two-way street where, over the course of your work life, you develop long-term relationships with other business professionals (and social contacts) so that you can both help, support, and guide each other. It may be that today you are in need of referrals for potential job opportunities. Tomorrow, one of your network contacts may need you for a referral to an attorney, accountant, or publicist. Strong networking relationships are always reciprocal. That is the beauty of networking. It was never intended as a desperate plea for a job.

The real beauty of networking is that it is exponential. The more people you network with, the more new contacts you will get and the faster your network will expand. Suppose you contact ten people this week and ask them all for the names of three other people you can network with. Next week, your list of contacts is at 30 and you will ask each of them for three more names. The following week, you have 90 contacts and chances are one of them may know of just the right opportunity for you.

Networking really does work, but you have to work at it. Your network contacts are not going to seek you out. Rather, you have to be proactive and contact each person directly. Phone or in-person contact is great whenever possible; e-mail contact will do if for some reason you cannot meet in person or talk on the phone. Either way, your mission is to collect information and more contact names—information about companies that might be interested in a candidate with your qualifications and contacts who might know of other opportunities or other leads. And be sure to remember to use the latest technology to help advance your efforts—online networking groups. They are growing daily in popularity and can offer a real boost to your networking and job search efforts.

The whole key to success in networking is to ask for help and *not* for a job. Rarely will any of your network contacts have just the right job for you. If they do, they will mention it. You do not need to ask. Instead, your network contacts will have ideas, recommendations, and referrals, and that is precisely what you want from them.

When we approached our experts to share their knowledge of networking and how to optimize your results, we were delighted with the diversity of recommendations they shared with us. Read on to learn how you can enhance your networking performance.

□ □ □

# Networking 101

**Dr. Clint Gortney**
*Managing Director*
*The Gortney Group, Manassas, VA*

To begin our networking discussion, we turned to a pro—Dr. Clint Gortney—to get his insights on how a candidate should build an effective networking campaign. Regardless of the amount of experience a job seeker has, the level he or she has reached in his or her career, or the type of position that he or she is seeking, networking can be an extremely difficult task. Here's what Clint recommended as the best strategy for formulating a networking campaign that can be implemented effectively and professionally.

Clint began his discussion with a startling fact: Almost all *good* jobs are not advertised; they are found through networking! Even in this electronic age, when we hear so much about online resume postings, resume scanning, resume e-mail campaigns, and more, there is still nothing that works better than the tried-and-true practice of talking to people.

To best outline and clarify the process of networking, Clint broke it down into two groups: candidates who know what they want to do and candidates who do not. This important distinction impacts the ways in which each of these groups should network for the best results.

## For Candidates Who Know What Type of Position They Are Seeking

Begin your networking process by asking people you know whether they know anyone they would recommend you speak to about new career opportunities. You need only one or two contacts to start building your network. Remember, the purpose of a networking meeting is *not* to find a job, but to build a network and learn useful information.

When you place your networking call, ask for 15 to 30 minutes of the person's time and be sure to tell them the name of the person who referred you (be sure you have that person's permission). When you arrive at the networking meeting, and after the usual initial pleasantries, provide a copy of your resume and then tell them who you are and what interests you. Listen carefully and ask questions only if you need to. Remember, you are there to get information, and the more they talk, the more you will learn. If you do ask questions, ask the person about his job, his achievements and challenges, why he chose the company, what his career plans are, and other information about him and his career. Remember, people always like to talk about themselves!

End each networking meeting by asking who else you should talk to and try to get three to five names (with full contact information). Thank the person for his time and insights, and ask whether you can call him back as things develop. Most important, be sure to honor the person's time. If you asked for 30 minutes, finish in 30 minutes. If things are going well and it is appropriate, they will give you more time.

*Never ask for a job while networking!* When a person likes you, he will most likely bring up the topic if he knows of a position that might be right for you. Let him start that conversation; not you. In fact, many positions have been created for candidates after a networking contact or informational interview!

## For Candidates Who Do Not Know What Type of Position They Are Seeking

Even if you are not sure what type of position you are most interested in, the same basic networking principles apply to you. In fact, the networking contact/informational interview can be extremely helpful in researching various industries and professions, building your knowledge, and subsequently making an informed decision as to your career path.

If Clint is working with a candidate who does not know what they want to do, he will ask a few people that he knows if they would do an informational interview with the candidate. Once there, the candidate shares his background, interests, and more; the network contact provides feedback regarding career options. Clint strongly urges his candidates to refrain from a lot of conversation. Rather, he wants them to listen and take notes. He also recommends that the candidate bring his or her resume along and ask for any feedback. Clint believes this strategy is extremely helpful in shortening the time it will take the candidate to develop a career strategy.

## Rules for Success

Clint shared his basic rules for success:

- For those of you who know what you want to do and those of you who do not, the most important thing to remember while networking is to always ask, "Who else should I talk to?" And, of course, be sure to thank the networking contact for their time. These people are now part of your personal network and you can contact them again in the future to talk about jobs—for them or for you—and a host of other topics. Now that the networking contact knows you, they are accessible to you throughout your working life.

- As a general rule, significant contacts are generally found at about stage three or four in a networking round of interviews. It is uncommon to find something on the first round of interviews, so do not be disappointed. That's how the process works.

- People looking for jobs should be as serious about the time they spend networking as they would be about spending $150 per hour for a career counselor. If you're paying that much money, you pay close attention. Do the same in your networking efforts; they are just as valuable.

- When you make a networking appointment, keep it! Be on time and send a thank-you note after the meeting. Thank-you notes should say something about your meeting; or if the person has written a book or quoted something important to you, say something about this in your letter. Your networking contacts are an information resource and you need to invest your time, effort, and energy in the process.

- Never ask for a job when you're networking! When you just ask for advice, people want to help you and provide you with information. They have no investment in the process except to help you. Never bring up the subject of a job. If you do, your networking meeting instantly becomes a job interview with an entirely different dynamic.

- Approach the informational interview as seriously as the employment interview because you never know when a meeting might turn into something that leads to an opportunity. Dress properly, watch your posture, carry a nice briefcase, and take notes.

No skill is as important as building a strong network. With so many people being displaced in the workforce, it's hard to build relationships in companies today. Instead, you will find much greater success in building a personal network of professional contacts who can be there to support you throughout your entire working life. Keep in touch with your network as things change in your career, let them know what is going on, and they might be able to help you turn things around more quickly and more successfully. Remember, your network is the most powerful tool in your job search kit!

□ □ □

# Networking Is the Norm

**Mary Jo Shackelford**
*President and Co-owner*
*Exselleration, LLC, Washington, DC*

When it comes to networking, Mary Jo Shackelford is a winner! The Cofounder and President of Exselleration, Mary Jo consults with firms nationwide to provide her expertise in networking, contact management, and global marketing. She firmly believes that networking is today's norm...for finding a new job, for landing a new account, for making new business contacts. It's all about who you know and who you can get to know. Here is Mary Jo's sage advice and guidance that we have summarized for you. These lessons are critical because networking to find a new job has become the norm!

## Lesson #1: What Exactly Is a Network?

A network is a collection of personal and professional contacts that you have established and maintain a relationship with on an ongoing basis. This group of contacts can be called upon for assistance in achieving your professional goals, aspirations, needs, and expectations. In turn, you provide that same level of support and contribution to assist each of your network contacts to achieve their own goals, aspirations, needs, and expectations.

## Lesson #2: Building a Network

Developing a powerful professional network takes time, energy, and discipline. Most importantly, as you progress in your career, you will need to differentiate between your network and your company's network. They are *not* the same. You must devote the time and energy to develop your own network, both within and outside of your company and industry. A strong network includes contacts from diverse backgrounds, positions, companies, and industries. To make this happen, you need to embrace every opportunity to meet new people. Once you make each new connection, you will need to nurture that contact so that he or she becomes a solid player in your professional network.

To begin the process of building your network, attend every professional meeting and event related to your specific industry/profession that you can find. The time invested and contacts made at these functions will be invaluable as you build your career and credibility within your chosen field. Expand on these groups to include national conventions and meetings as well. This will allow you to develop contacts outside of your local geographic area. Soon you will have a national network working for you and with you.

Take classes to improve your skills as well as to further expand your network. These new contacts in the educational field can act as references for your ability to learn and master new skills, while once again enlarging your circle of contacts.

As you become involved in these activities, chose a specific organization that you would like to get more involved with. This does not need to be related to your career; it could very well be an organization that involves one of your hobbies or personal interests. Once you're involved and working with this group, you have again widened your network of contacts and further expanded your career resources.

## Lesson #3: Working Your Network

Working your network does not just happen. You are responsible for making your network a valuable asset to both you and your contacts. Here are some suggestions for building and sustaining a strong and viable network:

- Use your calendar (or PDA) to list your monthly and quarterly calls to members of your network. It is your responsibility to stay in touch! Be sure to note birthdays, anniversaries, and other important events in each contact's life so that you will be sure to acknowledge them.

- Watch for community events in which members of your network may be involved. For example, if one of your contacts is the president of a volunteer organization that is holding a fundraiser, acknowledge that event in some way. Even if you cannot attend, a simple note congratulating your contact on a successful fundraiser will be greatly appreciated and remembered.

- Acknowledge your network contacts for success in their careers, such as major account wins, promotions, and media coverage. They will be flattered that you noticed and even more committed to helping you.

- Support your contacts when they need you. If one of your contacts is having a particularly difficult time, be sure to call them and see whether you might be able to help in some small way. It is always nice to hear from people when things are going well, but not many of us think to call when things are looking down. This type of call will instantly and forever set you apart from the crowd.

- Stay in touch with each of your contacts and be sure to update them on any major changes in your situation. This gives you an opportunity to contact them and, if your change involves a new position or joining a new group, might help your contact expand his or her own professional contacts.

- Use e-mail, phone, letters, and notes to stay in touch with contacts that you cannot see on a regular basis.

- Take the time to clip articles that might be of interest to your contacts and forward to them. They will be impressed, not only that you thought of them, but that you took extra time to send it!

Use Mary Jo's advice wisely and you can begin to develop a strong network that will help guide and shape your career in the years to come. What's more, your network will serve to strengthen your personal credibility and professional visibility, provide you with new contacts, and present great new opportunities. Use it wisely and your network will be your strongest resource and most valuable tool throughout your career.

□ □ □

# Finding the Right Networking Contacts

### Jeannine Nettles
*Agency Recruiter/Human Resources Specialist*
*State Farm Insurance, White Plains, NY*

Knowing who to network with and how to find those people can be an extremely difficult task. To shed some light on the subject and provide you with thoughtful insights, we asked Jeannine Nettles to share her recommendations with us.

Step one in the networking process is to identify the companies that appeal to you. This should not only be companies for which you are interested in working, but also companies to which you want to contribute. Being a part of an organization needs to be a mutual experience and you will gain the most value if you are an active part of the equation.

Once you have identified the companies you would most like to work with and for, get to know people within the organization with whom you have some common interest. You will find that you feel more comfortable talking about yourself and your career when you are familiar with a particular person. Really learn from that person and his or her experiences. Show your interest in them, their work history, and their achievements. How did they grow into that position? What were their career choices? What insights can they offer to you? You can then apply your career choices based on the information you received and begin to develop the best process for yourself to land a position with that company.

Just like developing any other relationships, when you are working to build your network contacts, appreciate the fact that it might take some time. Networking does not happen overnight, so don't get discouraged. Because building relationships does take time, when you have found a company that you enjoy and are intrigued by, you will be more focused and patient while building the relationships. Any type of success takes time and networking is no different.

When developing your contacts, you must work hard to meet lots of people. Sometimes these contacts can result in leads for actual positions. Many hot jobs are not advertised on the Internet or in newspapers. In fact, the very best jobs generally come as a result of networking contacts. You need to have a genuine interest in the people and the organization you want to become a part of. If you can accomplish this, you are well on your way to your next great opportunity!

□ □ □

# Be Resourceful and Creative

### Dr. John Sullivan
*Principal*
*DJS & Associates, Pacifica, CA*

We were honored to have the opportunity to interview Dr. John Sullivan, a professor from San Francisco State University who now operates a private corporate advisory service. John is extremely well known for his expertise in careers and employment and, in particular, his unique appreciation for the art of networking. Here is what he shared with us.

## Showcase Your Work

John believes that the very best way to network is to showcase your work. You need to get yourself and your work in front of the right decision makers so that they can truly see what you can do. Consider contacting members of associations to which you belong, sending them a personalized letter and a sample of your work, and asking them for their guidance and assistance. Or consider submitting your work to one of hundreds of listservs on the Internet. On these sites, you can post information and request professional feedback. If you can get someone to look at your work, you are actively building your professional network.

## Building Your Network

Frequently, people will tell you where to go to network—where everyone else goes. Don't go there! Instead, find new ways to attract and build your network, and you will find success much faster. If you and everyone else you know constantly go to the same networking contacts, they will run out of ideas, referrals, energy, and time.

Whenever you are attending a conference, look closely at the name tags of the other participants. In fact, it is best to arrive early at the conference, review the list of name tags on the table, and then watch who picks up which tag. You will then know who is who and who you want to network with. Then, practice the art of small talk so that you feel comfortable approaching these people and starting a conversation. That is step one in building and expanding your network.

## Questions to Ask Your Contacts

Another important consideration is that your speed of hire will be significantly enhanced if you can solve a problem. When you are meeting people for the first time, ask them what the biggest problem is that their company is facing. If appropriate, tell them you have dealt with a similar problem before and might have the answer. Then follow up by e-mail, snail mail, or phone to share your recommendations with them. Even if you do not have the answer to their problem, think of something substantive to share with them in your subsequent communications. Care about an issue and show it!

You can also inquire about where the growth is in their company or industry. Where are new hires coming from? How often do they hire? What types of people do they hire? Each network contact can potentially provide you with a wealth of information about their company and their industry. All you need to do is ask.

## Be a Consultant

Another great networking strategy is to join a company on a consulting basis. This provides you with immediate employment (perhaps short in tenure, but nonetheless, a job and a paycheck) and sets the stage for internal networking that can often result in an offer for a full-time, permanent position. Do not assume that taking a consulting position will be a dead end. To the contrary, it can be the start of a great new career!

## Two Unique Strategies

John also shared two very unique and creative networking strategies with us:

- Identify a company that you are interested in working for and send your business card and resume to the CEO by overnight mail. Then, a week or two later, send your resume to the company's human resources department and let them know that the CEO has your resume. You have a much better chance of being offered an interview if HR already knows that the CEO has your resume in hand.

- See where people park their cars and write down their license plate numbers. In many states, a quick phone call or Internet search will give you the name of the person who owns that vehicle. CEOs often arrive early and leave late, so see whose car is in the lot at 7 a.m. or 7 p.m. Then return to the parking lot on another day, walk past the CEO, and simply say hello. That's it. The following week, do it again, but this time ask, "Aren't you Joe Smith?" (or whatever the name of the person is). Then move on. The next time you encounter Joe, he will remember you and talk to you. Then, at that point, you can share the fact that you have a great new idea, a new project you are working on, or whatever, and ask if Joe might have a few minutes to spend with you. This strategy can be extremely effective.

The point of John's advice is that networking does work, but that in today's marketplace, a unique approach to networking will help you stand out from the crowd and get noticed. If you rely on only the traditional networking channels, your results might be slower and less effective. Expand beyond your normal reach, try new things, and watch for great success!

□ □ □

# Building Your Confidence

### Drew Farren
*Operations Manager*
*Corning's Recruiting Center for Excellence, Corning, NY*

Confidence is perhaps the single most critical component of effective networking. Regardless of your particular circumstance (for example, laid off, fired, relocated, quit), if networking is going to work for you, you must be confident of your professional skills and competencies. To help you learn how to build your confidence, we turned to a real pro, Drew Farren, an expert in networking, recruitment, and workforce management. Here's what he had to say.

Let's begin with the fact that 70 to 80 percent of all positions are filled through networking. Knowing that, it is your responsibility, as a job seeker, to know how to network with confidence, enthusiasm, and charisma. Here are some resources to establish your core network:

- **Develop a list of the top ten companies you would like to work for.** It is much better to start with a manageable number like ten instead of a larger number like 50. That sounds like so much work. If you start with ten this week, you can add another ten next week, another ten the following week, and, before you know it, you will have reached 50 or more. Break it down into smaller, more easily manageable tasks and you will find that you have much greater control and confidence.

- **Once you have your list of ten companies, find someone at each company that you have something in common with and then work to build a relationship with that individual.** As we all know, if you can find an ally on the inside who will promote your candidacy, your chances of employment with that particular company are dramatically increased.

- **Online networking has become a very efficient tool for finding names and contact information.** In fact, virtual networking and online networking resources have exploded over the past few years. To find company-related information, try these Web sites:

  - http://networking4.eliyon.com

    Search by company to find the names and positions of people who formerly worked for that organization.

  - http://center.spoke.com/invitation/basic.spoke

    Search by company to find names and positions of people who currently work within a company.

  If you want to expand your online networking efforts, visit these sites for business or social networking groups:

  - www.ryze.com/networks.php
  - www.linkedin.com
  - www.itsnotwhatyouknow.com
  - www.tribe.net

  Not only are all of these Web sites great ways to build new contacts, but these contacts can also be extremely valuable in generating other new contacts within their professional networks.

- **When networking, it is vital that you ask questions.** That truly is what networking is all about—collecting information, identifying new opportunities, making new contacts, and getting new referrals.

- **Build top-tier networking contacts with directors, vice presidents, and other senior-level executives.** Middle-level managers might not be focused on the bottom line like a senior-level manager. Every day that a position is not filled with the right person, it costs the company and negatively impacts its bottom line. Network with a decision maker who understands this and is motivated to fill a position.

- **Network from the top.** When you use a referral's name, that person should be known and respected. The person you have contacted through the referral will assume that you know that person and they will pay closer attention to you and your interest in the company.

- **Get used to being passed around!** It is not a bad thing; rather, it is the process of networking.

- **Write and distribute a monthly newsletter to your network.** It needs to be only one or two paragraphs to keep people in your network informed as to your progress, where you have interviewed, who you have met, and more. You can also ask for advice or assistance on how they might be able to help move things forward for you, help get you interviews, and help you find a great new opportunity. Normally, if you ask for advice, people will respond.

- **Do not let your network dry up.** If you do, people might not want to be a part of it anymore. Contact your network on a routine basis, either through direct phone calls or e-mail, get together for a networking breakfast, or send out e-mail announcements that include information or opportunities that might be valuable to your contacts. This is a great way to create a pipeline of networking by sharing job leads, and it can be especially effective for senior-level professionals.

- **Don't be afraid to pick up the telephone!** All too many people feel that this is a burden and they are uncomfortable doing it. Get over your fear and move forward or you won't have a network! Remember, there are only six steps of separation between you and the person/company you want to know. The only way you are going to get to know these people is by networking—assertively, consistently, and confidently.

- **Find common ground with your network contacts.** Networking is like going on a blind date. When you sit down, unless you have something in common to discuss, there will be no second date.

- **If networking truly is difficult for you,** consider reading *How to Win Friends and Influence People* by Dale Carnegie or *Sales Dogs* by Blair Singer. By doing so, you will learn the basics of how to establish relationships, win new friends, and actively sell yourself and your skills. An engineer who tends to be quite analytical can become a very good networker by reading this information and then putting into action what he or she has learned.

- **Learn to expect rejection, which, believe it or not, can be very positive.** Receiving 20 rejection letters shows that you are active in your search. What's more, the feedback you get with these rejections might be just what you need in order to sharpen your networking skills, improve your job search capabilities, and learn how to better sell and market your qualifications. Take the negative and turn it into a positive!

- **Judge yourself by goals and not by time.** If you network with 10 new companies per week, you will add 10 new people to your network each week. By the end of the month, you will have established 40 new contacts if not more. All weeks will not be the same—some will be more productive than others. Judge yourself by how many contacts you are able to make and not by the amount of time that it took.

- **Have two different elevator speeches prepared—one about your career and the other about who you are.** Both should be about 30 seconds in length. Use the STAR method to highlight your background and help you answer the infamous question, "Tell me about yourself." The STAR method focuses on

  - S = Situation
  - T = Tactic
  - A = Action
  - R = Results

  In essence, what you want to do is describe a situation, your tactical approach, your specific actions, and the positive results you delivered. By using this format, you can quickly prepare scripts that communicate precisely what you want your network contact to know about you.

In summary, building a network that will work for you and with you takes time, patience, and effort. However, once that network is built, it can be the most valuable resource you will ever have in your career. As such, to optimize your results, you must manage your networking efforts with confidence, energy, and an unending drive to find your next opportunity. It truly is out there waiting for you.

□ □ □

# Maximize Your Networking Efforts

**Raphael J. D. Sebastian**
*Vice President*
*WorkplaceDiversity.com, Livingston, NJ*

Networking is a very complex process that must be handled in a structured, sequential manner and not on a helter-skelter basis. To better understand how to maximize your networking efforts, we turned to an expert, Raphael Sebastian, for his insights and recommendations. Here's what he shared with us.

## The Networking "Game"

Networking is *not* a spectator sport. You have to put yourself out there and get in the game. In order to effectively network, you must have a sound strategy and commit to an approach that will work best for you. You cannot look at it as though it is something distasteful. Rather, try to think of networking as a game—a relationship-development game where the more "live" contacts you make the higher you score. Since it is a fact that "who you know" is critical to furthering your success in everything that you do, you need to meet as many people as you can to build an active network of contacts.

Most people approach networking the wrong way. First, they say hello, hand over a business card, and then tell people what they want or need from them. If you approached a dating relationship in that same way, you would certainly be rejected. Instead, you need to introduce yourself and enter into the conversation on the human level. You should be cordial and kind in the early stages of the conversation. Ask the person about themselves and their needs. Listen actively. See how or if you can help them. Your goal is to get them to buy into you as a person before you share your needs with them.

In talking to the person, you want to find an opportunity to share the skills and value you potentially can offer. By listening well, you will learn what the person or organization is looking for and you can then align yourself with them. Before you go to a meeting or an event, you should do your homework to learn who is going to be there, what the key players will be looking for, what is important to the participants, and how their needs and goals fit with your needs, objectives, and values. You want to find possible synergies so that you can make a meaningful connection, just like dating. Suppose, for example, that you are a man who has just started dating a woman who is an extremely religious church-goer and you are not. In the long run, this relationship might not work because your values are not aligned with hers in an area that might be very important. The same can be said of a company that is looking for a candidate to work long hours and weekends. If you value your leisure time and prefer not to make such sacrifices, the opportunity may not be the right opportunity for you. Do your homework!

## Following Up

To network effectively, you must follow up. This is where most people fall short by doing what Raphael calls "just-in-time networking," or networking only when the need for a new job or something else is imminent. Networking is a basic sales skill. Everyone needs to, and has to, sell themselves at some point. Great salespeople are always trying to expand their Rolodexes. And, just like a great salesperson, you should, too. In fact, you need to try to make contacts on a regular basis and reach out to them before you need something from them. That's known as nurturing your database and it will keep your contacts alive and healthy. The bottom line is that if you are not following up, you are really not networking.

A good technique is to record relevant information about your contacts on either an index card or in a contact-management system on your PC. You can even use the back of their business cards. Every contact counts and you must follow up appropriately with all of them. The information you record will really help you follow up and remember key things about each contact. *Do not rely on your memory.* Instead, write everything down to remind you of names, contact information, action items, spouses, personal items, and more.

When reaching out to nurture your networking contacts, you can send just brief one-line e-mail messages to wish them a happy holiday, refer them to a great article, congratulate them on a particular achievement, or ask whether there is anything that you can do for them. Remember, networking is a two-way street—you do for them and they will do for you. People are delighted to get e-mail messages with information for them and no questions to answer and no action items to pursue.

## Who to Network With

Raphael brought up an outstanding point when he commented that all too frequently people look only at titles when deciding whom to network with. If the title is significant, they will proceed. If it is not, they bypass that person, often making a huge mistake. Remember that all contacts count. Look at the example of walking into a company. Typically, the first person you meet is a receptionist or the administrative assistant to one of the company's executives. Although he or she might not have a big title, they can still be tremendously valuable to you in your networking or job search efforts. They might be the influential gatekeeper that you have to get past. They might have a strong relationship with the decision maker. If you fail to nurture that contact, or if you are rude to the assistant, you can bet it will get back to the decision maker and you will, most likely, be out of the running. If the administrative assistant thinks you are a jerk, anyone he or she talks to about you will also think you are a jerk! Be nice to everyone...that's what networking is all about.

## Other Practices to Remember

When making a networking phone call, make sure there is a smile in your voice and start the conversation with an upbeat, positive opening. Sell yourself, but remember that networking is really all about the other person. When you identify with the other person's needs, you instantly start to develop the network contact and the rapport that you need. When networking, small talk is a big deal.

Even in our fast-paced culture, people do not always feel that everything has to be just about business. People like to feel they are engaged in conversation, and you need to pave a smooth path to that comfortable conversation. You have about one minute to sell yourself to someone you do not know. This is when your elevator pitch can be extremely important. An elevator pitch is a 30-second memorized story about who you are and what you do. Your elevator pitch is *not* a job description. Rather, it should communicate a positive message about your accomplishments and how they will benefit the person or organization that you are dealing with. You can also communicate how your skills and accomplishments might help the organization overcome a specific problem it has encountered.

Be careful not to ask for too much too soon. If you are making a telephone contact and the first thing you ask for is a face-to-face meeting, it might be interpreted that you are moving too fast and want to close the deal already. Your first network contact is much like a first date—you want to develop a relationship before you attempt to close. One of the most critical components in developing those positive relationships is your ability to listen well. People love to be really heard by candidates, so be sure that you teach yourself good listening skills. They will be invaluable.

In summary, to be an effective networker, you must know what the company is looking for and what you bring to the table. Do not necessarily start with the human resources department within a company. Very often the best people to network with are line managers, professional staff, and support staff. In fact, receptionists and secretaries often know everything that is going on in a company, yet are often overlooked as great networking resources. Be sure to network with everyone. You never know where that one great opportunity will come from.

□ □ □

# Networking with Associations

**Nels B. Olson**
*Managing Director—External Affairs*
*Korn/Ferry International, Washington, DC*

When we wanted expert advice on networking, we looked to the best of the best—Korn/Ferry International—one of the world's largest and most successful search firms. Once inside Korn/Ferry, we wanted the best of their best, which is how we met Nels Olson, a well-respected Korn/Ferry employee and a member of the executive recruiting team that recruited for President George Bush's administration. Here's what he shared with us about how to develop and leverage association contacts to optimize your networking efforts and results.

Nels strongly advises that senior-level executives become active and involved in trade associations, professional associations, and interest groups. Executives can utilize these organizations as prime networking tools if they develop key relationships at the right level, because these associations can guide executives in discovering changes and opportunities in their industries. To make these contacts work best for you, consider the following:

- **Attend association trade shows.** These events are generally in a casual setting, which is the best place to develop new knowledge and build new relationships. Because they are largely social gatherings, the pressure is off, people are relaxed, and you should have the opportunity for great conversation.

- **Take a leadership role in an association.** When you do this, you will be able to network through a leadership role and at a leadership level. Whether your goal is a secretarial position or an assignment in the executive office, your leadership role within an association can be invaluable in developing new relationships. Get involved, become visible, make contributions, and people will take notice.

- **Mentor someone new in the association.** Provide guidance and suggestions, facilitate their new contacts, and give back to the industry or profession that has given so much to you. These types of relationships can lead to wonderful new opportunities for you.

Aware that we were interviewing one of the brightest in the search industry, we extended our initial interview past the question of how best to use associations and asked for additional valuable insights from Nels.

Nels warned that there are certain pitfalls that senior executives must watch out for when building their contact networks. First and foremost, they should not try too hard and appear desperate. They must build their self-awareness skills and know how the push/pull balance works in networking. CEOs and senior executives who do not easily build relationships or try too hard can rub people the wrong way. For senior executives who find networking to be particularly challenging, Nels recommends that they work with a coach to help them develop better interpersonal, delivery, and relationship-management skills. People can come around quickly when they are provided with the right skills and when those skills are used in the right environment.

Senior executives need to be open to new ideas, new opportunities, and new adventures. They need to be involved in a culture where they can thrive, contribute, and feel good about themselves. They need to have a career plan in effect for themselves and know where they want to go, when, and how. Then they need to use networking—with associations and in countless other venues—to learn, expand their knowledge, and make those opportunities happen.

Just as important as everything mentioned above, Nels believes that senior executives need to proactively manage perceptions of themselves. People do not always do a good job of marketing themselves and often do not have a strong sense of self. To be sure that they are networking to their best ability, executives must be aware of how others perceive them—how they look and how they speak, the way they walk into a room, how they shake hands, the amount of eye contact they make, the words they use, their body posture, and so much more. The better a candidate knows himself, the better able he or she will be to build networking relationships that will be critical to long-term career success.

□ □ □

# It's a Lifelong Process

### Gerry Crispin and Mark Mehler
*Authors, Speakers, Writers, and Consultants*
*CareerXroads, Kendall Park, NJ*

Some of you might recognize Gerry's and Mark's names as the authors of the great online job search book, *CareerXroads*. Knowing that their expertise spans the entire range of the careers and employment industry, it was difficult to decide what to interview them about. Once our discussion got going, however, it was obvious that the process of lifelong networking was a concept they consider critical to one's success—today and in the future. Here's what they shared with us.

Networking is a lifelong process, not something you do just when you need a job! It is all about building relationships—with everyone you can and anywhere you can. These are relationships that you probably will not use today but that can be of tremendous value to you in the future.

When Gerry was a young adult, he would track down authors and thank them for the information he learned from their articles and books. He would tell them what he learned and ask them for their advice on how to become a successful published author. This is precisely what networking is all about—building relationships that will benefit both you and your network contact for years and years to come.

Mark is particularly concerned that college students and young adults do not focus on lifelong networking, but rather, devote their time and energy to networking to find a job. They often look upon these relationships as stepping stones to something bigger and better. Mark believes that colleges must do a better job of educating their students about how critical the process of lifelong networking is to the future success of their careers.

One of the best things about networking is that it is exponential! The more people you bring into your network, the faster and larger it will grow. Be curious and talk to everyone. Alumni associations, professional organizations, professional networking groups, and social networks are great places to meet people. Even your neighbors, mailman, Realtor, and local librarian have contacts and can often be a big help to you. And you never know who you might meet standing in line at the grocery store! Your list of potential networking contacts is endless.

When communicating with your network contacts, know what you want to do and be passionate about it. Your level of energy, optimism, interest, and enthusiasm will be contagious and will encourage your network contacts to really work for you!

□ □ □

# The Do's and Don'ts of Networking

**Jeannine Nettles**
*Agency Recruiter/Human Resources Specialist*
*State Farm Insurance, White Plains, NY*

To end our chapter with some practical networking guidance, we again turned to Jeannine Nettles for her valuable insights on the do's and don'ts of networking. Here are her recommendations:

## Do's

- Do be as friendly as possible. Start a conversation, be approachable, and find topics of mutual interest. In an event or meeting situation, be prepared to meet new people, but also be prepared to meet them virtually anywhere—at a gym, at the grocery store, or on the street. Then be prepared to talk about what you are trying to accomplish. This way, people can gather all the information they need about you. You never know where you could meet someone who knows just the right opportunity for you.

- Do have business cards prepared with your complete contact information (phone numbers, mailing address, e-mail address).

- Do have something for people to take away. Typically, a recruiter will take a person's card and reference that information for later retrieval.

- Do have personal business cards made without your current employer's information.

## Don'ts

- Don't just hand out your business card unless you know that it is the right forum in which to do so. There are specific events that are designed for business card exchange and you need to know the proper forum for each event. Sometimes it is not appropriate to talk about new opportunities.

- Don't rush things. Networking takes time.

- Don't just join any company. Rather, make sure it is a company that has the same values as you do and a company in which you are quite interested.

□ □ □

## Authors' Best Networking Advice

1. **Networking really does work!** Although most job seekers hate to network, it is by far the most effective job search strategy that anyone can employ. In fact, statistics prove that somewhere between 70 and 80 percent of all jobs are filled through networking contacts. Whether you like it or not, networking must be an integral part of your job search campaign and your lifelong career-management efforts.

2. **Ask your network contacts for help and not for a job.** Most of your contacts will not have a job available for you at the time you contact them. And, to be honest, that is not really want you want from them. What you do want are three to five additional contact names, people who might be aware of opportunities or might be well networked with others who could be of benefit to you. Remember, people will be much more inclined to offer you help than to offer you a job!

*(continued)*

(continued)

3. **Communicate with confidence, passion, energy, and enthusiasm.** People really want to help other people who are passionate, enthusiastic, and confident. They know that if they refer you to one of their colleagues, you will make a good and positive impression. Be sure that your communications—written and verbal—demonstrate the degree of passion and excitement that you want to showcase in all of your job search efforts.

4. **Informational interviews are a great networking tool.** Ever thought about working for that large electric utility down the street? What about the local soft-drink bottler or regional CPA firm? You might have given these companies and others like them some thought, but not really known enough about what they do or who they hire. If so, call and ask for an informational interview and *not* a job interview. Most people will be happy to extend a few minutes to you to discuss their company and what they do. Then, once you have collected that information, you will be in a much better situation to determine whether that company is right for you. What's more, you will have made a great new contact that you can add to your network!

5. **Network everywhere.** When most people think about networking, they think about their professional contacts and that's it. However, that's not it and, in fact, there are probably scores of individuals that you know outside of work who can be of value to you in your networking efforts. Consider the FedEx delivery person, your local pharmacist, or an insurance sales associate. Each of these individuals that you deal with on a routine basis knows lots of other people that you do not know. Be sure to expand your networking efforts beyond your business life to embrace your local community. You never know when your spouse's best friend (who you know only from social gatherings) might have just the contacts that you need.

6. **Join organizations.** Professional and trade associations, civic organizations, and other groups are often an excellent source for networking. Just think about the number of people you could meet by joining and attending the monthly

meetings of the local chapters of the American Management Association, American Chemical Society, Society of Association Executives, American Red Cross, or any one of hundreds of other organizations. The contacts you can make will serve you well throughout your career.

7. **Volunteer.** Volunteering is also an extraordinary way to meet new people outside of their normal working environments. Have you ever thought of volunteering for a Habitat for Humanity project? If not, you should consider that or any one of a number of other charitable organizations. Often the people involved in these projects and organizations are local business leaders giving back to their community. Get to know these people!

8. **Create an organized networking plan.** Being organized is one of the most critical aspects of networking. As your network grows and grows, the number of contacts you have will increase at a phenomenal rate. In order to keep track of all of your contacts, the follow-up communications you have promised, the new contacts to connect with, and more, you must have a workable system in place. If you forget to follow up as promised, you will have left a less-than-favorable impression with your contact and he or she might question the seriousness of your job search and your networking relationship with them.

9. **Write a networking newsletter.** One of the best ways to stay in touch with your network, let them know what is going on with your job search and your career, and offer them support is to write and distribute a newsletter. You can consider doing this once a month or once a quarter. Begin your newsletter by sharing information that might be of value to them and then follow up with a brief summation of your job search to date. You can also ask for additional leads and referrals, contact names at specific companies, industry data, and more. As long as you share information with your contacts—information that can be valuable to them—they will be delighted to receive your newsletter and respond to you with valuable insights and contacts.

*(continued)*

*(continued)*

10. **Be realistic.** More often than not, it will not be until your third or fourth tier of network contacts that you really start to get some action in your job search. This is the norm, so do not be discouraged. Just as with everything else, there is a process to the art of networking and you must be patient and realistic in your expectations. Do not set yourself up for disappointment by expecting extraordinary results too early in your campaign.

## Career and Job Search Survey Results

### Question:

Are you more likely to consider a candidate if he or she has been recommended or referred by someone you know?

### Results:

56 percent reported that they would interview the candidate out of courtesy to the person they know.

44 percent reported that they would interview the candidate because they perceive the candidate as qualified.

0 percent reported they would not interview the candidate because it would make them uncomfortable.

### Conclusion:

Networking effectively and generating employment referrals will result in interviews.

# CHAPTER 6
# How to "Nail" Your Interviews

## In This Chapter

- Tools and Strategies to Impress Your Interviewer
- Making a Winning Impression
- The Most Common Mistakes Interviewees Make
- How Hiring Managers Determine Whether a Candidate Is a Good Match
- Asking Questions During an Interview
- Taking Notes During an Interview
- Listening to Understand
- Can You Recover from an Interview Faux Pas?
- When Suitability Is the Issue

- Building Rapport with the Interviewer
- Letting the Real You Shine Through
- The Importance of Body Language and Eye Contact
- The Power of Endorsements and References
- Writing Powerful Thank-You Letters
- Top 14 Strategies to Nail Your Interviews
- Authors' Best Interviewing Advice
- Career and Job Search Survey Results

Many job seekers believe that once they have reached the interview stage in their job search, they are halfway home. If only it were that easy. Getting the interview is just one step in a series of many steps you must take to reach the final job offer. And, in fact, interviewing is a multi-step process within itself. You can generally expect to go through two, three, four, or sometimes even more interviews before a final offer is made.

At the interview stage, you have only just begun the excitement of your search! That's when things really kick into high gear and you must be poised to sell yourself. Without grandstanding or being overbearing, you want to communicate your knowledge, skills, accomplishments, and fit for the position. Powerful interviewing is not simply a matter of answering questions as they are asked. Rather, it is about your ability to subtly take control of the interview, build a strong rapport with your interviewer, and present your most notable accomplishments as they relate to that company's needs. It is about positioning yourself as someone who takes control of a situation, solves problems, and delivers results.

Just as important, interviewing is a two-way street. You are not only there to answer the interviewer's questions about you and your experience, but you are also there to ask questions. Come to each interview prepared with appropriate questions about the company, the industry, the people, the products, the politics, the values of the organization, and more. Do your research well before the interview, get to know the company and its mission, and understand the corporate culture. It will be important to your interviewer to determine whether you can be part of the existing team.

Although interviewing can often be a somewhat intimidating situation, confidence in one's self and one's capabilities is perhaps the most important message you can communicate. If you want a company to take a risk and hire you (after all, you are a virtually unknown commodity), you must exude confidence in your ability to perform. It is this strength in personality, energy, and vitality that will attract a company to you and entice them to bring you aboard.

Our collection of interviews in this chapter is particularly strong, and we thank all the corporate HR executives, hiring managers, and recruiters who contributed. Our focus was on identifying what each expert considers to be the most critical strategies for interview success. Here's what they had to say.

□ □ □

## Tools and Strategies to Impress Your Interviewer

### R. Douglas Hardin
*Senior Vice President—Federal Systems*
*IntelliDyne, LLC, Falls Church, VA*

To uncover the tools, strategies, attitudes, demeanor, and mannerisms that will truly impress a hiring decision maker, we asked Doug Hardin to share his interview strategy with us. Here's how he summarized his step-by-step process.

Doug begins each interview session with a detailed discussion of the company and its operations. He wants his candidates to understand that working for IntelliDyne is a real commitment. It is a tough job in an intense, 24/7 environment and requires real dedication. He is candid with his candidates and he expects the same in return from them. Both parties need to evaluate whether this is a good match to ensure a successful hire.

Early in the interview, Doug also asks his candidates to tell him about themselves. In response, he wants candidates to share information about their background, jobs, projects, accomplishments, technical qualifications, and more that is relevant to the particular job at hand. If a candidate has experience in other related areas, it is fine to mention, but the focus must be on relevant skills and experiences.

Next, Doug focuses on questions that help him determine whether a candidate has the right qualifications for the position. He asks direct, and often difficult, questions. "You've had several jobs. Which one was the hardest and why? Please give me specific examples of situations that made it difficult and how you managed those challenges." But the bottom line is that Doug does not care about which one was the hardest. What he is attempting to do is use the questions to learn about the candidate, how they think, and what they do.

He will also want to know which job was the best job and what was so good about it. From a candidate's answers, he can ascertain what his or her challenges were and what that person can do. He will learn about the culture in which the candidate thrived and compare that to IntelliDyne's culture.

Much of Doug's evaluation of a candidate is based on character, integrity, and attitude. "It is extremely difficult to evaluate a candidate's technical capabilities in an interview. I won't know that until the candidate is hired." Candidates should be ready to talk about values, character, culture, and more. Doug wants to know what "culture" means to them and what values they hold dear. It is his belief that values impact performance, productivity, and cultural fit. That, in and of itself, is what will sell Doug on a potential candidate.

Doug's interviewing process is a breath of fresh air in today's market! When you interview with him, you will not have to come back for multiple interviews. You might have one additional interview, at which time you will meet others in the organization, but that's it. The process is streamlined and efficient.

□ □ □

# Making a Winning Impression

## Mary McMurtry
*Field Employment Manager*
*Southwest Airlines, Dallas, TX*

To further expand our discussion on how to make a winning impression during an interview, we turned to Mary McMurtry. We learned a wealth of information about how candidates can positively position themselves, along with lots of interesting facts about the unique and inspiring culture of the Southwest Airlines organization.

Like Doug Hardin of IntelliDyne, Mary believes that cultural fit is of paramount importance. "The culture of an organization is a living, breathing entity," Mary commented. "In fact, I work hard to demonstrate our corporate culture to prospective hires by greeting them in a friendly manner, shaking their hands, and asking if they were able to find the office easily." She displays a caring attitude and expects the same from her candidates.

Mary and her group utilize behavior-based interviewing techniques, believing that a candidate's past behavior is indicative of his or her future performance. She might ask, "Tell me about a time when..." when talking about the job so that she can compare what the candidate has done in the past with what will be expected of him or her in this position. She also frequently asks, "What attracts you to this position and what makes it exciting for you?"

Mary recommends that whenever a candidate responds to a question, he or she shares the whole context and paints a picture that is clear, accurately reflects the situation, and focuses on his or her contributions. "Be thorough and concise with your answers so that the recruiter and manager fully understand your background. If you don't do this, the recruiter or manager might not probe deeply enough to truly appreciate your experience."

Honesty is also a critical hiring criterion. Mary will thoroughly probe to determine whether the candidate is being 100 percent honest—in the interview and on the application. If they see a question about criminal history, even regarding speeding tickets, candidates need to be upfront. Background checks are done on all new hires, and if the candidate does not reveal this information on the application, it could be a deal-breaker.

When hiring, Mary and the hiring manager work cooperatively. If the candidate is applying for a position in Information Technology, Mary and her recruiters might look for something different than the hiring manager or direct supervisor of the candidate does. The hiring manager generally focuses on the hard skills, while recruiters tend to focus on soft skills. Therefore, if the candidate is seeking a specialized position, the interview can be a delicate ballet between the two. After the interview is completed, Mary will meet with the hiring manager to share ideas, evaluate each person's candidacy, and work toward making a decision.

When nearing the end of an interview, Mary often asks, "Of all the candidates I have interviewed today, what do you believe makes you the best candidate?" Now is the time to toot your own horn by summarizing your background, work ethic, personality traits, notable achievements, technical qualifications, and more that so strongly position you for the job.

Once a candidate has been hired, Mary and her staff continue to follow up to be sure they've made a wise hiring decision. If things are not going as well as hoped, they will go back, review the hiring process, and attempt to immediately and expeditiously address any problems, concerns, or inconsistencies. For example, if a candidate assured the interviewer that working nights and weekends was no problem, but once hired it did become a problem, Mary would meet with the new hire to discuss and resolve the situation.

Mary's most critical advice to job seekers: "It's your show and you need to make the most out of the 30 minutes or so that you have been given. Work hard to impress me and I will gladly move your candidacy forward."

□ □ □

# The Most Common Mistakes Interviewees Make

**Lou Adler**
*CEO*
*The Adler Group/CJA, Tustin, CA*

We were fortunate enough to interview Lou Adler, an expert on interviewing and trends in job search, about what he considers some of the most common mistakes job seekers make during their interviews. Here's what he shared with us.

## Not Preparing Enough

Fundamentally, the biggest mistakes candidates make is they do not prepare enough! Ask yourself how much time you spent preparing for your last interview and see whether you are like most people who admit to spending only an hour or two preparing for a job interview. That simply is not enough. Just think how much time you would devote to preparing a business presentation and ask yourself why an interview presentation should require any less preparation.

To succeed in an interview and win the interviewer's confidence, you must be able to answer the question, "So, why are you here?" And the only way to effectively answer that question is through an intense commitment to preparation, learning as much about the company and the position as you possibly can.

When you are well prepared for the interview, you will exude confidence. If you are nervous, my best advice is to fight through it, remind yourself that you are prepared for the interview, well qualified for the position, and capable of responding to any and all of the questions the interviewer might ask.

## Not Knowing Your Greatest Selling Points

Once you have learned as much as you possibly can about the company and the position, your next step is to review and write down your 10 to 12 greatest selling points for that company—the greatest values you bring to them and your ability to meet their objectives. There will be occasions when the interviewer does not ask the right questions to bring out those skills in your discussion. It is your responsibility to be sure that you introduce those 10 to 12 skill areas into the conversation so that you are certain to communicate all the essential information. Write down and practice a detailed explanation or example of each of your 10 to 12 skill sets, being sure to highlight accomplishments within those specific areas and not just generalities. If you are qualified, prove it!

## Not Asking the Right Questions

Candidates must ask hiring managers the right questions in the interview, things such as key responsibilities of the position, key performance objectives, lines of reporting responsibility, performance measurement processes, success factors, and more. When the job seeker asks these types of specific questions, he or she is able to determine what is important to the interviewer and then use that knowledge to determine which skills, accomplishments, responsibilities, and more are most on target. By customizing answers to each company's specific needs, job seekers will be able to more favorably position themselves against other candidates and get the offer.

## Not Asking for the Job

When the interview is nearing its end, the most important thing that any job seeker can do is to ask for the position and inquire as to the next step in the interviewing process. As this point, each job seeker's goal is to schedule the next interview and move the process along.

## Asking About Salary

Just as important, do not ask about salary. If it is a first or second interview, it's too early in the process to be discussing compensation. Rather, inquire as to how performance will be measured and close the interview with a summary of how you will meet (or exceed) those performance requirements. Communicate that you are already thinking as part of the team and not solely interested in what's in it for you.

Remember, when you are interviewing, you are selling a solution: you. By researching the company's Web site to learn all that you can, you can package your experience as a solution to that organization's needs. Without specific knowledge about the company, you cannot accomplish this and your interview becomes just one among many others—not distinct, not memorable, and not a winner. Develop rapport with your interviewer, engage him or her, share the knowledge you have learned about the company, ask great questions, and you will immediately distinguish yourself from all the other applicants. Then leave the interview knowing that you have planted in the interviewer's mind the idea that you can do the job and that you are the #1 candidate.

□ □ □

# How Hiring Managers Determine Whether the Candidate Is a Good Match

**Robert B. Kuller**
*CEO*
*Process Powered Consulting, Audubon, PA*

Moving forward in the interview process, we asked Robert Kuller how he decides whether an applicant is right for his company and the position for which he is interviewing. He shared some really interesting and insightful information with us.

Bob uses the following criteria to determine whether a candidate is right for a position within his organization:

- Ability to think critically and independently
- Ability to make decisions
- Ability to work collaboratively
- Strong experience and record of accomplishments
- Strong technical qualifications
- Strong ethics

His interview process can best be described as behavioral-based. Bob uses a portfolio of potential work scenarios that he outlines for each candidate, and then asks them to respond with what they would do, how, and why. In essence, he is trying to identify the specific behaviors and actions that a candidate will demonstrate in a specific situation. By doing so, he is able to ask meaningful questions and, in response, get substantive answers from each candidate.

Here are some sample questions that Bob might ask in a specific interview situation:

- You walk into an organization and its product-development and lifecycle-management departments have significant problems. Most critical are specific quality and documentation issues. Which would you attempt to address first?

- What happens if your boss thinks X and you think Y? How do you go about expressing your thoughts and ideas, and how do you present your alternatives?

- You have two major projects due next Friday and there is simply no way that you are going to meet your scheduling objectives. What do you do?

It is important to note that Bob is not looking for a right answer. Rather, he is focusing on how the candidate thinks and the process he or she will use to solve problems. His objective is always to identify candidates who can present multiple viewpoints, look at a total situation, think critically, and act rationally.

Most significantly, by utilizing this behavioral-based or scenario-based interviewing process, Bob is attempting to determine whether each candidate meets his six hiring criteria as outlined previously. To clearly communicate his points, he detailed why these six criteria are so critical to his hiring process.

## Critical Thinking/Independent Thinking/Decision Making

All too many people do not have the skills needed to be effective decision makers, and managers must make positive decisions. When Bob interviews, he is attempting to elicit responses that demonstrate that the candidate is assertive enough to make critical decisions.

Any candidate in a job interview needs to take a certain amount of control over the interview. This means affirming and taking a good offensive (as in sports) to not just answer questions with two-line responses, but to be specific about situations, circumstances, and results so that the candidate is sure to communicate what he or she has accomplished and how.

If Bob were to ask a candidate, "How do I know you are capable of making quality-based decisions," he wants to hear an answer that demonstrates where and when this candidate has made quality-based decisions based on real-life experiences. He does not want a quick, textbook answer.

## Collaboration

Bob attempts to get a clear understanding of each candidate's specific management style. He wants to know how they work and encourage a group. Are they collaborative in spirit? Are they a team builder, or is their style more dictatorial? Bob wants to know that the candidate is open to the opinions of others and able to distill the really great suggestions from the mediocre ones, sell those great ideas to the group, and motivate them to move forward and excel. These types of issues are particularly critical in a company whose management style is open, interactive, and team-based.

## Experience/Accomplishments/Technical Qualifications

If a candidate is an effective interviewer, he or she will have communicated a great deal about their experience, qualifications, and accomplishments throughout the entire interview process. They will respond to questions using real-life examples and will have given the interviewer a good sense of who they are, how they think, and what they can make happen. Bob will then follow up with any additional questions to get specific information that might not have been addressed earlier.

In discussing the infamous "tell me about yourself" question, Bob is not looking for answers that can be found on a resume or in a cover letter. Rather, he wants the candidate to tell him what he does not know or what he cannot know from the resume. In essence, he wants the candidate to answer the question, "What is exciting about you?" He wants to know why each candidate believes he or she is a great candidate for the position, more about his or her specific skills and qualifications, and a demonstration of his or her strong ethical commitment. If a candidate answers this question well (Bob usually asks it early in the interview), the interview gets off to a great start. If the candidate does not answer well, he or she is starting the interview from 50 feet under and that is a difficult place from which to ever recover.

Pay close attention to Bob's six top hiring criteria as you prepare for your interviews and give yourself a competitive edge. If these are the things that are most important to him, you can be assured that they are of importance to the vast majority of hiring executives.

## Strong Ethical Fiber

Ethics is critical for today's organizations, both large and small. In turn, Bob wants a candidate to convey that he or she can be trusted and knows the difference between right and wrong. He is interested in knowing what a manager would do if an employee lied on an expense report about a $15 expenditure. For Bob, stealing $15 from a company on an expense report is still stealing, and he would like to know whether a candidate feels the same way. Knowing a candidate's thoughts on ethics will show a reliable pattern of what to expect. What would the candidate do in a situation like that?

□ □ □

# Asking Questions During an Interview

## Shaun Smith

*Manager—Employment*
*Memorial Sloan-Kettering, New York, NY*

Shaun Smith has hired scores of candidates over the years. We asked him what types of questions he likes a candidate to ask and how much of his hiring decision is based on the questions that the candidate does ask. Shaun responded with the following.

First and foremost, Shaun believes it is each candidate's responsibility to ask the right questions at each interview. These questions should pertain to the company—its mission, goals, and values—and to the specific responsibilities of the position. He believes that the most effective interviews are two-way conversations between the candidate and the interviewer. "Put yourself in the interviewer's shoes and think about how important the interaction is," comments Shaun. "It is certainly much easier to interview a candidate who responds, asks questions, and communicates that they are interested in the position."

Here are a few important guidelines for asking questions during an interview that Shaun shared with us:

- **Do not ask questions that have already been covered in the interview.** On occasion, Shaun has identified someone he believed was a great candidate, but his sentiments changed when the candidate starting asking questions that had already been discussed previously in the interview. Do this once and it is okay; more than once and it demonstrates that the candidate was not paying attention.

- **Do not ask too many questions.** Shaun believes that five questions are appropriate. Any more is too many. In most cases, interviews are timed and interviewers can become impatient and watch the clock.

- **Prepare your questions well.** Begin by thinking about what stage in the interview process you are in. For example, technical questions will not be answered at the human resources level. Then consider the specific conversation that has transpired during your interview and base your questions on that information. Tune in to the key points that the interviewer has focused on and ask relevant questions. This will confirm to the interviewer that you were listening and are interested.

- **Always have questions.** There is nothing worse at the end of an interview than not having any questions to ask. This can communicate to the interviewer that the candidate is not particularly interested or attentive. This will virtually end an individual's candidacy, particularly if the hiring manager was not too certain about the candidate to begin with.

The Q&A section of the interview should help the interviewer truly understand the candidate and what's in his or her mind. Shaun commented that there have been occasions when he was not particularly interested in a candidate. However, the questions the candidate asked were so good and so on point that it positively changed his perception of that individual.

□ □ □

# Taking Notes During an Interview

### Viola W. Bostic
*Deputy Executive Director*
*National Federation of Community Development Credit Unions,*
*New York, NY*

As career professionals ourselves, we are constantly asked whether it is appropriate to take notes during an interview. To get an insider's perspective on how companies view this, we turned to Viola W. Bostic.

Viola believes that taking notes during an interview is extremely important. She states that the best way to start is to ask the interviewer whether they mind if you take notes. More than 99 percent of the time, the interviewer will not mind at all and, in fact, be impressed with your level of interest in the company and the position.

Viola stresses the importance of writing down words and short phrases that will remind the candidate of specific conversations and topics of discussion. She doesn't recommend that you write full sentences or paragraphs of information. If a candidate does this, his or her focus is on note-taking and not on the interview itself. It is critical that the candidate continue to maintain steady eye contact with the interviewer as he or she is jotting down notes. Viola advises all job seekers to be sure to write down items such as

- All the key points of the conversation
- The key issues and challenges impacting the company

- The key hiring criteria for the position
- Any other information that they might want to refer back to

Following the interview, the candidate can use the notes to write a powerful thank-you letter that addresses all the key points. This task, in and of itself, will position the job seeker as a strong candidate in Viola's perception. "I'm torn between thank-you notes that are e-mailed or handwritten, and recommend that you use whichever is most appropriate for the time frame involved." If the interviewer and company are ready to make a decision by the end of the week, an e-mail thank-you letter is appropriate. Otherwise, Viola recommends a handwritten note mailed via regular mail. Note that Viola prefers a handwritten note on nice stationery and not a typed letter. Her perception is that this is much more personal.

One final comment that Viola shared with us is each applicant's need to *read* the interviewer, watch his or her body language, and pay attention to the flow of the conversation. If a job seeker is able to do this, he or she will be able to better control the interview and set the stage to favorably position him- or herself for an offer.

□ □ □

# Listening to Understand

## Rocky Parker
*Human Resources Officer—Associate Services*
*Nationwide Insurance, Columbus, OH*

Something that all of us hear about when we discuss the subject of job interviews is how critical it is to really listen to what your interviewer is sharing with you. To understand just how important this is, we asked Rocky to describe how he can tell whether a job search candidate is really listening and what impact that has on him. Here's what he shared.

Rocky begins each interview with a five- to ten-minute chat to set the stage. He welcomes the candidate, helps the person relax, and verifies that both are on the same page about the job he or she is applying for. Then the interview proceeds.

About 45 to 50 minutes later, when the interview is winding down, the one thing that most impresses Rocky is hearing the candidate repeat back to him key information that he has shared. A candidate who talks about the job and culture in a meaningful way based on the information learned tells Rocky that he or she was really listening to him.

And it is not just that the candidate listened, but that they really heard and understood what was said. There is a huge difference between listening and hearing, and really listening for understanding is becoming a lost art today. So many times, people are so busy strategizing the next thing they want to say while other people are talking that they do not listen and they do not understand. This happens frequently today in meetings of all shapes, sizes, and purposes.

If a candidate does not echo back to Rocky the things he or she heard during the interview, or if he or she does not seem to have been listening for understanding, the candidate might not be viewed as strongly as another candidate who did. Take your time, listen carefully, understand, ask intelligent questions, and repeat critical information, and you will instantaneously position yourself as one of the strongest candidates for the job.

One last but extremely critical comment that Rocky shared during his interview was what he considers to be his interviewing strategy: *Hire for attitude...train for skills.* If he has two candidates, one with adequate skills but a great corporate culture fit and the other with excellent skills but only a moderate corporate culture fit, he will almost always hire the one with the best fit. Skills can be learned on the job or in the classroom; attitude cannot. Be sure that you have the right attitude to take your career to new heights.

□ □ □

## Can You Recover from an Interview Faux Pas?

**Katherine Virdi**
*Director—Human Resources*
*IntelliDyne, LLC, Falls Church, VA*

When we interviewed Katherine Virdi, we asked her to respond to a particularly difficult question: "Can a candidate recover from an interview faux pas?" This is a question that we are frequently asked, and here's what Katherine told us.

A candidate can definitely recover from an interview mistake! Keep in mind that the interview is the first impression for both the company and the candidate. If a candidate makes a mistake, he or she should acknowledge the error, apologize if appropriate, and move on. If it is just one mistake, it might not even be a factor in the final decision-making process.

Everyone is human and everyone makes mistakes. In fact, Katherine shared with us that she has certainly made a few mistakes in the past when interviewing. If the candidate deals with the mistake well, it demonstrates his or her ability to handle a stressful situation and can, in fact, leave the interviewer with a positive impression.

Two of the most basic and common interview mistakes are

- Arriving late for the interview (or not showing up at all)
- Dressing inappropriately

You would think that candidates would understand how critically important these two factors are in making a positive first impression. However, that is not always the case.

For candidates who are caught in traffic, get lost, or cannot find a parking space, call! Tell your interviewer that you are going to be X minutes late and ask whether they would like you to proceed or whether they prefer to reschedule. Courtesy goes a long way! Then be sure to apologize when you arrive and move on. For candidates who simply do not show up for the interview, unless it was a true emergency situation, your chances are shot with that company. You have clearly demonstrated, before you even arrived, that you cannot be relied upon.

For candidates who dress inappropriately, you have an uphill battle. Keep in mind that this is your first impression and there is tremendous emphasis on appearance and how you present yourself. If you are interviewing for a position where you will have direct client contact, how you present yourself is of vital importance. Take a few extra minutes to iron your clothes, comb your hair, roll down your sleeves, and project a positive and professional first appearance.

□ □ □

# When Suitability Is the Issue

**John Martin**
*Senior Vice President*
*IQNavigator, Denver, CO*

Throughout much of this chapter, we have focused on how to interview well and position yourself as a strong candidate. One thing we have not yet addressed is how to handle concerns that your interviewer might express about your suitability for a position. For a decisive answer, we turned to John, and this is what he told us about how he prefers the situation best be handled.

When John is interviewing a prospective candidate, but has concerns about that individual's suitability for the position and the organization, he will communicate those concerns to the job seeker. They might range from issues relating to corporate culture to the specific skills and qualifications required for a position. If John does communicate his concerns, they are important to him and the candidate must address them in order to move forward in the interviewing process. A quick brush-off simply will not do.

John recommends a brief yet direct response. The candidate does not need to launch into a lengthy discussion, but should share a few sentences about a relevant past experience that will hopefully help John overcome his concerns. If the concerns are legitimate, John wants to know how the candidate has overcome those issues in the past—the specific actions taken and the results.

Do not immediately assume that you are out of the running if an interviewer does express concerns about your candidacy. Rather, take a moment or two to acknowledge those concerns, address them effectively, and then move on. You *can* overcome objections and win the offer!

□ □ □

# Building Rapport with the Interviewer

### Chrisi Rogers
*Manager—Employment and Employee Relations*
*National Rural Telecommunications Cooperative (NRTC),*
*Herndon, VA*

To learn how a candidate can build rapport during an interview, we wanted to find an expert whose focus is on rapport and candidate fit, and not necessarily on the specific functional qualifications of a position. That led us to Chrisi Rogers and her great advice.

Chrisi feels rapport is built when a candidate is well prepared for the interview. Candidates should research a company and the specific position and then use common sense. Chrisi expects that a candidate's depth of knowledge will vary according to the level of position for which they are interviewing. Chrisi does not expect a candidate interviewing for the position of receptionist to have the same level of knowledge about NRTC as she expects the candidate for a top leadership role to have.

Just as important, Chrisi wants the sense that the candidate is being authentic during the interview and not providing the answers the candidate believes Chrisi wants to hear. Chrisi is fair in her interview manner and style and expects the candidates to be honest and direct. She comments that it is fine to take some time to respond to an interview question; but although a short delay is acceptable, the candidate should not take too long. She wants candidates to answer her interview questions with meaning and not simply grasp at straws for the answer. In fact, she says that it is perfectly acceptable to tell an interviewer that you want to think about that answer and get back to them later. Further, candidates should be honest if they do not know the answer to a specific question and simply say as much. Honesty is always better than attempting to fabricate an answer.

A good deal of the time that Chrisi spends interviewing is devoted to experience-related and performance-related questions because a candidate simply cannot make up that information. She also believes that if she asks questions that help the candidate feel confident early in the interview process, it will make them feel more comfortable and, in turn, they will be better able to answer the tougher questions she asks later.

Chrisi spends time asking *relationship* questions about favorite bosses, conflict management and resolution, projects that might not have gone well, and more. She believes that her style is unusual in that she is not affected as much by candidates' body language during the interview. She appreciates the fact that interviewing might be stressful and that the body language a candidate displays during the interview might not indicate his or her body language during nonstressful situations.

Candidates should know what they want. To get the job, Chrisi prefers that candidates know why they want the job. Before a candidate starts to make a transition or begins to seek new employment, he or she needs to know what he or she wants in life—the right job and the right fit. It is not, and should not be, just about money. A candidate can learn a skill but not a trait: "You can teach a person to answer a phone, but you cannot teach them to *like* answering the phone." Candidates must know themselves, as well as their truths, motivations, and pleasures in order to find the right position with the right company.

Chrisi relies on her instincts when interviewing a candidate. This instinctive aspect of the interview process begins the moment a candidate contacts her, whether by phone or in person. Every interaction indicates whether a candidate will be a good fit for the organization. For example, the way the candidate greets the receptionist can indicate how the candidate treats people in varying positions within the organization. Chrisi often speaks with the receptionist about the candidate's reception and attitude because the receptionist likely has had more direct contact with a particular candidate than anyone else in the company besides her. In fact, candidates should be aware that the interview really starts the minute they enter the parking lot. Who knows whom they might meet in the parking lot, elevator, or hallway?

One final note: Ask good questions. Insightful candidates ask questions about an organization's culture, workforce, mission, and goals. If a candidate truly seems interested in the company, asks intelligent questions, and displays the right body language, rapport will naturally build and the candidate will position him- or herself as the ideal candidate.

□ □ □

# Letting the Real You Shine Through

**Thomas J. Lynch**
*President*
*Mobilecube2, Inc., Conshohocken, PA*

When we interviewed Tom Lynch, the first thing he told us was that what is most important to him—in his roles as both interviewer and hiring manager—is his ability to identify the *real* person he is interviewing. So we asked Tom how he was able to accomplish that.

Tom believes that the interviewing process is similar to the sales, marketing, and business development process—it is a pipeline, and the first part of the qualification process is to find out who the person really is. During the interview, a qualified interviewer is gathering the facts, evaluating the applicant, and understanding how he or she communicates. Are they able to communicate their capabilities in an interesting and enticing way, without telling everything? Tom has used this sales and marketing strategy himself in the past with great results when interviewing for a new position, and has also been quite successful when using it to hire candidates for his team.

Tom finds his candidates through recruiters and networking. He uses the phone to screen potential hires and looks for the real person to emerge through his validation process. Even before the interview, he is gathering information from the resume. "I focus on the path the candidate has taken, the firms he or she has worked for, the referral systems they have in place, and the actions they have taken." Tom is more interested in the quality of the person and his or her experiences than what degrees they might have.

The next step is the one-on-one interview. Tom does not use a scripted interview. Rather, he questions the candidate to determine whether the information on the resume is accurate and whether the person has the skills and abilities to fill the position. His interactions and dialogue are focused on who this person is, both at work and outside of work. Do they give back, do they volunteer, are they family-oriented, and the like? What makes a candidate tick and motivates them? He likes to know their goals and hobbies to see whether they are self-generating people (able to motivate themselves) and whether this will translate into their career and job.

One final note: Tom also focuses heavily on how the candidate will interact with customers and internal staff they will be working with. Thus, their communication style during the interview is a key indicator of how well they will communicate with others.

Once Tom has identified that a candidate has the right skills and qualifications, will work well with his team, and has the moral fiber he is seeking, he will then make an offer, negotiate the package, and expediently move the hiring process along. His goal is to create an efficient and unencumbered interviewing process that benefits everyone involved.

□ □ □

# The Importance of Body Language and Eye Contact

**Katherine Virdi**
*Director—Human Resources*
*IntelliDyne, LLC, Falls Church, VA*

We went back to one of our experts on interviewing—Katherine Virdi—and asked her to comment on how important body language and eye contact are during an interview. Her thoughts are quite interesting.

As a human resources executive, body language and eye contact are of critical importance. While the candidate and the hiring manager are discussing the technical components of the job, Katherine is focusing on the candidate. Is he or she open when spoken to, and is he or she looking directly at the person who asks the questions? Or, if in a group interview situation, do they look around the room and address everyone there?

IntelliDyne is well known for the diversity of its workforce, and Katherine is aware of the cultural differences that impact eye contact and other behaviors. Conversely, she also expects her candidates to be aware of American cultural norms and attempt to function within that environment. For example, men from certain cultures tend not to look directly at women in a room. Candidates must work to overcome this and give equal time and attention to female representatives of the company. In summary, as Katherine is watching an individual's behavior, eye contact, and body language, she is attempting to determine how each candidate will fit into the company, team, and organizational structure.

It is also important to note how critical a candidate's fit within the corporate culture is. Each company has a mission, goal, and vision, and everyone that works for the company must move in the same direction. Companies will not grow unless they are moving forward as a team. In turn, Katherine needs to be sure that her new hires are not rogue employees who do things their own way. As an individual, each candidate must keep the company's vision in focus, promote that vision, and work collaboratively as part of the team. The reality for Katherine is that nine out of ten times, if the fit isn't right between employee and company, she will need to let people go and rehire. For her, this translates to lost resources and lost revenues, so making the right hire the first time is critical.

□ □ □

# The Power of Endorsements and References

**Denise Males**
*Director of Recruitment*
*Major League Baseball, New York, NY*

There is often much talk about the use of endorsements or recommendations during a job interview, and we were curious as to how much clout these really carry. To get an insider's view, we talked to Denise to get her feedback on how endorsements can help someone to join a new company or earn a promotion with their current employer. Here is what she shared with us.

Denise believes that endorsements can be another powerful interviewing tool for both the internal and external candidate. In her perception, having endorsements makes the candidates appear more prepared and thoughtful about the interviewing process, and is an additional step that others might not take. At a minimum, it certainly will not hurt. Endorsements can be supplied to a company either as an addendum to your resume or as separate, stand-alone letters that are forwarded directly to the company by the individual offering the endorsement. To realize their full impact, endorsements must be written and not simply verbally communicated.

For external candidates, it is important who the references are. The higher up, the better; the bigger the title, the better; the more well-recognized the company, the better. Brand-building does work! References from bosses and peers carry the most weight with her. References from family and neighbors, unless there is a professional connection, do not work. If you worked in a family business and your reference is your aunt, Denise will not put much weight into what the reference has to say. Bottom line, Denise wants to know about a candidate's performance at work from an impartial third party.

For internal candidates, assuming all other things are equal, references can be the differentiator that positions the candidate above others and results in the offer. However, Denise recommends that internal candidates be careful about whom they select as a reference. If a reference is a top performer within the organization, great; if the reference is only a marginal performer, not so great. Remember, Human Resources knows these people and their reputations. Candidates must be careful that they select someone whose work is respected and whose recommendations get noticed.

Suppose there are ten candidates interviewing for a position and five of them are really good. In that situation, references can really make a difference. And, in fact, if one of those five has great skills but does not interview particularly well, the reference can help improve their standing. Or suppose a candidate is extremely quiet during an interview yet has received a glowing recommendation from his or her reference. This, in conjunction with the candidate's other attributes, carries weight with Denise and will help tip the scales in favor of the candidate.

Candidates never know what that one thing is that might make a difference in getting the job. It could be something they said in the interview, their references, or something else they provided. Use everything you have to favorably position yourself and let others help you succeed!

□ □ □

# Writing Powerful Thank-You Letters

**Wendy Enelow**
*President*
*Career Masters Institute, Coleman Falls, VA*

Another extremely important part of the interviewing process is your thank-you letter. Our chapter would not be complete without a discussion about thank-you letters. No longer are they just a formality; not just a quick, "Thanks for the interview...can't wait to hear from you." Thank-you letters (which I refer to as *second-tier marketing tools*) can have tremendous value in moving your candidacy forward and positioning you above the competition. Although much of what you include in your thank-you letter might have already been communicated during your interview, there is nothing more effective than the written word to etch those thoughts into your interviewer's mind.

You can use your thank-you letters to

- Overcome the interviewer's objections
- Reiterate your specific expertise as it relates to a company's specific challenges
- Highlight your core professional competencies and successes that are directly related to that company's needs

## Overcoming Objections

If, during an interview, the interviewer raised a specific objection as to your appropriateness as a candidate, use your thank-you letter to respond to, and overcome, those concerns. Demonstrate that it is not an obstacle, but rather an opportunity, and that you are fully prepared to meet the challenge.

For example: You are interviewing for Director of Business Development for a well-established company in Minneapolis. Although you are extremely well qualified, they are concerned that you have never lived in the area and have no network of local contacts. Eliminate their concerns by explaining that your network of professional contacts is nationwide and, in fact, you know John Doe of the XXX Company, have a longstanding relationship with an economic development director in the area, and so on. Your contacts will serve to expand the company's already-established network.

## Reiterate Your Specific Expertise

If, during an interview, the company communicated its specific needs, issues, and challenges, use your thank-you letter to demonstrate how you can meet those needs and eliminate those challenges.

For example: You are interviewing for Vice President of Finance for a distressed company that must take immediate action if it is to survive. They need a candidate with proven success in fast-track turnarounds and revitalizations. Consider presenting your experience in a format such as this:

---

With 12 years of experience as CEO of high-volume manufacturing companies, I have consistently delivered strong and sustainable financial results. Highlights:

- In 2003, led the turnaround and return to profitability of a $125 million food-products manufacturer, rebuilt customer credibility, and negotiated a $10 million corporate line of credit.
- Between 1999 and 2002, restored profitability to a $50 million garden products manufacturer that had multimillion-dollar losses for the previous three years. Today, the company boasts profits at more than 22% annually (7% over industry average).
- In 1998, consulted with a Fortune 50 company to create a strategic turnaround program for all 35 of its production facilities worldwide. Following implementation, the company realized an immediate cost savings in excess of $25 million annually.

---

## Highlight Your Core Professional Competencies

If, during an interview, the company communicated its ideal qualifications for a candidate, use your thank-you letter to outline how you meet or exceed each of those qualifications.

For example: You are interviewing for Director of Technology and Product Development with a high-tech venture and the company has clearly communicated its four essential candidate qualifications. Let them immediately *see* that you have those four qualifications with a letter format and structure like this:

---

**New Product Development**
Include a two- to three-sentence paragraph with a strong overview of your total experience in new product development, and then include a list of three to five bullets highlighting specific projects, achievements, operations, and so on.
- Projects, achievements, operations
- Projects, achievements, operations
- Projects, achievements, operations

**Technology Commercialization**
Include a two- to three-sentence paragraph with a strong overview of your total experience in technology commercialization, and then include a list of three to five bullets highlighting specific projects, achievements, operations, and so on.
- Projects, achievements, operations
- Projects, achievements, operations
- Projects, achievements, operations

**Team Building & Leadership**
Include a two- to three-sentence paragraph with a strong overview of your total experience in team building and leadership, and then include a list of three to five bullets highlighting specific projects, achievements, operations, and so on.
- Projects, achievements, operations
- Projects, achievements, operations
- Projects, achievements, operations

**Global Business Development**
Include a two- to three-sentence paragraph with a strong overview of your total experience in global business development, and then include a list of three to five bullets highlighting specific projects, achievements, operations, and so on.
- Projects, achievements, operations
- Projects, achievements, operations
- Projects, achievements, operations

---

## Letter Length

And, finally, the all-important "how long should a thank-you letter be?" question! Of course, as with anything else in job search, there is no definitive answer, but one or two pages is the norm, depending on the amount of information you want to communicate. Thank-you letters do *not* have to be only one page if you have valuable information to include!

Remind yourself that you already have the company's interest or you would not have been interviewed, and use your thank-you letter as a tool to *close the deal*. Remember, the entire process of job search is marketing and merchandising your product—you. There is no reason that writing thank-you letters should be any different than any other part of your job search activities!

□ □ □

# Top 14 Strategies to Nail Your Interviews

**Steven Broadman**
*Senior Recruiter*
*Convergenz, Tysons Corner, VA*

As our final interview for this chapter, we turned to Steve Broadman of Alliance Consulting, a firm specializing in the placement of contract/temporary technical personnel for specific project assignments. We asked Steve to outline the top criteria for successful interviewing, and he provided us with an excellent summary of the top 14 strategies to "nail your interviews."

1. **Sell yourself.** Understand that, as a candidate, you are a salesperson with a great product—you! It is your responsibility in the interview to market and merchandise that product with interesting and telling information about the value and expertise you bring to that company. Highlight your success stories in a non-arrogant manner and present yourself as a winner.

2. **Be overdressed for the interview.** You can always apologize later if you are overdressed. However, you can never overcome a situation where you are in a t-shirt and everyone else is in a tie.

3. **Know the company and the position.** You can never do enough research. The more prepared you are—the more information you have about the company and its mission, vision, products, services, cultures, employees, and more—the better the interview will progress and the more impressed the interviewer will be.

4. **Know what the company wants from you.** Have a clear understanding of the specific skills and knowledge the company is seeking in a qualified candidate and devote a great deal of your interview to highlighting your qualifications as they pertain directly to that company's needs. Extraneous information is largely a waste of time.

5. **Sometimes it is okay to tell your interviewer that you are nervous.** If you are at the right professional level and are nervous at an interview, it is okay to let your interviewer know. It can help break the ice and turn your interviewer into a friend or parental figure. It can help set the tempo in your favor. However, if you are an executive-level candidate, Steve recommends that you do *not* let your interviewer know because nervousness is not benefiting of the level of position you are seeking.

6. **Find common ground.** If you can find areas of commonality between you and the interviewer—projects, people, places, and companies that you both know—it will be great. Companies like to know that candidates are knowledgeable and well connected. If an interviewer knows some of the people you know, it can work in your favor because references can be checked with people the interviewer knows and trusts.

7. **Ask good questions.** How do I fit into the needed vision of the group? How will my success in this role be measured? How do I compare with the other candidates you've interviewed? How well do I meet your expectations? Ask intelligent, thought-provoking, and on-target questions.

8. **Ask challenging questions.** It is okay to ask a challenging question of your interviewer. For example, "Of the top three competitors, you rank third. Why?" This question will communicate your interest in understanding more about the company and demonstrate your knowledge of the marketplace.

9. **Overcome problems and challenges.** If you have had a problem on the job, do not be afraid to share it. Tell your interviewer what the situation was, what you did, and what you learned. Communicate that you will never get into that situation again and that you know the signs to look for to avoid having the same problem. Show you are a winner by highlighting how you overcame a problem in the past and succeeded.

10. **Never talk negatively about anything—no matter how bad the situation.** Always have something good to say about your past employers, bosses, and co-workers. If you talk negatively, your next employer might think that you will talk about them in the same negative way at some point in the future.

11. **Pay attention to your body language.** Body language can vary between cultures, and candidates must be aware of the differences that might exist. Regardless of your cultural or ethnic background, it is important to smile, make direct eye contact, and have a great handshake. What's more, if your interviewer is an animated person, it would be helpful to imitate his body language and look alive. Be a mirror to that person; it shows a keen interest in his or her style.

12. **Positively frame your job search.** Because Steve works with candidates on a project-by-project basis, it is not unusual that candidates will have periods of unemployment. Rather than tell your interviewer that you have spent the last three months, six months, or whatever looking for a job, it is much more favorable to say you completed a very difficult project and took a couple of months off to catch up around the house. Or perhaps you did some traveling, took some classes, or volunteered, and now it is time to get serious about getting back to work.

13. **Ask for the job at the end of the interview.** You can say, "This position sounds perfect for me. If given the opportunity, I can guarantee you that I will shine." Even if you are not sure that you want the job, ask for it...you never know. By showing interest in the position and enthusiasm for the company, you might very well position yourself for other opportunities in the pipeline.

14. **Send a thank-you note.** If you are in a technology field, using e-mail for your notes is fine. In other industries and professions, you might want to consider a handwritten thank-you note on nice stationery. It does leave a lasting impression! Use your thank-you note to reiterate your interest in the position, highlight a few key qualifications, respond to any objections, and ask additional questions. Most importantly, use your thank-you note to prompt the interviewer to contact you again—for another interview or an offer.

□ □ □

# Authors' Best Interviewing Advice

1. **Prepare in advance.** There is not enough that we can say about the importance of preparation before an interview. It is critical that you get to know the company and its products and services, mission, values, culture, people, and more. Fortunately, now that most companies have Web sites, it's quick and easy to find that information. There is no excuse for not being prepared!

2. **Be yourself.** If you go into an interview attempting to portray yourself as someone other than who you are, it will never work. The real you will come through—maybe not during the interview, but certainly on the job. Represent yourself truthfully and you will be much more likely to find the *right* job with the *right* company.

3. **Take control.** Although you don't want your interviewer to notice that it is happening, you want to take subtle control of the interview so that you are certain to communicate what you have established as your agenda—your skills, achievements, projects, and more that are of most interest and value to that company.

4. **Ask questions.** It is your responsibility to ask intelligent and thought-provoking questions of your interviewer. You want to learn as much as possible about the company, the people, the politics, and more so that you can make a rational decision about whether the company is right for you.

5. **Understand that interviewing is a balancing act between two parties with two different agendas.** Your goal is to get a job offer; the interviewer's goal is to solve a problem (fill a job). Your challenge—in each interview—is to find the right place where you can balance the interview between focusing on your strengths, qualifications, skills, and experiences with your ability to solve the company's problems. If you can find that perfect balance, you will indeed position yourself as a well-qualified candidate.

6. **Use the right language and keywords.** This is particularly important if you are interviewing for a position in a new industry or for a new type of job. By using keywords and

keyword phrases appropriate to the position and the industry, you will be perceived as someone who already knows what is going on, understands the business, and can acclimate to the new organization.

7. **Use the "big-to-little" strategy to answer questions.** Suppose your interviewer asks about your experience negotiating mergers and acquisitions. Begin your response with the big answer: "For more than 15 years, I have led M&A activities for IBM's international division...." Then follow up with little examples—specific mergers and acquisitions that you have negotiated, transacted, and managed. The big-to-little strategy is particularly effective because you can use the same structure and thought process to respond to so many different questions.

8. **Be positive about everything you say.** Never utter a negative word—about a company, a person, a project, a customer, or whatever. An interview is the time to be upbeat and enthusiastic, share successes, discuss challenges, and more. It is not the time to badmouth anything or anyone.

9. **Save the salary discussion for the very end.** The last thing you want to do is talk money first. That is a topic you want to delay until the company is ready to make you an offer. Never bring up salary during an interview. Obviously, there will be times when your interviewer brings it up. For details on how best to answer those types of questions, refer to Chapter 7, "How to Negotiate Your Best Salary."

10. **Ask for the job.** Although chances are the position will not be offered to you at either the first or second interview, it still is appropriate to tell your interviewer how interested you are and that you would like the job. With each subsequent interview, you can reiterate your interest and ask for the job. If you don't ask, they might not offer!

## Career and Job Search Survey Results

### Question:

What is the most common type of interview structure that you use—one-on-one, group, telephone, e-mail, or video?

### Answer:

| | |
|---|---|
| Most common | One-on-one interviews |
| Second most common | Telephone interviews |
| Third most common | Group interviews |
| Fourth most common | Video interviews |
| Least common | E-mail interviews |

### Conclusion:

Be prepared for any type of interview situation but realize that one-on-one, live interviews are the most common and telephone interviews are the second most common.

# CHAPTER 7 How to Negotiate Your Best Salary

Finally, we've gotten to the chapter with the good stuff—MONEY! After all, isn't that why 99.9 percent of us work? Of course, we enjoy what we do and take pride in it but, bottom line, most of us are in it for the money. If it weren't for the money, we would be hanging out, sailing, golfing, building a race car, writing a novel, breeding show dogs, or any one of thousands of other fun and fulfilling activities instead.

So, if we have established the fact that you are in it for the money, why is money such a difficult conversation to have with a prospective employer? Well, the answer is easy. They want to pay you the least that they can, whereas you want to make the most that you can. And, of course, no one wants to be the first one to mention an actual salary figure. So now you have two parties, you and your interviewer, both of whom want to talk money, yet no one wants to be the first to bring it up. It's a rather convoluted situation, wouldn't you say?

Fortunately, having the money conversation is so much easier with recruiters. When you work with recruiters, everyone is upfront. The recruiter will tell you what the position is paying (or, at least, a range) and you will tell the recruiter the salary range you are interested in. Remember, it's the recruiter's job to match the right employee with the right employer, and compensation is a big part of that match.

Most important to remember is that we are not just talking about salary, but about your entire compensation package, which might include any combination of the following: salary, bonus, insurance coverage, vacation, stock options, pension plan, tuition reimbursement, car expenses, professional memberships, child care, deferred compensation, and so much more. In fact, the list of potential benefits you can negotiate is extensive and now includes such innovative concepts as telecommuting, work sharing, flex time, and more. With each passing year, we see the evolution of new employee benefit programs and other incentives.

When you're poised to negotiate your salary, you need to look at the entire compensation package. Maybe the salary offer is less than you had expected, but the benefits are great. Does that compensate you enough? Or perhaps the salary is a little higher than you expected, but the benefits are few and far between. In either instance, you have to make a decision about whether you will be satisfied with the company's offer—a month or a year from now as well as today. Don't just accept any opportunity because you need a job. Rather, accept the opportunity that is right for you—right job, right company, right culture, and right compensation.

The only winning salary negotiations are those from which both parties walk away satisfied. You have got a great new job with a good salary and good benefits. The employer has a great new employee who will, hopefully, make some valuable contributions to the company. As trite as it might sound, it truly is a win-win situation for everyone.

The experts we approached to interview for this chapter are all accomplished in the fine art of salary negotiations. They understand the process—from both the employer's and the employee's perspectives—and have shared their insights so that you can be better prepared and more effective in negotiating your best salary.

□ □ □

# Top Nine Strategies for Negotiating Success

**Kurt Mosley**

*Vice President—Business Development*
*The MHA Group, Irving, TX*

Kurt Mosley has a wealth of experience in health care staffing and consulting. When we approached him to interview for this book, he offered to share his expertise by outlining his top nine strategies for negotiating success. Here is what he had to say:

1. **Set realistic expectations—your high and your low salary requirements—before you ever start to negotiate.** Know your baseline and be aware of your value in the market. If your expectations are too high, you will instantly price yourself out of the running.

2. **Timing is important when discussing salary.** If the topic comes up once or twice early in an interview, try to put it off until you know more about the position and your fit. You can negotiate from a far better place when you understand what will be required of you on the job and how well you will fit into the company's corporate culture.

3. **When negotiating your compensation, remember it is not just about salary.** Rather, it is about the entire package you will be receiving. Salary negotiations are much like buying a car—the price of the car and the options that come with it. You need to find out about all the benefits that are included in the compensation package and all the other perks that might come along with it. Although perks might not be hard dollars, they certainly can have substantial value for you. Never state your current salary without including your benefits as part of that number. The sum total of everything is what your compensation is and will come into play when a new employer is considering the compensation they will offer to you.

4. **Never offer to accept a salary that is less than what you are currently making.** In Kurt's opinion, this instantly lowers your credibility in the employer's eyes. However, there might be situations, particularly if you are changing professions or industries, where you might need to take a lower salary in order to successfully make the transition and position yourself for future promotional opportunities with a salary more closely aligned to what you have been making.

5. **Never accept counteroffers.** Consider the following scenario. You are thinking about looking for a new position and your current employer is well aware of your job search. They counter and you accept. Sounds great, doesn't it? But it's not. Your current employer now knows that you are looking for a new position and chances are likely that they will start looking for your replacement. When the ideal candidate presents himself or herself to the company, you might find that you are out of a job. Accepting a counteroffer confounds the situation and is not recommended.

6. **When you get an offer of employment, get it in writing.** And the more comprehensive the document, the better. You want the document to include information not only about compensation, but also about benefits, stock options, guarantees, and other critical information. What happens to your stock options if the company is sold? If you resign within a specific time frame, what happens to your options and long-term benefits? Know what you are signing up for!

7. **When you receive an offer, make a decision within 48 hours.** After a 48-hour period, both parties' interest starts to wane. It's like "groceries to garbage": If your groceries are not in the refrigerator for four, five, or six days, they turn to garbage.

8. **If the company is not yet ready to make an offer, do one of two things.** Ask whether you can check back with them within a specific time frame. Even if the answer is no, it's okay. Now you know to move on. Or, if you are considering other offers, let the company know this. Tell them you are intrigued by their company and the position and would be delighted to receive an offer. Ask whether it is okay to call back within 48 hours to see whether a decision has been made.

9. **Use the Internet to research salaries—in particular industries, professions, and locations.** All this information is at your immediate disposal, so be sure to use it!

□ □ □

# Negotiating $1000 a Minute

**Jack Chapman**
*President*
*Lucrative Careers, Inc., Wilmette, IL*

One of the most widely read and well-respected publications on salary negotiations is a book titled *Negotiating Your Salary: How to Make $1000 a Minute* by Jack Chapman (2001; Ten Speed Press). To be sure that we were giving you the very best advice possible, we asked Jack whether he would be kind enough to share a few key points from his book with us. He gladly accepted our invitation and this is what he shared with us.

The foundation for Jack's book is what he refers to as his five salary-making rules to guide every negotiation:

1. Postpone until offer.

2. Let them go first.

3. Be quiet.

4. Give your researched response.

5. Clinch the deal, then deal some more.

## Postpone Until Offer

How many times have you responded to an advertisement that asked for salary history or salary requirements? How many times did you include that information in your cover letter? Jack recommends that you never include that information and, in fact, that you go to considerable lengths *not* to provide that information early in your discussions with a prospective employer. And that is tough!

Companies want to know what your current salary is (or most recent salary) and what your salary expectations are. In fact, this is often basic information that they use to screen potential hires—screen you out either because you make too much or too little. Too much and they assume they cannot afford you. Too little and they assume you have not reached the level of responsibility they are seeking in a candidate. Either way, it is a no-win situation.

The very best of situations would be that you could discuss the ballpark salary range early in the interviewing process and save the details for the end. One great strategy for making this happen is a preemptive strike where you, the job seeker, bring up the salary topic. Spend the first few minutes in your interview building rapport and answering questions. Then bring up salary and ask what the company is offering to pay for the position. Unless it's totally out of the realm of reason, your response should always be, "Okay. We can work around that." That should allay the company's fears that salary might become a problem and allow you to move your interview process along.

If you are able to postpone the details of salary negotiation until an offer has been made, you have given yourself a significant advantage. The company has already decided that you are the right candidate and that they want you. All of a sudden, they might be willing to make the pay scale flexible and even practice creative budgeting to make it happen.

## Let Them Go First

If you followed Rule #1, you were able to postpone negotiations until the company made you an offer. They want you and it is their responsibility to sell you on the company, the job, the long-term opportunity, the compensation, and more. Let them make the first offer and you can then negotiate from there.

## Be Quiet

Jack's best advice is that when you hear a figure or range, repeat the figure or top of the range with a contemplative tone in your voice and then be quiet. Up until now, your enthusiasm for the job has been unbounded. Now, be quiet, count to 30, and think about the offer. Does it meet or exceed your current salary? Is it what you expected? Can you and your family live comfortably?

While you are doing this, the interviewer might become a bit nervous and concerned about whether you are going to take the position. They think to themselves that they have come this far and do not want to lose you now. The result of this 30 seconds is often a raise—a raise before you have even started your new job! Other times, you will get an explanation of why that is all the company can pay. Listen, be quiet, and think. Is this right for you?

## Give Your Researched Response

If you are going for the top salary possible, you should complete your market value research: Know the approximate market value for the position and calculate two different figures before going into the interview. The first figure is the highest you are worth and the second is the lowest you will accept. So, after the silence of Rule #3, and perhaps your first raise, respond to the interviewer with a comment about the salary being too high, too low, or just right.

A salary offer that is too high sounds like a great deal, but do not get in over your head! Your goal should not be to get every penny you can, but rather, to be paid a fair dollar that matches your performance. If your employer is making the mistake of overpaying you, their expectations might be too high and they might feel ripped off if you do not produce. Be forewarned! Accept the salary happily, but make sure their expectations of you are achievable.

If the offer is too low, do not give up. Express your sincere interest in the position and the company, but also bring up the salary research that you have done. Your research might have told you that positions like this one pay in the ___ to ___ range, so ask your interviewer whether he or she can meet that range. Do not be afraid that if you tell the interviewer the salary is too low that you will be out the door. In most instances, this is not the case. Remember, they have already decided that they want you. Move the negotiations forward and you will generally find common ground.

Chances are slim that a first offer will be just right. If it is, great! Accept the offer, negotiate the details, and prepare to start your new job. Most likely, however, the employer has come in with his lowest number while your goal is to negotiate for the highest figure in the range. Again, keep the negotiations moving forward and you will find the truly *right* number.

## Clinch the Deal, Then Deal Some More

Now that you have closed the deal, it is time to negotiate for more, and the list is a long one. Consider your own parking space, a flexible schedule, more vacation time, a higher-percentage bonus plan, more frequent salary reviews, paid memberships in professional associations, car and expense accounts, additional insurance coverage, personal days, relocation costs, deferred compensation plans, profit sharing, stock options, child care, pension plan, tuition reimbursement, and more. Chances are that you will not get everything that you ask for, but you will get some. Go for it!

Jack wanted to be sure that we ended our interview by addressing one critical fact of salary negotiations: The rules for managing your salary discussions with recruiters are totally different. With companies, you want to wait until the very end. With recruiters, salary discussions happen at the very beginning and that is okay. When you are working with recruiters, they are being paid to make the right matches between candidates and companies; and, obviously, compensation is a key consideration. Understand that all of the information above is for use when negotiating directly with companies. With recruiters, Jack's best advice is to immediately lay it out on the table so that the recruiter is well aware of your salary expectations and not wasting anyone's time.

□ □ □

# Your Timing Must Be Perfect

### Claire M. Donegan
*President/CEO*
*Career Search, Wayne, PA*

When we wanted to speak to a pro on salary negotiations, we immediately thought of Claire Donegan. In the recruitment business for years and years, she has an excellent knowledge of the employment market and how all the pieces work harmoniously. We focused our interview on the best time to negotiate salary and compensation.

"Salary negotiations should *never* take place during the first interview. The first interview is the time when you (the candidate) and the prospective employer should be getting to know each other. You should be interviewing the employer as well as the employer interviewing you." A candidate needs to sell themselves and their qualifications before they can begin any discussion of compensation. Salary negotiations should begin only once there is serious interest and an offer has been made.

There are two distinct ways in which a candidate can manage their job search. They can either work with a recruiter or go it alone (networking, ad responses, Internet postings, and more). Depending on which strategy you are using, or perhaps you are using both, the way in which your salary negotiations will be managed will differ.

"When working with a recruiter, your salary negotiations will be handled by that recruiter." Great, isn't it? Once you are scheduled for an interview, the recruiter will prepare you for the interview. Part of that preparation should be handling the question, "What is your salary range?" "I advise my candidates to tell the employer that 'Claire from Career Search has given me the salary range for the position and I am well within that range.' If an employer really pushes my candidate for more information, I tell them to repeat the range I have given them." Whatever a candidate does, they should *never go over that range*. "Even if you have a strong urge to tell Mr. Employer that his salary is too low, do not do it. Tell your recruiter why you feel the salary is too low and what a fair salary should be for that position. Once an offer is made, your recruiter is equipped to negotiate your salary on your behalf. Should an employer offer you a job on the spot and you feel the salary is too low, contact your recruiter and let the two of them work out the details."

Working on your own is different. You are responsible for your own salary negotiation. "Again, I do not suggest negotiating salary during your first interview. I still believe it is the time to get to know Mr. Employer and whether or not the position is a good fit for you. If an ad requires salary information, I suggest you state your current (or most recent) salary and include a statement that your salary requirements are negotiable." Mention your desire to find the *right* position with the *right* company, and even though salary is important, it has to be the *right* fit.

"Once an offer is made to you, then is the appropriate time to start negotiating." You have the offer; now it is just a matter of working out the details to everyone's satisfaction. Ask for what you want and ask for what you deserve. But most importantly, ask for a fair-market-value salary based on the position, the industry, the company, and the geographic location.

□ □ □

## Lay the Money on the Table

**Jim Oddo**
*Staffing Manager*
*Oxford Health Plans, Inc., Trumbull, CT*

There will be instances when, no matter how hard you try to delay the salary conversation, it simply cannot be avoided. Your interviewer insists on specific information that you have to share or you will not get anywhere with that person. To get an expert's perspective on why this strategy is so important to certain hiring managers, we turned to Jim Oddo, who has no qualms about it—he wants to know what salary a candidate expects at the very onset of his discussions.

## Pre-Screening Interview

Starting with the pre-screening interview, Jim wants to know four key things about each candidate:

- The type of position they are seeking
- Their salary expectations
- Their salary history (hopefully, it has been progressive)
- Their reason for exploring the marketplace

Salary does not have to be a specific number, but he wants a range that would be acceptable. He believes that if everyone is upfront about money, the process will run more smoothly—for his recruiters, line managers, and candidates.

Jim also wants to know the reasons for the candidate's interest in a career move. Is the move related to career growth or unemployment, or is the candidate simply looking for a better paycheck? At Oxford, they understand money is a motivating factor; however, they hope it is not the only factor. Career growth, work environment, long-term income potential (not just what you can squeeze upfront), and job stability are factors that should be considered top priorities. Getting excited about the job and the company is a much better strategy for positioning yourself as a top candidate.

What's more, Jim expects all of his recruiters to state the position's salary range during their initial discussions with each candidate. Knowing that you fit into that range is important early on so that no one is wasting anyone else's time.

## Your Role as the Candidate

If you, as the candidate, know the salary range and are okay with that range, Jim expects that if an offer is made, you will accept it. If you are asked the salary question and put it back to the recruiter simply by saying, "Well, what are you paying?" Jim is not satisfied. He wants the candidate to ask about the level of position and responsibilities and ask probing questions that will help him or her better understand the position. This gives Jim valuable information that will help him formulate a judgment on salary. Jim is also fine if a candidate asks about salary increases or promotional opportunities that might be available if he or she moves into the position at the stated range.

Jim is delighted when a candidate is comfortable discussing his or her salary history. With that information, he can make a case to senior management on the candidate's behalf to help justify his or her expectations. Candidates need to understand how an offer is put together. Jim and his recruiting team work with a hiring manager to identify the candidate of choice. Then hiring managers often go to their bosses to get the budget approval to extend an offer. Jim wants that to happen only once. If a salary expectation is discussed upfront, the process moves along quickly and smoothly, and there is never a need for hiring managers to go back to their bosses and say, "Remember when the candidate said they would take this amount?"

## You Lose!

Jim feels a poor negotiating tactic is one in which a candidate rejects an offer at the end of the process that he or she said would be acceptable at the beginning of the process, especially if the understanding of the position requirements has not changed. In this case, the reaction from senior management can be negative. Even if the candidate gets what he or she wants, he or she will now be starting off the new position on a less than positive note—not the place you want to begin your next job.

## What If You Win?

Jim believes it is extremely important that candidates set themselves up to win. The higher end of the salary range is set for high-end results and top performers. If you accept a position at the higher range, you will be expected to perform at that level. Be careful: You might set yourself up for failure if you are not ready for the challenge. Think long-term rather than how much money you are going to make today. Perhaps starting a level or two lower might be the best place for you to start, grow, prosper, and win.

Candidates need to know their likes and dislikes, and whether a particular opportunity is right for them. They need to know what level of compensation they expect today and tomorrow. They should talk about their goals and expectations, and if they reach their goals, what type of additional compensation they will receive. Jim is always impressed when candidates ask about long-term opportunities because they are communicating their long-term commitment to the position and the company.

Candidates must also work hard to build trust and confidence with the recruiter and hiring manager. If the offer comes in at $75,000 per year, and that is competitive for the position, and you want to eventually earn $100,000 a year, that's okay. You might not get your $100,000 today, but it is your long-term goal. As long as it is realistic and there are opportunities for growth within the organization, your goal might very well come to fruition over the long haul. Carefully consider what money you might be able to sacrifice today in order to position yourself well for a long-term opportunity. Jim expects his candidates to be upfront with their long-term goals so that both parties can be sure they are in agreement and pursuing a mutually beneficial employment commitment with each other.

## And, Finally...

A candidate's tone and appearance are important when negotiating salary. If you are discussing your salary requirements in person, your nonverbal communication is critical. It is always important that your tone of voice be pleasant, not defensive, and that you remain calm and confident throughout the entire process. Keep your eye contact strong, and don't fidget or look around. Jim can instantly tell if you are uncomfortable by your body posture and eye movements. Let yourself be assured and in control, keep the pitch of your voice smooth and even, and be succinct. It is not necessary to make the salary conversation long and drawn-out. A simple sentence or two will usually do.

□ □ □

# Don't Forget to Ask For...

### Bill Welsh
*Controller*
*Equinox Fitness, New York, NY*

We approached Bill Welsh for this book because of his extensive knowledge of compensation, including salary, benefits, bonuses, training, retirement, flex time, incentives, stock options, perks, and other components of the package. All too often, candidates *forget* to ask for these types of incentives, all of which should be factored in when negotiating a total compensation package. Here's what Bill shared with us.

## The Most Important Items

Bill began his interview by highlighting the two things he considers most important during negotiations: salary and stock options. In fact, stock options can potentially be larger than an annual bonus, depending on the size and success of a particular company. If a company is a high-growth organization, stock options could be worth hundreds of thousands of dollars. So stock options are something a candidate should never overlook or omit when negotiating compensation.

Bill recommends that you look at both the short-term and long-term compensation potential with each company. For the long term, you are looking at five years or more before your options might be worth anything. Although stock options now are reflected on a company's income statement, they are still an excellent incentive for companies to offer because there is no immediate cash outlay for new hires.

Here are a few other items that are important to consider during your negotiations:

- **Signing bonus.** Ask for a signing bonus! You have everything to gain and absolutely nothing to lose. The worst case is that the employer says no but still extends you the job offer.

- **Car allowance or commuting allowance.** Consider asking for a $500 per month allowance. Small items such as this don't show up on the company's radar screen and, as such, are wonderful incentives. More than $500 might appear excessive.

- **Spousal health insurance.** Ask the company to pay for your spouse's or partner's health insurance. Again, you might not be able to negotiate this, but it certainly is worth asking for. Note that as a company gets bigger, extra perks become less available.

## Consider Organization Size

It is important to consider the kind and size of organization that you will be working for. There is a vast difference in the range of flexibility among the various types of companies. Consider this:

- **$25 million mom-and-pop company.** These types of companies often have no rules, so you can ask for what you want and often get it. There are much fewer restrictions in a company of this size.

- **$100+ million company.** These companies typically have a financial or lending institution behind them and are not owned by one person. There are more restrictions on salary and compensation in this type of environment than in a smaller company. So Bill recommends asking for what you want and expecting to receive part of it.

- **Large corporations.** Large-size companies generally are mature, and have solid and steadfast rules with virtually no exceptions. There is not much room for negotiating in this situation.

## Other Things to Ask For

Remember, anything can be accomplished when negotiating. If a company says, "We do not offer car allowances," respond with "That is a pay cut for me." Then see whether there is something else the company can offer in exchange. Here is a list of perks and benefits you might want to consider asking for:

- When you leave one position for the next, your new employer will not allow you to get on the insurance plan for 90 days. Ask your new employer to pick up the cost of the COBRA insurance that you are eligible for over those 90 days. This way, there is no lapse in coverage and you do not have to take a pay cut to pay for it yourself.
- Cable modem (if your job requires it)
- Health insurance (for you and your family)
- Commuting or car allowance
- Reimbursement for car insurance
- Reimbursement for train pass
- Extra vacation time
- Flexible working hours
- Cell phone (although Bill believes that companies are moving away from paying individual cell phone bills)

## Final Tips

A few final tips you will want to consider when negotiating your compensation package:

- Know the bare minimum that you will accept for the position.
- Do not live on total compensation—live on base salary. You can set the extra money aside as savings, investment, college tuition, or whatever your specific needs are.

- When you receive an offer from an employer and you know that the company and the position are right for you, waiting to accept the offer does nothing for you. If it is right, accept it. If you want to wait 24 hours and sleep on it, that is fine. Do your calculations and whatever else you need to do, but if it feels right, accept the offer within 24 hours. If you need to wait a couple of days to accept, you are sending a negative message to the employer and that can blow the entire deal. Do not let that happen to you!

□ □ □

# And There's More: Employment Agreements and Contracts

### Shelly Goldman, CPCC, CEIP, CCM
*President*
*The Goldman Group Advantage, Reston, VA*

After interviewing Bill Welsh and hearing all the wonderful information he had to share about negotiating for benefits and other employment perks, we felt it was important to continue with that discussion and take it one step further. Shelly, who has a wealth of experience in this particular area, shares some information she considers essential for most job seekers.

Before you begin any new position, it is essential that you know the terms of your employment. What's more, we both strongly urge that you get everything in writing—your compensation, benefits, and any other written contracts or agreements that will be part of your terms of employment. Do this before you ever sign on the dotted line!

There are many different types of employment agreements and contracts you might be asked to sign. Generally, these documents are in place to protect the employer and hold you accountable to the employer; other times, they might provide a certain degree of safety and security for you, the employee. More often than not, the employer will ask you to sign these documents, but there might be occasions when you initiate the request. To better understand what these documents are and how important they are to the hiring process, let's explore each document in detail.

# Letters of Offer, Employment Contracts, and Executive Contracts

These three documents are quite similar and state the terms and conditions of your employment, compensation package, title, and any other relevant information. Letters of offer can be extended to any employee at any level. Employment contracts and executive contracts are generally designed for the senior-level executive and are prepared in greater detail. In fact, it is common practice for executives to receive both a letter of offer and an executive contract.

Most contracts for senior-level executives include the following:

- **Terms of employment.** This denotes the specific time frame or term of your employment. Usually the term is one year, but can be for several, and will be renewable at the end of the agreed-upon term. Your negotiated benefits should also be addressed in writing in this document. It should be clear that they will be rolled over if your employment contract is extended. This is extremely important because you will want to keep your severance, stock options, bonuses, and other negotiated terms. An important note: If you are promoted and do not have an employment contract, you might want to consider one. Or, if you already have one, it might need to be updated to reflect your change in position and the resultant changes in compensation and benefits.

- **Termination clauses.** If you do not have a specific term of employment in your agreement or contract, does this mean that you will be considered an "at-will" employee? Many states have laws that allow companies to dismiss an employee without notice or reason, unless you have a contract that states otherwise. Whenever possible, as a senior-level candidate, you want to negotiate your terms of employment, including justifiable reasons for termination and the benefits you will receive if terminated.

- **Compensation.** Compensation is *not* just about base salary. It is also about cash incentives, commissions, bonuses, expenses, retirement plans, stock options, signing bonuses, relocation clauses, savings plans, severance packages, clauses to protect your base salary from any possible decreases, health and insurance benefits, computer and telephone services, equipment reimbursement, memberships, parking benefits, automobile benefits or expenses, outplacement assistance, and career coaching/counseling, just to name a few.

- **Title.** Be sure that your contract clearly spells out the title of the position for which you are being hired.

- **Reporting structure.** Be sure that your contract specifically states the job title of the person you will be reporting to directly.

- **Responsibilities of the position.** Responsibilities and duties of the position should be thoroughly documented. This should include where you will be working; who will report to you; and what divisions, organizations, roles, and tasks you will oversee.

## Non-Compete Agreements

Non-compete agreements are exactly as they sound; namely, agreements that state that as an employee of the hiring company, you will not work for a competitor of that company for a stated period of time or within a specific geographic location. A non-compete agreement is designed solely to protect the employer. If at all possible, it is best that employees *do not* sign non-competes. If it is a condition of employment, you might not have an option if you want the job. Sometimes, when companies are acquired or merged, you might be asked to sign a new or revised non-compete. There are many ways employers develop their non-compete agreements, some more enforceable than others. Much of this depends not only on the way the non-compete is worded, but on the state in which it was executed. Different states operate under different covenants regarding non-compete agreements.

It is worth trying to negotiate *not* having to sign a non-compete agreement if at all possible. If you have no choice, the next best step is to modify the agreement. For example, if there is a clause stating you cannot work for a competing company within 100 miles of your employer's location, see whether this can be modified to 50 miles. Another modification that works in your favor would be to include in the agreement that if you are fired, the non-compete is null and void. Do your best to ensure that the agreement includes only companies that are in exactly the same business as your employer. Any peripheral types of industries should not apply. If an employer's intention is maintaining its client base when you leave, you might be able to get them to agree to a non-solicitation agreement in lieu of a non-compete. By doing so, you will not be prevented from working with a competitor of the employer and the agreement will be less restrictive.

## Non-Disclosure Agreements

Frequently, non-disclosure agreements are given in conjunction with non-compete agreements. Once again, the non-disclosure agreement protects the employer from the employee revealing confidential company information or trade secrets, protects customer information, and might prohibit an employee from even talking about anything that has to do with the company, its products, and its services.

## Points to Remember

In closing, Shelly stresses how important it is for every job seeker to remember the following:

- How you and the employer act during the negotiation process will tell both parties what they can expect from each other regarding future behavior.

- There are both positives and negatives to signing agreements and contracts.

- The greater the risk in your employment situation, the greater the need for you to have a solid employment contract in place should you find yourself without a job.

- Hiring companies like to make non-compete agreements as restrictive as possible because the more limiting the agreement is for the employee, the better able they are to protect their interests.

- Although difficult to enforce, non-compete agreements at times can create difficult situations for the employee and leave you unable to work in your chosen profession or tied up in legal issues and court. Fighting non-competes can be emotionally draining and financially costly.

- You might need to agree to some terms of a contract or agreement you could do without or find objectionable. If you try to change the terms of the agreement, the best time to negotiate is after the offer is extended and before you accept the job. If you find your employer unwilling to change the terms, you will need to make a decision to either sign the agreement or turn down the offer.

- Be upfront from the start about what you want. You want to be perceived as someone who is direct and can be counted on. If things become too complicated and the employer feels you are not negotiating from a place of good faith, your offer could be rescinded. The employment negotiations are not over until you and the employer execute the agreements and contracts. Enjoy the process, but do not get too comfortable and forget what it is all about.

- The more marketable or atypical your skills and the more the employer wants you, the more influence you will have to negotiate in your favor.

- When negotiating a contract or agreement, it is wise to hire an employment attorney who is an expert regarding employment law in their specific geographic area. Each state has its own particular laws, and you need to hire a professional who knows them well to best protect your interests.

☐ ☐ ☐

# It's Not Over Until You Sign on the Dotted Line

**Denise Males**
*Director of Recruitment*
*Major League Baseball, New York, NY*

All too often, people receive a verbal offer from a company and, even though the written offer has not yet arrived, they halt their job search immediately and start announcing their news to everyone they know. Wondering whether this truly is the best strategy, we turned to Denise for her objective insights and recommendations on how to handle a verbal offer with no written offer in hand.

First and foremost, Denise warns every job seeker that "it's not over until it's over." Put more directly, she recommends that every candidate continue interviewing until such time as the company has presented a written offer of employment.

If it takes a week or so to get a written offer to a candidate, Denise warns that there might be a reason. At times, companies will tell an applicant that an offer is coming, but might simply need time and want to keep the candidate interested. There might be a variety of reasons why a written offer takes a while to arrive, but in today's age of instant fax and e-mail communications, waiting a week for an offer generally tells you that something might be going on within the company. Perhaps the company is waiting for budget approval, but has not received it yet. Or they might be experiencing internal changes and are waiting to see what will happen.

The candidate owes it to him- or herself to continue interviewing. Something could change with the company, or something could change with the candidate. Perhaps the candidate will go on additional interviews and find the job of his or her dreams—a better fit, more money, more challenge, or more opportunity.

Then there is always the possibility that the offer never comes. If this happens and the candidate has other irons in the fire, it will help to make him or her feel more empowered and less vulnerable. Continuing to interview will protect the candidate. If he or she had halted the job search and the offer fell through, the candidate would feel even worse. Keep interviewing, keep control of your search, and you will be able to handle the disappointments with much more ease and grace.

If the potential employer tells the candidate that they want to hire him or her, but the written offer will not be coming for a few days, the candidate should let them know that he or she is fine with the wait, but he or she does have other interviews scheduled. The candidate might find that by letting the potential employer know the situation or the interest other companies have in him or her, the length of time to receive the written offer might be decreased because the company won't want to lose a well-qualified candidate. The candidate should be polite when talking with the employer about having other interviews scheduled or when sharing other offers he or she has or is expecting. If the employer realizes the candidate is active in his or her job search and that there are other firms interested in the candidate, it might increase the employer's level of interest in that person and, in turn, expedite the delivery of a written offer.

□ □ □

# Win the Game

**Rich Sierra**
*President/CEO*
*Health Care Recruitment, Pembroke Pines, FL*

We first met Rich Sierra at the Kennedy Information Expo in New York City in November 2003. When we asked him for his guidance on the topic of salary negotiations, he outlined what he considers to be the six keys to interview success:

1.  Do your research.
2.  Be realistic.

3. Understand the employer's point of view.

4. Be creative.

5. Do not negotiate in bad faith.

6. Do not win the battle and lose the war.

We then asked Rich to explain each of these concepts and how they come into play in the art of salary negotiations. Here's what he had to say.

## Do Your Research

To effectively negotiate your salary, you must know what the market pays for the position and the years of experience you bring. This begins the actual salary-negotiation process. People often feel they are worth a specific amount of money, but that might not be what they will get paid. There is a range for each position and the market will pay only what you are worth. You must carefully research your profession, the company, and the location of the company to determine what your actual salary range will be.

## Be Realistic

Everyone wants a raise in salary, but you must understand that there are variables that will always impact what you are paid. There are four primary considerations a company evaluates when determining what salary they will offer to you. These include

- The company's budget for the position
- Market conditions
- The economy
- The other candidates vying for the same position

You must take these factors into account and put them into the equation when you are determining what salary you want. The more people understand these points, the better equipped they will be to negotiate an equitable salary instead of sticking to a specific figure that they have in mind.

## Understand the Employer's Point of View

Negotiations are not one-sided! An employer has a position open as a result of a specific need at that moment in time. And they have allocated a specific budget for that position. Candidates are able to create a win-win situation when they take this into account and are not confrontational during salary negotiations.

## Be Creative

This is extremely important. There are many ways to negotiate compensation, and it is not just about salary. You might want an additional $5,000 and the employer might not be able to give that to you in salary. But they might be able to offer you time off, pay for you to attend a professional conference, or offer that $5,000 in a bonus. There are also many other benefits that are not attached to salary (for example, flexible work schedules, a four-day work week, telecommuting). Although these might not be reflected in your weekly paycheck, they certainly are of value to you and your family. Employers have a limit on what salary they can offer, so look at the many perks that are being offered and then make an appropriate decision.

## Do Not Negotiate in Bad Faith

The employer wants to hire you in good faith, but might not be able to offer you the salary that you want. If they hire you reluctantly because they've given you a higher salary than they planned, they hire you in bad faith. You might get that extra $5,000, but the relationship might then start out on a sour note. Negotiations must be done in a spirit of cooperation with the goal of a positive outcome for both you and the employer. No one likes to lose a negotiation. The employer is taking a risk by hiring you and endorsing you. Sometimes you have to give up money to retain that relationship. Remember, this is the beginning of your relationship with that employer, not the end. Look long-term when building relationships and negotiating employment opportunities.

## Do Not Win the Battle and Lose the War

The employer will remember if they were put into a corner when negotiating with you. If they pay a specific amount of money to bring you on board when a demand was created for more salary, more will be expected of you. You could make your first mistake, but you will not be around to make a second. If the employer needs you and hires you, but then another person shows up after you have already started your position, the loyalty might not exist. You are not the be-all and end-all...everyone is replaceable.

Most important, if you and the employer are too far apart on salary negotiations and the employer's range simply does not work for you, walk away. Do not settle for something that you will instantly be dissatisfied with. That is certainly a no-win situation for both you and the company.

□ □ □

# Authors' Best Salary-Negotiation Advice

1. **Know what you are worth.** Critical to negotiating your next salary is knowing what you are worth. This depends on your previous compensation, the industry, the position, the level of responsibility, and the geographic location of the job. Never enter into salary negotiations without already knowing your monetary value in the marketplace.

2. **Research the market and the industry to know what the position is worth.** Another key component to determining your worth is knowing what comparable positions pay in your industry. Take the time necessary to research this information so that you will be fully prepared. If you receive an offer that is lower than you expected, you can then explain to your interviewer that you have researched the industry and the local employment market and believe that $_____ is the appropriate salary for the position. Can they meet that?

3. **Never be the first to bring up salary during an interview.** The saying goes that "the first one to bring up salary is the one that loses." Although that might not be true, you are well advised to never bring up the topic of salary. At some point, your interviewer will broach the subject and you can discuss it then. However, never be the one who makes the first move.

4. **Try to delay your salary discussion as long as possible.** If your interviewer wants to talk about salary in the first five minutes of your first interview with the company, make every attempt possible (using the advice in this chapter) to put the conversation off for as long as you can. It is much better to establish mutual interest between you and the company, saving the salary discussion for much later when you both already know that you are a good fit. This will generally give you much greater latitude in asking for what you are worth and what you want.

5. **Ask for everything.** You never know until you ask. If you are being offered an attractive position, you are quite interested in the company, and they are quite interested in you, that is the

*(continued)*

*(continued)*

time to ask for everything and anything that you want—more money, better benefits, more flexibility, a more impressive job title, or whatever. If you do not ask, you might never receive.

6. **Never respond with an excited "Yes!"** Picture this: You are sitting in your interviewer's office, excited about the prospect of a new job, and thrilled when the interviewer offers you a salary $12,000 more than what you are currently making. Your first reaction, obviously, is to immediately accept the offer. However, the best strategy is to be contemplative. If you think about the offer for a minute or two, there will be many instances when your interviewer will up the offer instantly. Just think—you already got a raise and you have not yet even started!

7. **Be confident.** If you exude confidence and accomplishment, companies are much more likely to offer you a higher compensation. They want to hire winners, and you have clearly demonstrated that you are a winner. Do not be shy. Tell them what you are worth and why. You might be amazed at the results!

8. **Get it in writing.** We would all like to believe that we operate from the same level of integrity, but it never hurts to protect yourself. Be sure to get a written employment offer that details your job responsibilities, goals, and compensation before ever accepting a position.

9. **Let your recruiter work for you.** If you are working with a recruiter, chances are that they will negotiate on your behalf. Prior to the interview, the recruiter most likely already told you what the position was paying. If the offer comes in a little lower than your expectations, tell your recruiter and detail why you feel that you are worth more compensation. In 99 percent of the cases, the recruiter will go to bat for you. Remember, many recruiters are paid a percentage of your first year's salary, so they are just as motivated as you to increase that number.

10. **It is okay to walk away.** If an offer is not right for you and the compensation is not enough, walk away. Sometimes there is no room for negotiating, and it is okay to say no. Not every opportunity or every offer will be right for you.

## Career and Job Search Survey Results

### Question #1:

Do you expect candidates to negotiate regarding their salary, benefits, and work schedules once you've made an offer?

### Results:

82 percent reported that they did expect a candidate to negotiate.

18 percent reported that they did not expect a candidate to negotiate.

### Conclusion:

Negotiate when an offer is made. In most circumstances, it is expected.

### Question #2:

On average, how much of a range do you have to negotiate a higher salary with a professional candidate (not hourly personnel)?

### Results:

64 percent reported that they can negotiate up to a 10 percent higher salary.

20 percent reported that they can negotiate up to a 20 percent higher salary.

18 percent reported that they have no limit on salary negotiations.

0 percent reported that they have no authorization to negotiate higher salary.

### Conclusion:

In virtually all instances, the interviewer has the authority to negotiate a higher salary.

# CHAPTER 8 How to Move Your Career Forward

The final chapter of this book focuses on what you can do—today and in the future—to take control of your career and move forward. The competition has never been fiercer, and it is up to you to develop and work your own career plan. That plan might be focused on growth and promotion with your existing employer, or it might be concentrated on identifying alternative career opportunities in new and growing industries. Regardless of your personal career preferences, your challenge is the same: to develop a career plan that leverages your strengths and qualifications, meets your personal and professional goals, and provides you with self-satisfaction and self-fulfillment.

There is no single strategy for lifelong career management. The only guiding principle is that the process is dynamic and constantly changing. The goals that you establish for yourself when you are 25 will change dramatically by the time you reach 45, and that's okay. You have to understand that your career plan will change and evolve as you learn, grow, expand, and explore. That's part of what makes your career exciting.

What's more, companies keep changing, growing, divesting, acquiring, relocating, downsizing, and more, all of which is outside your control. It might be that you had planned to spend your entire career in the aerospace industry, an industry that has been fraught with lay-offs, downsizing, bankruptcies, and consolidations over the past two decades. When you were laid off eight years ago, you had to change your career plan in response to the changing marketplace. No longer were the opportunities in aerospace unlimited; rather, they were virtually nonexistent. In turn, you had to realign your career plan, investigate new opportunities, and pursue a new career path. Being responsive to market conditions is a huge consideration when planning your career and all the subsequent turns and twists it will take.

Many companies focus on similar characteristics when looking for candidates to hire or employees to promote. They want individuals who have innate leadership capabilities, are strong communicators, can build and lead teams, and are not daunted by challenge and failure. They want problem-solvers who offer innovative solutions and are able to transition those solutions from concept into action. In essence, they want people who excel and achieve; and if you can position yourself as such a contributor, opportunities will come your way.

Perhaps the most important concept to discuss in relation to lifelong career management begins with a simple question: "Who do you work for?" If you answered with the name of your company, you are wrong. You work for yourself—for ever and for always. No matter who writes your paycheck, ultimately you are working for yourself and your family. Never lose sight of that, for it should guide your entire career.

Our collection of interviews in this chapter is with a wide representation of business executives, hiring managers, recruiters, and human resources professionals. Each has shared what they consider to be the most vital information for moving your career forward, accepting new opportunities, and reaching new heights. We now turn to their sage advice and guidance that you can apply when managing your career over your entire working life.

□ □ □

# Characteristics, Skills, and Abilities of Promotable Employees

### Coleen Smith

*Vice President, Global People Development and Staffing,*
*Education and Training, Employee Relations, and*
*Best Place to Work*
*Colgate-Palmolive, New York, NY*

In attempting to uncover the true skills and qualifications that will allow employees to stand out in the workplace, we wanted to interview a human resources executive from one of the most widely recognized and well-respected companies in the U.S. We were fortunate to be able to speak with Coleen Smith, who provided a wealth of information about what her company looks for in promotable employees. Here's what she shared with us.

For years and years, Colgate-Palmolive, just like virtually every other company in the world, focused a great deal of their employee development on functional competencies. It was the work that mattered, first and foremost. Today, however, the corporation is putting more emphasis and focus on developing leadership skills in order to help employees advance and succeed. The company's focus is on finding new hires and retaining employees with strong ethics and integrity. Coleen believes that an employee's ability to perform well within the organization goes beyond just education and experience. The employee's true ability to succeed will depend largely on his or her ability to not only manage a group of people, but to manage with respect. Colgate wants people that other people want to work for.

When Coleen is evaluating an employee's long-term potential and fit with the company, she assumes their ability to do their job is a given. Therefore, she focuses on what it is about them that will shape them into future leaders: the leadership model they subscribe to, their ability to build positive relationships, their ability to communicate well at all levels of the organization, and how they give feedback to their managers and supervisors.

Coleen said that when she talks to employees, she pays close attention to how they describe things and how they talk about what they did. Did they manage with respect? Are they ethical? Do they use team-oriented language? Are they thoughtful? Do they listen well? Her focus is not just on what they know and what they have done, but on the way in which they were able to accomplish those things.

This information allows her to form a realistic impression of that individual's leadership competencies and style.

It is also critically important to Coleen that an employee be able to answer very simple questions such as why they work for the company, what is best about their job, and who the people in the company are that they want to work for. For senior-level executives interviewing for even higher-level positions, Coleen wants to know that they are very knowledgeable about the company strategy and key priorities, but she also wants to know their compensation and benefits package, the value of stock options they have, and other specifics that demonstrate they are truly committed to, and understand, the organization.

Because 75 percent of Colgate-Palmolive's business is outside the United States, it is imperative that the company value unique contributions and have the ability to recognize excellence in areas other than just operations and projects. That is where strong leadership competencies can really come into play. It is a much different situation to manage an employee sitting next to you than it is to virtually manage groups of people who are geographically dispersed. That is a talent the company looks for, values, and attempts to build internally through its leadership-development efforts. Further, she evaluates an individual's ability to operate effectively within a truly global context. That means working well across multiple countries with people from all over the world.

When interviewing an employee seeking a promotion, Coleen works hard to ask questions that truly demonstrate the individual's level of integrity. She often uses a behavioral-based interview style in an attempt to delve into an employee's true self and attempt to identify whether that person has the same preferences, styles, and values as does the company. Colgate is a global company and many positions are travel-intensive. It is imperative that there is a strong match between the employee and the company to ensure a long-term and successful relationship, and to ensure that new employees are well aware that their position may require extensive travel. She recommends that employees prepare three to five points of conversation that will truly reflect their leadership capabilities and position themselves for a spot in the company's succession plan. If they are able to accomplish this and communicate those few essential points, they will be perceived as more prepared and more interesting candidates.

Statistics have shown that 75 percent of employees leave a company (any company, not necessarily Colgate) because they do not have a good relationship with their boss or are not supported by their boss. Having a boss who is a coach and mentor is what people look for. In turn, business managers and leaders must focus on developing their people in order to motivate and retain quality employees.

Colgate has established an outstanding reputation as a great company to work for because of its commitment to managing with respect, developing internal candidates, and creating a corporate culture where people enjoy working. When a company is able to achieve this, people work better together, there is respect for one another, and employees want to stay. And, as we all know, employee retention and promotion is one of the most vital components of any human resources professional's position.

In summary, Coleen shared some key leadership qualities of Colgate people:

- Integrity
- Managing with respect
- Common sense
- Dealing with ambiguity
- Keeping it simple
- Communicating
- Power management (the more you have, the less you should use)
- Being humble
- Understanding no one is perfect

□ □ □

# Positioning Yourself for Recognition and Promotion

**Gwen Weld**

*General Manager—Worldwide Staffing*
*Microsoft Corporation, Redmond, WA*

Working to get yourself recognized by your current employer and positioning yourself for a promotion can be a daunting task. To better understand how you can differentiate yourself within the workplace, we interviewed Gwen Weld, an 18-year employee of

Microsoft. Gwen first shared her insights on what she and Microsoft look for when hiring a new employee or promoting an existing employee:

- It must be readily apparent that an individual has future potential to contribute to Microsoft beyond the current position for which he or she is applying.

- An individual must have the capability to learn and develop as the industry and technology change. No business will survive and thrive without talented employees.

- Grow and develop within the framework of your job and the specific organization you work for.

- Do your best work—always and forever.

Just as important, a couple of the key values that Microsoft embodies are the following:

- Open and respectful with others, dedicated to making them better, and inspiring others around you to be great.

- Self-critical—questioning and committed to personal excellence and self-improvement.

- Willing to take on big challenges and see them through.

With that said, when Gwen is evaluating internal candidates for promotion to positions of higher responsibility, she looks at the candidate's ability to

- **Take a leadership role and take a stand.** This demonstrates that you have a firm conviction, the guts to voice your opinion, and the confidence to drive things forward and make them happen.

- **Build relationships with good people and allow them to challenge you to think and stretch.** This will make you a better person and allow you to be seen in a different perspective. Early in her career, people asked Gwen to do things she did not have the skills for. She was willing to take the risk, grow, and learn new things. Her advice is to partner with different colleagues, figure out the appropriate course of action, and push the envelope.

- **Step outside your comfort zone and acquire new skills.** When you do this, you will gain confidence and be ready for new challenges. When you step outside your comfort zone, people will view you differently and ask your opinion, even if it is not your particular area of expertise. Do it and you will get recognized.

- **Look for new opportunities.** People want to overachieve and, when given the right challenge and opportunity, they can do so. If the challenge wanes, look for new and different things to do, make new contacts throughout the company, and be visible.

- **Be patient.** New skills take time to learn, and you must be willing to devote the time and energy to your own development. Earn the right to be seen and differentiate yourself. Strive to perform above those who already have skills in new disciplines.

Gwen is constantly looking for new opportunities to stretch her top performers. Each year, she focuses on a select group of top-performing employees to determine what new skill sets they can learn to accelerate their development and advance within the organization. She is also acutely aware that the current discipline or function in which an employee works does not have to be a career for life. By expanding the skills and competencies of each of these employees, she is often able to position them for leadership roles in other job functions and organizations than their original career track.

□ □ □

# Standing Out from the Crowd

### Mark Jaffe
*President*
*Wyatt & Jaffe, Minneapolis, MN*

Even though you might get along exceedingly well with your co-workers, the workplace is always competitive. When a promotional opportunity comes up, you might find yourself competing against one of your most valued colleagues. With that said, we wanted to interview someone who could provide us with insights and guidance as to how an employee can stand out from their peers, get noticed, and position themselves for a promotion. We turned to Mark Jaffe, a talented and well-established recruiter, to learn from his wealth of experience.

Mark believes the single best way to distinguish yourself from others is by taking on tasks that others have failed at or been daunted by. When you take on a difficult task, immerse yourself in that new project, new role, or new business, and attempt to perform miracles (or, at least, get strong results).

The best job is often *not* with the company with the most prestige, the best title, or the most money. Rather, it is the place where you will get the most recognition and acknowledgement for your efforts and your contributions. When looking at new jobs and/or promotions with your existing employer, you might have two or three different opportunities to select from. Focus on the one where you believe you can have the greatest impact and make the greatest difference. Even if you fail, you will be acknowledged as someone who took on an impossible challenge. If you succeed, you have done a great job, made a huge difference, and established an outstanding reputation for yourself.

When thinking about your career—today and in the future—it is important to decide whether you want to be a generalist or a specialist. Twenty years ago, the wisdom was to be all things to all people. That has changed today and specialists are becoming the norm. By positioning yourself as a specialist, you are solidifying your reputation as someone with specific expertise. In essence, you are defining your brand and giving yourself a competitive edge by doing specific things better than anyone else.

Here's an analogy that Mark used to make his point. Suppose you are a patient who walks into a clinic with what you think is strep throat. You need a culture taken and any doctor on call will do. A generalist is just fine. Now, compare that to a situation in which you have been in a major car accident, you are in the emergency room, and you need a specialist—someone who can perform life-saving intervention. Although there will always be a place for generalists, it is often the specialist who has the most notable reputation and most visible presence.

Mark also recommends that you take risks. When he reviews a resume for a potential hire and sees that there have never been any significant failures in their career, he is not particularly interested in that candidate. If this individual has never encountered failure, adversity, or conflict, how does Mark know how he will deal with it? He considers these individuals to be high-risk hires. Rather, he would prefer to recruit a candidate who has been *injured* a few times and knows how to handle such situations. Taking a risk is how you become an authority, and it is that risk-taking attitude that creates high energy throughout the entire management chain.

Companies want leadership and executives who know how to do that. When candidates go for job interviews, they need to share what they really think and not what they think that company wants to hear. When you are in the running for a position that pays

$300,000 a year, $400,000 a year, or more, you must have your own point of view and be able to communicate it effectively throughout all levels of an organization. You certainly do not want to be audacious or perversely controversial, but you do want to communicate what you think to a prospective employer. Forget that you were trained since early childhood to keep your opinions to yourself. For executive job seekers, your opinions do count. Be forthright, authoritative, and have the guts to tell people what you really think and believe.

Package your truth in sophistication and distinguish yourself as a problem solver, risk taker, and top performer. Clearly communicate that you are the person who is willing to say, "The emperor has no clothes on," so I think we need to do this a different way. Trust your instincts, gain respect, and, if you are right enough times in your lifetime, you will develop a strong and sustainable reputation as an authority who really does make things happen.

□ □ □

# Communicating Who You Are

### Marie-Anne Martin
*Chief—Human Resources Planning and Development Section*
*United Nations, New York, NY*

Whether you are interested in a promotion with your current employer or looking to transition your skills into a new organization, one of the most critical factors in your success will be your ability to communicate well. To understand just how important communication skills are in any environment—from the most established of all corporations to the unique global infrastructure of the United Nations—we asked Marie-Anne to share her insights with us.

## Communicating with Power

In order to move your career forward, you must have outstanding communication skills and strategies in place. They will be especially important and will make your move easier (obviously) if your reputation within an organization or within an industry are already strong. If your reputation is not good, moving from one position to another will be even more difficult. Remember that a reputation might not be true to you; it is very often a perception.

For the sake of this interview, let us just assume that you have an outstanding reputation as an employee, that you are well respected, and that you are consistent with the positive messages. These things demonstrate that you are serious about what you do and more.

## Communicating Through Networking

To make a successful career transition, your objective must be to make yourself look good. Network within the organization and contact the human resources department. HR can assist you with internal opportunities if you simply communicate to them that you would like to make a career move and need their help.

If you are seeking to relocate or move to another firm either within or outside your current profession or industry, let people know through your networking efforts. Both formal and informal connections work well. Let people know that you are interested and have a willingness to move. Ask people to introduce you to others who might be interested in someone with your specific set of skills. If you are looking to move within a different area of work, develop different types of network contacts with people in different departments. Take courses and connect yourself with someone who has already done the work. If they have experience in what you want to do, they might be able to provide you with clear and concise information, contacts, and much more.

## Communicating Through Mentoring

A good strategy for advancement, information, and career progression is through a mentoring relationship. Many organizations have a mentoring program in place (the UN does). Your mentor can help in many ways and can also represent you within the organization. Generally, your mentor will be someone higher up in the organization and, therefore, will be privileged to information that you cannot get. They can also ask things of others that might not be appropriate for you to ask.

## Cross-Cultural Communications

If you are working in a culturally diverse environment, your actions and communications can have different effects on different people. You need to look at the cultural element and understand that each culture has a distinct set of values and attitudes. Often, cultures will clash and you must learn how to best deal with the differences and intricacies of each. A mentor relationship can be extremely beneficial in this situation.

## Corporate Communications

Know the written and unwritten rules of your organization or the organization you wish to work for. People need to know how to do things in an organization—even mundane things like how you dress can make a difference. If Friday is dress-down day, be sure that you dress down so that you are conforming to the existing corporate culture. Although you want to work to make yourself stand out professionally, not abiding by the cultural norms established by a company will not achieve this.

## Nonverbal Communications

You can also communicate in nonverbal ways. Body language and attitude are part of what you need to understand in order to communicate positive messages and show how you will fit in. Depending on the position, if Marie-Anne knows a person is interested in working in her department, she will look for how that person behaves consistently. She will ask her colleagues for references. She will want to know that this person can work well at all levels and that he or she has a consistently positive attitude. People talk within an organization. If you think you can keep something a secret, you are mistaken! Stay away from the rumor mill; it is not something you want to be a part of.

Projecting a positive image is very important. You want to have the image of someone who is dynamic, energetic, and willing to do whatever it takes. You want to get out of your office and meet people, be engaging, and smile. But remember: Don't overdo it! You do not want to be seen as too eager; it could be annoying and have the exact opposite reaction from what you want.

In closing, Marie-Anne stressed the fact that the best communication skills will not replace performance, qualifications, or experience. Apart from being a talented communicator, an individual must have a clear strategy in place—what do they want in their career, when, and where—and know how they are going to get there. Put the plan in place along with top-notch communication skills and you are bound to succeed!

□ □ □

# Recommended Career Development Strategies for the Upwardly Mobile Employee

## Stephen Lopez
*Vice President—Support Services*
*National Board of Medical Examiners, Philadelphia, PA*

When we interviewed Steve Lopez, we wanted to know what strategies he would recommend for individuals to advance their own careers (in addition to typical things such as training, seminars, and conferences). Bear in mind as you read his comments that he hires strictly for technical positions.

Steve began his interview with a reality check of the information-technology industry and the massive changes taking place. Over the past years, high-end IT jobs have been moving offshore. Once these jobs are gone, they are lost forever. Young people need to heed the trend and plan their careers in new and innovative ways.

Steve's career track itself is quite interesting. He knew right from the start that he did not want to be a hands-on technical person. Rather, his long-range vision was a position in management in the technology industry. Early on, he learned to master the jargon—both technical jargon and business jargon—a critical skill in moving toward the management goal he had set for himself. In addition, he pursued his MBA, realizing that a strong business education would help him move and expand his career. He also looked for new challenges outside his comfort zone, knowing that people have to think past that zone in order to move forward.

Almost immediately, Steve identified the huge disconnect in peoples' ability to communicate well between the business and technical sides of the industry. It was this disconnect that provided him with the greatest opportunity. As one who was able to bridge that gap and communicate on both sides of the fence, he instantly put himself in an extremely advantageous position to not only move into management, but also to protect himself from the effect of thousands of jobs moving offshore.

The moral of the story: Technical people need to expand their horizons and reach for positions as business managers and project managers. The traditional role of the programmer is disappearing quickly, and to maintain a firm stance within the industry, technologists must also become managers and team leaders.

Steve recommends the following career-development strategies for individuals who want to actively move their careers forward:

- Think about how you can move outside the barriers and boundaries you work within in your current organization.

- Look for opportunities to add more diverse responsibilities, no matter how full your plate is.

- Build in a new skill that allows you to develop as a manager of people, projects, and organizations.

- Pursue a graduate degree, a real market differentiator and competitive advantage in the technology industry.

- Accept opportunities to acquire offshore experience.

- Engage in activities that will enhance your value to, and visibility within, your company.

- Be patient and take responsibility for your career growth. Plan out your career for the next five to ten years, work your plan, challenge yourself to learn new skills and acquire new knowledge, and establish milestones to gauge your success as you move along.

Not only does Steve recommend these strategies, he knows that they work! By following his own advice, he was able to move from Engineer to Supervisor to Manager to Enterprise Architect to Associate Vice President and now, his current position as Vice President and a member of the Management Team of the National Board of Medical Examiners. Follow Steve's plan of action and you too will enjoy positive results.

□ □ □

# Be a Change Master

**Cynthia A. Hartley**
*Senior Vice President—Human Resources*
*Sonoco Products Company, Hartsville, SC*

In order to survive in today's volatile employment market, employees must be adaptable and learn to function within working environments that are constantly changing. We all know that the status quo does not exist anymore. Rather, the employee who truly thrives will be one who can embrace change. To learn how best to accomplish that, we turned to Cindy Hartley for her expert advice.

Cindy outlined what she considers to be the top four items that will facilitate a positive response to organizational change:

1.  **Keep communications open.** When change occurs, companies should keep employees informed of what is going on in order to make the transition easier. Often, however, it is difficult for a consistent message to reach every employee. Therefore, as an employee, you should ask for feedback. The more you know, the better able you will be to address the reasons behind the change and adapt more readily.

2.  **Be flexible and adaptable.** You will become a much greater asset to your organization when you are flexible and adaptable to change. When you know the facts about what is changing and why, you do not have to imagine the worst. It is human nature to think terrible things when you do not have the facts, another important reason to ask questions and encourage feedback.

3.  **Be open to different career directions.** Look carefully at your skill base and career path, and make sure that you are staying current in your industry and profession. If you do not do this, you are potentially boxing yourself in and will have a much more difficult time dealing with change. Conversely, when you broaden your skills and stay up-to-date, you will have many more options available in what you can do and what value you bring to your current employer.

4.  **Keep your attitude positive.** Do not take yourself and your situation too seriously. What is the worst that can possibly happen? And is that really the end of the world? The situation might result in a few bumps in the road for you, and at first glance, it might not seem very positive. However, when you approach the situation with a positive attitude, you might find opportunity and exposure to a new career direction within the company (or, perhaps, with another company). Companies value employees who put a positive spin on things and who have an upbeat and engaging attitude. Your willingness to be open to new things, new projects, and new people will create new opportunities for you. It's a guarantee!

□ □ □

# Job Titles, Accomplishments, and More

**Jane McLaughlin**
*President*
*LifeCycle Software, Ambler, PA*

Moving your career forward—within one organization or several—requires constant progression and acceleration. To learn how job titles and specific accomplishments can serve to propel your career, we turned to Jane McLaughlin, who shared her experiences in hiring and career development. Here's what she had to say.

First and foremost, when you increase your responsibilities over time and add accomplishments to your list of career successes, you *are* moving your career forward. Movement does not have to be jumping from one company to another. Rather, movement can be slow and steady, assuming an additional responsibility here and another there, and then delivering tangible results. When you move from Section Manager to Department Manager to Director, the message to prospective employers is that you have progressed based on your knowledge, performance, and achievements, and that you have become an expert in your chosen industry or profession.

One important item to note is that if you are interviewing with a company that is in a different industry than your past experience, you might need to explain your career progression and what it means to ensure that your interviewer fully understands and appreciates all that you have accomplished.

Other activities to consider participating in that will add value in helping to move your career forward include the following that Jane outlined for us:

- **You might also consider joining professional associations as a way to learn more about your industry and profession.** Through these affiliations, you can network with people outside your own company and learn what they are doing in their companies. What are their titles? Does your company offer the same titles and same career paths as others? This is important information that you will want to have when negotiating your next promotion, next job title, or increased responsibilities with your current employer.

- **Ask your company to send you to industry-related conferences that will help you stay current and informed.** Conferences are a great way to get an overview of the market and the industry, look at emerging trends, and amass information that will be critical in helping you plan your short- and long-term career moves. If you live in the Eastern U.S., look for conferences in Boston, New York, Philadelphia, Atlanta, and Washington, D.C. If you live on the West Coast, Los Angeles and San Francisco are big conference cities. For those of you in the Midwest, turn to Chicago.

If you commit yourself to staying current with your industry and profession, and if you can demonstrate your career progression through higher-level job titles, increased responsibilities, and more notable achievements, you will have positioned yourself to succeed regardless of the competition. Great employment opportunities abound. It is your challenge to find them and position yourself as the number-1 candidate.

☐ ☐ ☐

# Positioning Yourself for Workplace Prosperity

### Anne Fisher
*Senior Writer and "Ask Annie" Columnist*
*Fortune and Fortune.com, New York, NY*

We were fortunate enough to have the opportunity to visit with "Ask Annie" of *Fortune* magazine fame. When we approached her with the concept of workplace prosperity, she immediately focused our attention on a relatively new concept: inventing a position for yourself. What follows is Anne's advice on how to make that happen.

If you are currently employed but not happy with what you are doing, or you are happy but want something more, look closely at what your company is currently doing and where it is headed. Take the time to find out what management is saying, what they need today, and what they anticipate needing in the future so that you can favorably position yourself. People often think they need to look for a new job, but frequently that job already exists within their current organization. As the company is changing, employees who listen will have an opportunity to be part of that change and work their way into a new opportunity.

## Succeeding in Times of Change

Here is a telltale sign to watch out for that will indicate your company is ready to undergo change—sometimes small, incremental changes, and other times dramatic changes. There is new top management in the company or a particular operating division. Someone new will likely have their own ideas about changes and areas of growth in which to focus. You might have a new boss or new management team above your immediate boss. If so, this is a good time to be on the lookout for what they are trying to accomplish and what you can directly contribute to that process. In today's market, many people are cynical about companies' mission and vision statements because people often talk these to death, but do not listen hard enough to what they can bring to the table to make a difference and facilitate positive change. When people take the time to do this, they become part of the reason the goal is achieved. Talk to your immediate boss first—so that he or she does not feel as though you have gone behind his or her back—and let them know you would like to talk to the new management about how to support their vision, plans, and actionable goals.

If a new boss, new CEO, or new manager says they want _____, and you feel you could contribute to that, your immediate boss can be a true ally if, and only if, you have already developed a good relationship with him or her. If that is the case, go to the top person and tell them you believe their new project, new initiative, or new organizational change process is a great idea and ask how you can help. Some employees might feel this is too pushy; they think they should not rock the boat and should not call attention to themselves. Wrong! People must self-promote because only they know how and what they can contribute. If you do not self-promote, no one will do it for you.

Approach the decision maker and let them know you are interested in helping. It is often lonely at the top, and believe it or not, they need and want help. If you are able to do this and clearly communicate the value and expertise you offer, you might very well land a bigger and more responsible position. In turn, you will gain a whole new level of experience and a new way to get things done. Sometimes, existing managers and executives who are attempting to change the direction of a company might be less open to doing things in a new way. New management, however, can present a wonderful opportunity for people looking to share new ideas and move into new assignments.

## Bring New Ideas to the Top

If you read a trade publication or attend a professional conference, you can often find out what the competition is doing and what is interesting about their projects, products, services, and more. Go to your immediate supervisor first and then to top management to offer your suggestions for the company based on competitive trends. The more you know about your industry, the better able you will be to know what is going on, what trends are emerging, and where the other major players are headed. No matter how busy your schedule, make time to engage in these types of activities. The competitive intelligence you will gain can have amazing results for you and for your company.

If you have a good working relationship with your boss, share your new ideas. Employees are often afraid to share new ideas for fear that their bosses will steal the idea and get all the credit. If you are concerned about this, put your idea in writing. Send a one-page proposal to your boss outlining what you did (for example, attended a conference, read an article, identified new industry statistics) and what you are now thinking and proposing. E-mail a copy to your boss and to another individual higher up in the company. Be sure your boss is the first addressee in your e-mail message; other managers should be copied. That way, everyone knows it was your idea and it is clear where the credit should go.

## Try a Job That You Love

One factor that Anne considers most critical is long-range career planning to find a job that you truly love. For example, many people have ideas for small businesses, but do not know how to get started or do not know how to manage their time to launch a new venture while still employed. Anne has seen many successful small businesses that were started part time, often as a hobby. If you have an idea, or there is something you love to do, and you can find the time, start doing it now!

Your love or hobby can turn into a full-time job. It does not have to be all or nothing. You do not have to quit your current job to start working on something you love. Rather, if you can spend a few hours a week developing your business, it becomes a risk-free way of dipping your toe into what you would rather be doing. If you have the passion, you will find the time. It's that simple.

## Networking: Get Out and Talk to People

In her role as "Ask Annie," Anne receives a voluminous amount of mail. One big category of people that she hears from have been to Monster.com and other major job boards, submitted hundreds of resumes, yet received no responses and no interviews. In fact, in a recent Gallup Poll, approximately 80 percent of the people who applied for a job on a job board said that it was like sending their resume into a black hole. Anne's advice is not to waste your time with these activities, but rather get out there and talk to people. Over the years, she has found that most jobs you will want are not advertised anywhere. More often, jobs are created when employees in companies meet and build relationships with the right people. When doing this type of internal networking, Anne recommends that you ask for help, input, and information. This can be difficult, particularly the higher up in the organizational chain of command that you are. People in their 20s often network more effectively because their egos are not as fragile and they believe everyone can help. The higher up your position is, the harder it can be to reach out, ask for help, and use your network to your advantage.

When you network, you are getting your message out. Anne believes the higher up you go, the more likely you will be to get a job from someone you know. Although most people know this, many still find it difficult to pick up the phone and ask what is new, what is going on, and are there any opportunities. When you network, bring something with you to help the person you are networking with. Come to the meeting with an idea of what you are going to do for someone else. When you do this, you are not asking for anything. Rather, you are offering something, which leaves a long-lasting and positive impression. Keep yourself active and participate in networking, ask about a problem they are having, and offer a possible solution. People help people who ask what they can do to help them.

Although Anne believes that doing as much networking as possible is critical to your long-term career success, she feels that it is less effective in today's market where so much networking is constantly going on. She recently read an article in the *New York Times* that talked about how networking can sometimes backfire because so many people are all approaching the same sources. In turn, it becomes much more difficult to get your networking calls returned and your network working for you. The lesson to be learned here is to build an exclusive network of contacts who are not constantly approached by so many other individuals.

If you are able to follow Anne's advice, you will find that you have the power to move your career forward and prosper. The opportunities are there. It is your challenge and your responsibility to identify them, position yourself favorably, and continually demonstrate your value to an organization.

□ □ □

# For Young Professionals Only

**Bea Hardman**
*Director—Human Resources*
*Hyatt Regency Oak Brook, Oak Brook, IL*

We felt it was important to include some information specifically for young professionals—individuals just launching their careers or with less than a year or two of experience. We turned to Bea Hardman, who has extensive experience hiring and working with young professionals. Her insights communicate several powerful points that every young professional should heed:

1. **Be enthusiastic and passionate about what you do.** Be proud of your product, your company, and yourself. Be committed and give 200 percent each and every day. You want to go to work happily each day, loving your job, and knowing that you are contributing.

2. **Work diligently to gain the respect of your peers, other employees, and your supervisor.** Be a team player. Be straightforward and assertive, not aggressive. Leaders are kind and supportive, not fearful and intimidating.

3. **Get involved!** Offer to work on special projects, help other departments, or do whatever you can to expand your knowledge, get to know more people within the organization, and start to make a name for yourself.

4. **Look for a coach or mentor to provide guidance and help steer your career.**

5. **When you encounter a setback, don't dwell on it. Learn from the experience and move on.**

6. **Continue to educate yourself and share your knowledge with others.** Keep up-to-date technically and with issues, products, services, and more that are particular to your industry and profession.

7. **Learn to network well, be visible, and let others know you are available.**

8. **Maintain a financial focus at all times.** No one can run a business without being concerned about the bottom line.

9. **Give yourself time to learn and prepare for a promotion.** Younger people tend to be impatient and must realize that life-long career development and management truly is a *lifelong* process!

□ □ □

# You and Your Mentor

**Jack St.Genis**
*Chairman and CEO*
*Molecular Separations, Inc., Sarasota, FL*

One of the most effective things you can do to facilitate the progression of your career throughout your work life is to find a mentor, someone who will guide you, support you, and help fast-track your career. In deciding who could provide some realistic insights about the value of a mentor, we turned to Jack St.Genis, whose previous mentors have included such prominent business executives as John Delorean, Lee Iacocca, and others. Here's what Jack shared with us about the value of those relationships.

In large corporations, such as General Motors, Matsushita, NEC, and Raytheon, there is virtually no way to the top without a coach, mentor, or advocate. In large companies, middle management struggles to be seen by senior management. In order to obtain your goal, you have to have an ally with visibility who is willing to work on helping you increase your visibility. The same can be said about smaller companies, where most of the decisions come from the corner office and are controlled by a very small inner circle that, in many cases, is family. This is the toughest situation in which to find a mentor, unless, of course, you marry the boss's son or daughter! Look at the Young President's Organization roster; it is amazing how many names are the same as the company's name.

## The Way to the Top

The way to the top is twofold:

1. Make your boss, your potential best mentor, look good.

2. Do the job you have.

Bosses lose very few conflicts, and they have the ability to relegate the uncooperative to anonymity. Your boss can put you on projects that will make you a success or assign you to the "Charge of the Light Brigade." The result of the latter is a beautiful funeral (outplacement), but does not help to feed your family. Being pushed out to the parts depot in some remote little community that no one has ever heard of is the American version of being sent to the Gulag in Russia. Conversely, make your boss's star shine and help him or her get promoted, and you will form a vacuum that allows you to be sucked up right along with him or her when he or she is promoted.

The truth is, hard work is not enough to get you to the top, or more importantly, where you want to be (location, type of position, industry or product preference, and more). Salespeople have a slight advantage because their performance is usually measurable and visible at the top. The same is true with engineering innovation. But what happens at a corporation where increased volume is not the sales measurement, or innovation is nonexistent when you are assigned to fenders, axles, or power supplies?

Sales at large corporations with dominant market share are largely about sticking to a sales plan, and most of the time, about rationing products in short supply while maintaining an acceptable relationship with the customer. In engineering, it is about delivering projects within specification, on time, and on budget. There are more than 11,000 parts in a car, and you can be sure that the president of the automotive company does not know who designed or value engineered each one of them. So how can you stand out and get noticed? Your answer is to have a mentor who is looking for an innovation to make him or her look good.

## The Value of Having the Right Mentor

Here is a great story that will demonstrate the true value of a mentoring relationship. When John Delorean began his career, he was a designer in a sea of engineers in Detroit. Yet, he was able to get the General Manager of his division to notice him by hiding the ugly windshield wipers under the cowl of the hood. This got the car, and subsequently him, noticed by senior management and gave him gravitas with the General Manager. He then listened carefully to what would make this new model a success, and his boss a success, and he sought out the appropriate solutions. As a result, the General Manager was promoted to the corporate staff, and soon, John Delorean was promoted to the General Manager of the largest car division.

A word of caution: Be careful whom you choose for a mentor. Many company losers masquerade as performance players who can carry the ball for you. Most of them are out of plays and get little attention from above, so they are looking for adulation from those junior to them. The worst thing you can do is attach yourself to the over-the-hill (out-of-favor) gang. Look to see who really can do something for you if you perform for them.

The president's speechwriter, advertising agency account manager, or merchandising supplier sometimes has more influence than the boss' deputy. Outside suppliers, with close attachments to senior management, often can get you in front of the big guns more easily than those who have to go through the appropriate channels. Suppliers have much more influence on senior management than line managers like to admit.

Special teams, joint ventures, and charitable and civic projects will also get you significant visibility. Nothing will get you more prestige than having the CEO of a joint-venture company say to your boss that you are a real mover and shaker. Of course, your boss will have to take credit for having mentored you himself, but is that so bad?

If you want to see as close as we have come to human cloning, just watch an Admiral's Selection Board or a Fortune 500 company's Presidential Selection Committee. Many corporations, just like the military, want an exact replica of what they already have. Remember the transition pictures in *Fortune* magazine of Jack Welch with his successor Jeff Immelt? Both were wearing khakis with blue blazers and open-collared shirts. I bet there were two perfectly matched Hartman attaché cases on the desk behind them! It's easier to imitate than it is to innovate! When Lee Iacocca came to Ford with his cigar-smoking habit, the staff almost died from the smoke generated by those trying to develop a taste for cigars.

Find a true mentor and your career will soar!

□ □ □

# What Companies Value in Their Employees

### Karen Shadders
*Vice President—People*
*Wegmans Food Markets, Rochester, NY*

To learn more about who companies want to hire and what they value in their employees, we turned to Karen Shadders for her insights. As the Vice President of People at Wegmans Food Markets, Inc., she brings a wealth of information to us.

When Wegmans hires, they hire for potential future leaders because their professional, management, and executive staff is primarily grown from within. The four key things they look for when seeking to promote employees are the following:

1. **Results orientation.** Has the employee delivered results to the company? Wegmans looks closely at the employee's performance and contributions to determine promotability.

2. **Values that match the organization's values.** Wegmans wants to see that the employee holds the same five key values that the company does, and, as such, ensure a strong cultural fit. The five values are

   - Caring about people

   - Having high standards

   - Making a difference in the communities they serve

   - Respecting their peers and recognizing that each person brings something different

   - Empowering people through shared responsibilities

Wegmans' leaders know that their frontline employees are best connected to the customers; and, therefore, the leaders of the organization must be well connected to the frontline employees or they will not be successful. The professional staff must understand what is working well and what is not, and have earned the confidence of the people they work with. They must listen to what is being said and embrace a model of service and leadership. The people who embody these values will be successful at Wegmans.

3. **Ability to build relationships across functional teams.** During Karen's 13-year tenure with Wegmans, she has held positions in human resources, merchandising, store operations, and then back to HR. This demonstrates the tremendous opportunities for promotion and career development within the company, all based on an individual's ability to communicate well across diverse functional teams.

4. **Adaptability.** As Wegmans grows and changes, so do the people who do well within the organization. Part of how Wegmans helps them to grow is by providing cross-functional assignments. On-the-job learning is the most effective in their environment and provides employees with a diverse toolkit of skills and experiences. Karen believes that Wegmans is unique because they focus on doing the right thing, and their people know that it starts at the top. Building relationships across the organization while moving within the divisions and building trust along the way is *huge* at Wegmans and will positively position a candidate for future promotional opportunities.

☐ ☐ ☐

# Savvy Strategies for Promotion

**Rob Croner**
*Senior Vice President—Human Resources*
*Radian Group, Inc., Philadelphia, PA*

Rob spends a great deal of time working with mid- to senior-level managers in his organization. As such, we asked him to share his insights on how employees can best position themselves for promotion and career advancement. Here's what he told us was more important.

Rob believes that people often do not take enough personal responsibility for moving their careers forward. Rather, they expect their employers to do this for them. Usually, when they do take action, they look at moving away from their current employer and jumping to another opportunity. Yet, so many people could benefit greatly from networking within their own organizations and, if they took a proactive role, they would never feel the need to leave their current companies. People tend to be passive about their careers; they are reactive only when a situation arises that they must respond to.

Inevitably, there will be times when there is tension between an employee and his or her boss. If employees are good at what they do, most bosses will try to keep them in their current position. A good manager wants his employees to stay with the company, and is aware that employees want opportunities, the chance to do new things, and promotions. A good boss looks at each employee and works to focus on the long-term opportunities for that employee. In the ideal situation, a boss and employee can approach the subject of promotion in a thoughtful and cooperative manner.

## Action Items

Here are a few specific action items employees can initiate in order to position themselves for advancement:

1. **Create an internal network.** Most people within an organization are happy to spend some time with you and share information to help you learn how they do what they do and why they do it. It is a great way to build relationships and learn invaluable information about your company. Most relevant to our conversation here, it is an outstanding way to build visibility within your company and position yourself for a promotion to a higher-level assignment.

2. **Become involved in special projects.** When you do this, you expand your contacts throughout the organization, acquire new talents, and make new contributions. Be sure to focus on projects and opportunities that will allow you to develop new skills and position yourself for new opportunities that might come along.

3. **Think about the job that you want and market yourself for it.** You can consider a co-op or internship opportunity that will allow you to come in the back door. Once you are there, it is much easier to move into a position of greater responsibility because you already know the organization and how it works. This gives you a decisive competitive advantage over external candidates applying for the same position.

4. **Engage your manager in your career planning.** Many people are afraid to do so, yet they should not be. Take your boss out to lunch on occasion so that you can discuss your career goals in a nonthreatening environment and without constant interruptions. Do not communicate that you are unhappy in your current position (even though you might be); rather, focus your conversation on the fact that you are looking for growth and new opportunities. Your current boss can be your biggest ally in helping to move your career forward. Although you boss might be disappointed to lose you if you move on, he or she will receive favorable feedback for encouraging you to stay with the company.

5. **Meet with a human resources representative.** Your HR department can be quite helpful in your career discussions and will often lend direct support. They can help mentor your career and help you develop a step-by-step career-advancement plan.

## Promotions for the Poor Performer

One final comment that Rob shared with us had to do with work performance issues. If you are a poor-performing employee, earning a promotion will be more challenging. Rob finds that most people are not poor performers for technical reasons, but rather because of fit or chemistry issues with their boss, division, or company. Style issues frequently come into play.

In attempting to resolve these situations in the workplace, Rob looks at the root of the problem, where the confusion is, and how to improve communications between the nonperforming employee and his or her boss. Frequently, the expectations of the job were not clearly outlined at the onset, and thus, problems arose. Through clear communication, these issues can often be clarified and employee performance improved. In other situations, it will be best for an employee to move into a new position with the company that will provide a better fit. If you find yourself in this situation, it can be an excellent opportunity to meet other people in the company and work to move your career forward.

□ □ □

# When You Know It's Time to Make a Career Change

**Frank Leonetti, CBCP**
*North American Business Manager*
*Global Services, StorageTek, Lumberton, NJ*

When we wanted to speak with someone who could give us great insights into how an individual knows when it is time to make a career change, we approached Frank Leonetti because of his vast experience advising people, projects, and organizations in transition. Here's what he had to say.

Frank believes a person is ready to make a career change when they know what it is that they want. If they want to move into a position of more responsibility, they should ask themselves the following questions:

- Have they done their homework and really understand what is involved in that potential career move?

- Have they spoken to people in that current role and analyzed what it will take to be successful in that role, and do they have what it takes to succeed?

- Do they understand the industry, the products or services, the people, and the long-term outlook for both the company and the industry?

- Are they truly excited about a new opportunity?

If an individual can answer yes to all of these questions, the next step is to reach out to their family. Does their family understand what it will take from *them* in order to be successful? Their work hours might change, and that can have a significant impact on the family.

The last thing to consider in the equation is money. First, you must decide whether this new career is right for you and your family. If so, evaluate whether the increased compensation is worth the extra responsibility, time, travel, and more.

If you are considering an internal promotion to a position of greater responsibility, be sure that you are properly prepared and can answer the following questions:

- Who are the people above you?

- Who are the other people who want the same job? Do you know what value they bring to the position?

- Where is the company moving?
- Have you done all that you can to get to the next level?
- Have you built your network?

Things can change in an instant. Companies are merged, acquired, reorganized, revitalized, and more. You could potentially be out of a job through no fault of your own...just an innocent bystander. If you are well prepared and aware of the trends within your company and your industry, you will be able to better respond in such a situation and potentially be one of the few who is asked to remain with the company despite all of the transition.

□ □ □

# Surviving a Reduction in Force

### Coretha Rushing
*Senior Vice President—Human Resources*
*The Coca-Cola Company, Atlanta, GA*

Hundreds of thousands of workers have been directly impacted by the unprecedented number of reductions in force in companies throughout the U.S. and abroad over the past 10 years or more. Although some of these individuals have experienced positive results, for most, the outcome has been negative. To understand what employees can do to survive a RIF, we turned to a real human resources expert and asked Coretha Rushing to share her insights and wisdom with us. This is what we learned.

When companies want to look at their resources, internal structure, and operations, they often do efficiency studies. The results of these studies might be the identification of areas within an organization that a company can no longer afford. When this happens, the company will make changes, one of which might be a reduction in the workforce.

It is very difficult for people to do their best work under this type of pressure or when they feel they have no control. Feelings of helplessness or victimization happen for some. Others are still able to operate productively and successfully. What's important to remember is that you do not have to feel helpless or victimized. You have choice—how you respond and progress during this period of uncertainty is critical.

You might think that the only people to suffer in a RIF are those who are laid off. Not true! The people who still have their jobs after a layoff can suffer, too, and often wonder whether they will be next. Remember, if you are laid off, or if you are concerned about being downsized, you have decisions to make. First and foremost, you need to develop a plan that outlines the types of positions you would be interested in, along with a list of target companies for whom you would like to work.

So many times people find themselves in mid-career and forget that they once had a career plan. Coretha likes to ask people who are experiencing a company restructuring what they want to be when they "grow up." This is a time to remember that you can have control over your life and use this time of turmoil to check in on where you are now in your life and career.

Coretha's experience has shown her that people are afraid to ask the question about what they want to be because they might not know the answer. This can be a real wake-up call. In fact, that is part of the challenge for people when they realize they have a choice. People who ask this question and meet it head on will be able to position themselves better for new and greater opportunities. They will know how they can bring value to the organization and what specific skills they can offer.

People need to look at their life in total. It is easy for young people, fresh out of college or graduate school, to typically look at things in a narrow way. They have not yet thought of personal sacrifices that need to be made at times in their lives in order to reach the end result. Young people might need to make life and career decisions with family and friends, and they must take personality and spirituality into account because career management is not one-dimensional. Rather, by taking a holistic approach to career management and career reengineering, you will have a decidedly distinct and competitive advantage.

First, you must decide what is important to you. Are you looking for more balance and flexibility in your life? Are you looking for the trappings that come with certain jobs, or are you willing to sacrifice? Are you looking for the big house and expensive car? If you are, that's okay as long as you know that those are some of your primary motivators. However, you must realize that in order to attain those things, you might have to sacrifice along the way.

Typically during a restructuring, most companies are clear with their employees about the upcoming layoffs early. The unknown can be debilitating, but you have to stay grounded because you have work to do. Do not spend precious time worrying. Instead, pull out your resume, update it, and think about what specific actions you will take if you are laid off. Look at your financial situation to determine how quickly you will need to find another job so that you are prepared. Then get back to work!

People always have more going for them than going against them, even in a layoff situation. Regardless of what is happening at work, you must retain control of your work life. When you turn over your control, you turn over your power and find yourself in the passenger seat with no one at the wheel and the car headed for a brick wall. Do not let this happen to you!

If you are laid off, you still need to stay positive. No one wants to hire a person who sounds and looks like a victim. If you have been a valued employee and done your job well, it might hurt even more to be restructured out of a job. But you must remember that layoffs are not necessarily about who's the most talented. Companies often have to make very difficult decisions and top performers do get downsized when the deliverables or services they provide to the company are no longer required. When you have met or exceeded all of your performance objectives and delivered measurable value to a company, but they simply cannot afford you anymore, it is easy to understand why the layoff can be especially painful.

When Coretha was a Human Resources Executive at IBM, she was around when they experienced their first set of layoffs. People were lost and perplexed, not sure where to turn or what to do next. Coretha would spend a great deal of time consoling people, reminding them that things would get better and assuring them that when one door closes, another opens. Their one true challenge was to be sure that they did not let the open door go unnoticed.

In closing, Coretha stressed the importance of looking at new ways to leverage your best skills and reflect on what is positive about you as a contributing member of a team so that you can positively prepare yourself to make your next career move. And, most importantly, Coretha reminds us that it is not just large companies that offer outstanding career opportunities, but smaller and midsized companies as well. Don't overlook them!

□ □ □

# Before Looking for a New Job

**Michael A. Wirth**

*Director—Business and Application Development*
*Talent+, Lincoln, NE*

If you have decided to make a career change or apply for an internal promotion, there truly is a plan and process to it all. To provide you with that information, we turned to Michael Wirth, who shared his insights on what to do before looking for a job or considering an internal promotion. Here is his step-by-step plan of action:

1. **Decide what you want to do and who you want to be.** This step is critical in preparing yourself for the right career opportunities.

2. **Take a few career-assessment tools.** These can provide you with extremely valuable information about your skills, motivators, personality, career preferences, and more. What's more, many assessments are now available online, which makes the process of taking them much easier, faster, and less expensive.

3. **Do a career inventory search.** In essence, identify your core skills, competencies, knowledge, and areas of expertise. Then take it one step further and identify which industries and professions look for candidates with those precise qualifications.

4. **Ask others how they perceive you and your skills.** This is invaluable information in helping you prepare yourself for your next opportunity. Remember, people do not necessarily perceive you as you perceive yourself!

5. **Reflect back on your career and what you have enjoyed the most.** These functions, projects, roles, and responsibilities should be the foundation for your next career opportunity. Work consumes such a huge portion of our lives and you will be much more successful if you do what you enjoy and what satisfies you.

The preceding items are what Michael refers to as the must-haves in one's career. Then add to that mixture your priorities for salary, location, and corporate values. When you have amassed all of this information, you are then ready to launch your search. If you do not know who you are or what you want to do, a job search can be a tremendous waste of time. Create a job search plan that addresses all of the preceding five items and then work that plan to create your own career success.

When you decide to make a career change, it will change your entire life and the way that you look at your family, friends, customers, colleagues, supervisors, and the world. Think hard about why you want to make that change and then stay focused on that change. Read books, talk to people, get involved in different activities, and expand your circle of influence. The more you learn, the more people you meet, and the more information you acquire, the better prepared you will be to make a positive change in your life.

Experience does not beget excellence. Just because you do not have experience does not mean that you do not have the talent. Look inside and think about what you want to do and why. Can you do it well? Do you want to make the change because you want recognition or more money? Obviously, those things are important, but not as important as finding a job that you will find personally and professionally rewarding. We spend such a huge amount of our time working these days. If you are not fulfilled, those days, hours, months, and years can seem to go on forever.

□ □ □

## Authors' Best Advice for Moving Your Career Forward

1. **Know who the "professional you" is.** Your career will progress much more rapidly if you are in a position and industry that excites you and in which you excel. And the best way to determine this is to really understand who you are, what motivates you, what energizes you, and what gives you the most professional satisfaction. Taking the time to explore these concepts prior to launching your career will definitely put you in a stronger position for building and managing your career over time.

2. **Create a lifelong career plan.** Start developing your personalized career plan today. Include your short-term and long-range career objectives for type of position, type of industry, geographic preference, compensation, and more. And do not just make it an activity that you are going to work on this week or this month. Your career plan is a dynamic document that will change over time. You will need to devote

the time and resources to updating it on a regular basis. We recommend doing so every 6 to 12 months.

3. **Keep records of all of your achievements.** As part of your career plan, you will want to record all of your professional accomplishments, honors, awards, project highlights, and any other information about how you have succeeded. Not only is this information useful when preparing for a job search, writing a resume, and proactively managing your job interviews, it is also extremely valuable when you look back at what you have accomplished and what you have enjoyed. That information might provide you with baseline data for where to take your career next.

4. **Be flexible.** Change happens everywhere, in every industry and every market sector in the world. Those changes will most likely impact your career at one point or another. Be prepared and be flexible, knowing that to continue moving forward you might have to change your career direction as industries and markets change.

5. **Accept new challenges and new opportunities.** You might think to yourself that you are not too excited about your recent lateral move into a new department. Rather than be dismayed about your new responsibilities, look at them as challenges and opportunities to further expand your skills, knowledge, and expertise. With each new layer of qualifications that you add to your portfolio, you will be positioning yourself for better and greater opportunities that will come in the future.

6. **Find a mentor.** There are few things that you can do in your career that will be more valuable to you than finding a true mentor, an individual who has a vested interest in you and your success. In turn, your role is to support your mentor and make them look good, feel good, and excel. If you are fortunate enough to have this type of reciprocal relationship, it can take your own career to new heights.

7. **Know your employer and what they value.** If you are happy with your current employer and want to remain with the company, the best advice we can offer is to thoroughly understand what they value in their employees. If you know

*(continued)*

*(continued)*

the company's hot buttons, you can better prepare yourself for promotional opportunities within the organization.

8. **Know when it is time to move on.** When the day comes that you do not want to get out of bed and go to your job anymore, you will know that the time has come to leave. There is almost nothing worse than dragging yourself to a job each day where you are unhappy and unfulfilled. When you begin to experience those feelings, your subconscious is telling you something, so listen and act accordingly. There are virtually no jobs where someone is content to remain for the rest of their lives, and that is okay.

9. **Accept your failures and move on.** Everyone fails at some point in their lives, and the best thing that you can do is accept that we are all human. Do not gloss over the failure or attempt to change how people interpret it. If a product you designed does not work or a new customer-service program you developed was a bust, learn what you can from those mistakes and move on. No employer expects 100 percent perfection from anyone!

10. **Network at the top.** As we have communicated repeatedly throughout this book, there is no better strategy for planning and managing a successful career than networking. Not only can your network contacts be of tremendous value to you when you are in an active job search campaign, they are just as valuable to you in your lifelong career-management efforts. They can provide guidance, recommendations, insights, referrals, and more, all of which can be critical components to your long-term career success, advancement, and fulfillment.

Take control of your career and great things will happen! We guarantee it!

# INDEX